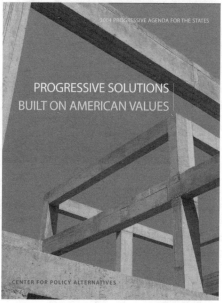

Progressive Solutions Built on American Values:
2004 Progressive Agenda for the States
Copyright © 2003 by Center for Policy Alternatives
ISBN 0-89788-200-8

The Center for Policy Alternatives (CPA) is the nation's
only nonpartisan nonprofit organization working to
strengthen the capacity of state legislators to lead and
achieve progressive change. Founded in 1975, CPA is a
501(c)(3) nonprofit, supported by foundations, unions,
corporations and individuals.

EDITOR	CENTER FOR POLICY ALTERNATIVES
BERNIE HORN	1875 CONNECTICUT AVENUE NW, SUITE 710
	WASHINGTON, DC 20009
CONTRIBUTING WRITERS/EDITORS	PHONE: 202-387-6030
SARADA PERI	FAX: 202-387-8529
NICHOLAS POLT	WWW.STATEACTION.ORG
LAURA DELLATORRE	INFO@CFPA.ORG
KIRSTEN LINDQUIST	
NANCY SCHWALB	
COVER DESIGN	
AMY CHOU	

December 2003

Dear Friends:

We are proud to provide you with a *Progressive Agenda* for 2004.

For the fourth consecutive year, the Center for Policy Alternatives has prepared this collection of 50 policy toolkits on a broad range of topics. Our intent is to equip state legislators with practical strategies and user-friendly materials so they can take the offensive, offering values-based alternatives to address our nation's most vexing problems.

As with all of CPA's programs, the focus of the *Progressive Agenda* is on state legislators and their quest to lead and achieve progressive change in the states. Last year was one of the most difficult years in history for state government. Faced with a stagnant economy, limits on revenue growth, and the ever-escalating human and community needs that have been consistently ignored by the national government, state leaders have been tested and are looking for creative ways to balance the competing demands of their constituents. The year ahead will be equally demanding.

The ideas and solutions presented in this collection of innovative state policies share a common vision of a society that respects and nurtures the potential of all people, and a government that is a positive agent in securing that goal. As this year's title suggests, this book presents an agenda built upon the basic values on which our nation was founded.

The Center for Policy Alternatives has its own "agenda" for 2004. First, we will expand and strengthen our leadership development programs for state legislators. In addition, CPA will enhance the size and power of our network of state legislators who are committed to leading and achieving progress in the states. And finally, in 2004 CPA will launch an initiative to become an organization that is representative of, governed by, and directed for state legislators.

State legislators are the vanguard of today's progressive movement. Their courage, sacrifice and hard work inspire all of us here at CPA, and we dedicate this *Progressive Agenda* to them. On behalf of the Board and staff of CPA, I wish you success!

Sincerely,

Tim McFeeley
Executive Director

Table of Contents

For progressives, the action is in the states. The federal policies of tomorrow are being enacted in the states today.

With the White House and Congress now firmly in the hands of conservatives, there are few opportunities to implement progressive policy ideas at the federal level.

Opportunities do exist, however, in the states—where state legislators are leading the fight for progressive policy solutions.

State legislators are proposing the nation's most far-reaching, proactive measures. They are making legislatures a testing ground for the newest political ideas. And they are winning progressive victories with cutting-edge policies—creating new healthcare programs, expanding anti-discrimination laws, strengthening the social safety net, developing new consumer protections, defending the environment, and most recently, reforming the tax system.

For progressives, the action is in the states. The federal policies of tomorrow are being enacted in the states today.

While legislators have become the vanguard of the progressive movement, they barely have the time or resources to do their jobs effectively. Forty-one states have part-time legislators, and in 22 of those states, legislators have no paid staff. Nineteen legislatures meet less than 80 days a year, and six convene only every other year. These same legislatures annually consider 150,000 bills and enact 75 times as many laws as the U.S. Congress.

Business groups and right-wing ideological organizations provide strong, coordinated assistance to conservative state legislators—furnishing them with bills to introduce, as well as talking points, witnesses, and lobbying support to enact those bills.

We offer this book, the fourth edition of the *Progressive Agenda*, to help legislators promote economic and social justice, individual freedom, stronger communities, a clean environment, and inclusive, open government.

Progressive Solutions Built on American Values covers 50 topics, includes 60 model bills, and lays out more than 100 of the most innovative progressive solutions being debated and enacted in the states.

It is a platform surveying a wide range of domestic issues—from corporate accountability to predatory lending, from prescription drug pricing to sentencing reform. And it doesn't shy away from hot button issues, addressing reproductive rights, gun control, the death penalty, medical marijuana, and same-sex marriage.

Of the major proactive laws enacted in the states in 2003, more than half resemble solutions featured in prior editions of this book.

This *Progressive Agenda* is designed to help legislators take the offensive. Progressives have been on the defensive for so long that many Americans seem to think we have run out of ideas. So every topic in this volume includes at least one—and often more than one—proactive, innovative solution.

We are proud to report that past editions of the *Progressive Agenda* have made a difference. Of the major proactive progressive laws enacted in the states during 2003, more than half resemble solutions featured in prior editions of this book. Some of the model legislation presented in this volume has become law almost verbatim.

Although the *Progressive Agenda* was written to support advocacy in state legislatures, most of the topics and policies apply to the federal and local levels as well. There's something here for anyone who is interested in domestic policy on any level.

Finally, we don't expect readers to agree with every policy solution offered in this book. We would be astonished if someone did! But we welcome the interest of everyone who is intrigued by one or many of our policy models.

—Bernie Horn

For dozens more policy topics and progressive solutions, see the Center for Policy Alternatives' website at www.stateaction.org.

Acknowledgements

The *Progressive Agenda* is a collaborative effort.   The organizations listed below drafted, edited or provided substantial information for policy summaries related to their areas of expertise.

Three organizations deserve special mention: the Center on Budget and Policy Priorities is the source of almost all discussion of corporate and estate taxes; the National Employment Law Project provided drafts for all three sections on unemployment insurance; and NARAL Pro-Choice America edited five reproductive health topics and provided model legislation.

Besides those listed as contributing writers and editors for this book, we would like to thank a former editor, Liz Cattaneo. Much of this work is based on previous editions that she shepherded to publication.

Contributors:

AFL-CIO Working for America Institute*
American Federation of State, County and Municipal Employees*
Ballot Initiative Strategy Center*
Campaign for Criminal Justice Reform
Campaign for Tobacco-Free Kids
Center on Budget and Policy Priorities*
Coalition to Stop Gun Violence*
Corporation for Enterprise Development*
Demos*
Gay, Lesbian, Straight Education Network*
Good Jobs First*
Human Rights Campaign*
Marijuana Policy Project
Maryland Citizens' Health Initiative
NARAL Pro-Choice America*

National Center for Fair and Open Testing
National Center for Lesbian Rights*
National Coalition to Abolish the Death Penalty*
National Council of La Raza
National Education Association*
National Employment Law Project*
National Gay and Lesbian Task Force*
National Immigration Law Center*
National Legislative Association on Prescription Drug Pricing
National Partnership for Women and Families*
Planned Parenthood Federation of America*
Public Citizen
Sentencing Project
Service Employees International Union*
State Environmental Resource Center*
Wider Opportunities for Women

*Designates members of the State Issues Forum (SIF), a collaboration of national advocacy organizations that work to advance progressive policy at the state level. The Center for Policy Alternatives, founder and chair of the SIF, convenes meetings and staffs the forum.

Balancing
State Budgets

Nobody likes to raise taxes or cut government services, but most legislatures will be forced to do one or both in 2004.

Balancing State Budgets

Summary

- Budget deficits in the states will likely exceed $40 billion in 2004.
- State budget deficits were caused by tax cuts, not by overspending.
- A wide variety of policies are available to increase revenues and cut state expenses.
- If progressives don't offer a program to balance state budgets, the conservative program—laying off government workers and slashing social services—will prevail.

Budget deficits in the states will likely exceed $40 billion in 2004.

The National Conference of State Legislatures estimates that over the last three years, states have been forced to address a cumulative budget deficit of nearly $200 billion.[1] The states' fiscal problems are expected to continue.

State budget deficits were caused by tax cuts, not by overspending.

Adjusted for inflation and population growth, spending of state-raised funds increased by only about two percent annually during the 1990s— substantially less than the increases in state spending over the past five decades.[2] Recent budget deficits are primarily the result of states' responding to the strong economy of the 1990s with large, permanent cuts in personal and corporate income taxes. In most states, if taxes were restored to pre-1994 levels, current budget problems would essentially be solved.

A wide variety of policies are available to increase revenues and cut state expenses.

Most states have now depleted their reserve funds and exhausted short-term accounting fixes. Nobody likes to raise taxes or cut government services, but most legislatures will be forced to do one or both in 2004. The following are 28 possible ways to close budget deficits:

■ **Tobacco Excise Tax—Increase the tax and cover more tobacco products.** One of the quickest and most popular ways for states to raise hundreds of millions of dollars is to raise the tobacco tax. Different state polls conducted across the country have found that Americans strongly favor large tobacco tax increases—raising cigarette taxes by 50 or 75 cents per pack. Since 2002, 31 states have increased their cigarette tax rates, raising the state average from 43 to 73 cents per pack. Twenty-eight state legislatures (AR, CT, DE, GA, HI, ID, IL, IN, KS, LA, MD, MA, MI, MT, NE, NV, NJ, NM, NY, OH, PA, RI, SD, TN, UT, VT, WV, WY) and the District of Columbia raised cigarette taxes. Voters in Arizona, Oregon and Washington increased their taxes by statewide referendum. States have also expanded the tax to cover chewing tobacco and snuff. Higher tobacco taxes save thousands of lives by reducing teen smoking, as well as adult tobacco use.

■ **Alcohol Excise Tax—Increase the tax.** All states impose a "sin" tax on alcohol, but most tax alcohol at low rates. The average excise tax on liquor is about $4 per gallon, while several state taxes exceed $6 per gallon. Some states tax beer and wine at much lower rates than spirits, based on the percentage of alcoholic content. States with the lowest alcohol taxes include AK, CO, IN, KS, KY, LA, MD, MO, NE, NV, ND and TX.

■ **Estate Tax—Decouple from federal estate tax.** States are losing billions of dollars in tax revenue because of a change in the federal estate tax enacted in 2001. Most estate taxes in the states are linked to the federal estate tax credit, which is being phased out over the next three years. As a result, state tax revenues are plummeting. Only 18 states are currently decoupled from the federal estate tax: IL, KS, ME, MD, MA, MN, NE, NJ, NY, NC, OH, OR, PA, RI, VT, VA, WA, WI.

■ **Personal Income Tax—Raise the rate for the highest incomes.** The simplest method of making income tax rates more progressive is to institute a surcharge, or new tax bracket, for individuals earning over $250,000, $500,000 or $1 million per year. The Connecticut legislature passed a "Millionaire's Tax" in 2002—a one percent surtax on incomes above $1 million that would have raised an estimated $140 million. However, the governor vetoed the bill. This kind of increase can be enacted as a permanent or temporary tax. During the last recession, four states increased top rates permanently, while five others increased those rates temporarily.

■ **Personal Income Tax—Implement a more graduated scale.** If taxes need to be raised, why not do it fairly? Of the 41 states with a personal income tax covering earnings, only 14 have graduated tax brackets that truly differentiate between lower and upper-income taxpayers. Six states have a flat tax rate—no income brackets at all. In 16 other states, the top tax bracket is $25,000 or less, giving very little meaning to the tax bracket system. In other words, about half the states are ripe for a fundamental reform of income tax brackets.

■ **Personal Income Tax—Eliminate or suspend exemptions, credits and/or deductions.** Virtually every state with an income tax has created or expanded income tax exemptions, credits and/or deductions over the past 10 years. Advocates should research tax loopholes—changes designed to benefit special interests instead of families—and the amount of revenue lost because of each loophole. Legislation can either eliminate the loopholes permanently or suspend them temporarily.

■ **Personal Income Tax—Tax non-resident gambling income.** Net gambling winnings are taxable as income, and state residents are taxed. But states can also tax non-residents who have gambling winnings in the state. CA, CO, IL, MN and NJ tax non-resident gambling income. The value of such a tax expansion depends, of course, on the amount of gambling activity in the state.

■ **Personal Income Tax—Implement a tax amnesty.** Over the past 20 years, 40 states have implemented tax amnesty periods in order to collect overdue taxes. Connecticut, for example, has offered tax amnesties in 1990, 1995 and 2002. The most recent amnesty collected more than $100 million in back taxes. A 2003 Illinois amnesty collected back taxes from almost 20,000 businesses and individuals. However, by offering amnesties too often, states risk lowering taxpayers' incentive to pay on time.

■ **Corporate Income Tax—Implement a more graduated scale.** Thirty states use a flat tax for corporate income. That means there is only one tax bracket, with no graduated scale at all. These states can adopt a graduated system, increasing the tax rate for corporate income over certain levels, e.g., $25,000, $100,000, $250,000, $500,000 and $1 million. For example, Iowa, Kentucky and Maine have graduated scales from $25,000 to $250,000, with tax rates ranging from 3.5 percent at the lowest to 12 percent at the highest. If necessary, a graduated scale can be implemented temporarily, by imposing a surcharge on corporate profits over a certain level—for example, a 5 percent surcharge on corporate profits over $250,000.

■ **Corporate Income Tax—Require combined reporting.** When filing tax returns, corporations that operate across state lines apportion their income among the states where they do business. Corporations use many strategies to artificially shift the reporting of their income to low-tax or no-tax states. Combined reporting is the broadest and fairest reform to stop the most common tax avoidance strategies. Because combined reporting requires corporations to add together the profits of related businesses before the combined profit is subject to apportionment, the company gains little or no advantage by shifting profit among its subsidiaries in different states. Combined reporting ensures that a corporation's state income tax liability remains the same regardless of the corporation's legal structure. Sixteen states use combined reporting: AK, AZ, CA, CO, HI, ID, IL, KS, ME, MN, MT, NE, NH, ND, OR and UT.

■ **Corporate Income Tax—Close the PIC trademark loophole.** Large corporations commonly shift the reporting of income by using a "passive investment company" (PIC), a corporate affiliate that is often no more than a file in a Delaware lawyer's office. The PIC holds legal ownership to the parent corporation's patents and trademarks and charges huge royalties to the parent company, shielding those funds from taxation. This tax dodge was made famous by Toys R Us, which charged its parent company for the use of the "Geoffrey" giraffe trademark, and other intangible assets. This tax loophole has been closed in 24 states. The following states could gain tax revenue by eliminating this income-shifting tactic: AR, DE, FL, GA, IN, IA, KY, LA, MD, MO, NM, OK, PA, RI, SC, TN, TX, VT, VA, WV, WI and the District of Columbia. Enactment of combined reporting also blocks the PIC trademark loophole.

■ **Corporate Income Tax—Redefine "business income."** The U.S. Supreme Court has limited the types of business income that are subject to apportionment among the states. To comply with Supreme Court rulings, most states define and tax "business income." But the commonly-used definition allows corporations to avoid taxes by declaring certain transactions to be "irregular" and therefore "non-business income," cheating states out of their fair share of corporate tax revenue. States can close the "non-business income" loophole by redefining "business income" to be as broad as the Supreme Court allows, that is, "business income means all income which is apportionable under the United States Constitution." Only six states (FL, IA, MN, NC, PA and TX) have adopted this definition. All other states with a corporate income tax could increase revenue by adopting this definition as well.

■ **Corporate Income Tax—Enact a "throwback" rule for "nowhere income."** A little-known federal law, P.L. 86-272, prohibits states from taxing corporate income if the corporation does not conduct a certain level of activity in the state. As a result, corporations often claim that a huge portion of their profits come from sales in those states where federal law prohibits taxation. For tax purposes then, the income seems to come from "nowhere." Twenty-five states have a "throwback" rule directing that if income from a product is not taxed in the state where it is sold, it is taxed in the state where it was made. The throwback rule is so simple it can be accomplished by adding a single sentence to existing corporate tax law. Twenty states (AR, CT, DE, FL, GA, IA, KY, LA, MD, MA, MN, NE, NY, NC, OH, PA, RI, SC, TN and VA) could gain revenue by enacting a throwback rule.

■ **Corporate Income Tax—Tighten rules on "silent partners."** Certain business entities such as S-corporations, partnerships and limited-liability companies are not taxed because their income flows directly to the partners, who are supposed to pay tax on that income. But many out-of-state partners do not report their earnings to the states where the partnerships earned profits. Often, states do not check to see if these "silent" partners reported any income to the state. Most states' efforts to check on pass-through reporting are inadequate, and millions of dollars of tax revenue is lost. Ohio and New Jersey are two states that have tightened the rules on pass-through entities in recent years.

■ **Corporate Income Tax—Eliminate or suspend exemptions, credits and/or deductions.** Over the past 20 years, states have created hundreds of different exemptions, credits or deductions to the corporate income tax in order to encourage or reward different types of businesses or business behavior. Advocates should research the corporate tax loopholes created since the early 1980s, and the amount of revenue lost because of each loophole. Legislation can either eliminate the loopholes permanently or suspend them temporarily.

■ **Corporate Income Tax—Accelerate sunset dates for tax exemptions.** A number of states have created corporate tax exemptions that sunset after a period of years. States can gain additional revenue by moving exemption sunset dates to 2004.

■ **Corporate Income Tax—Decouple from federal bonus depreciation.** States are losing billions of dollars in tax revenue because of a change in the federal corporate income tax enacted in March 2002. A new federal tax deduction, called "bonus depreciation," allows businesses to claim 30 percent depreciation for certain business machinery placed in service after September 2001. Last year, 30 states that had previously followed federal depreciation rules decoupled from the federal tax code, effectively disallowing the new bonus depreciation provision. However, AL, CO, DE, FL, KS, LA, MO, MT, NM, NC, ND, OK, OR, SD, UT, VT and WV stand to lose more than $1.1 billion over the next two years if they do not permanently decouple from the federal depreciation rules.[3]

■ **Corporate Income Tax—Reform the Alternative Minimum Tax.** It is all too common for corporations to use a series of tax loopholes in order to avoid paying any state tax at all. The federal government has an Alternative Minimum Tax (AMT) for these situations. Currently 13 states also impose a corporate minimum tax that is a fixed amount— ranging from $10 in Oregon to $2,000 in New Jersey. Seven states go further, requiring businesses to pay the higher of a tax calculated as a percentage of profit or a tax calculated on some other basis. In Texas, the alternative base is the business' net worth; in New Hampshire it is "value-added" within the business; and in New Jersey it is the business' gross receipts.[4]

■ **Sales Tax—Delete exemptions on some products.** Each state tends to have different sales tax exemptions. Some are progressive (e.g. exemptions for food and medicines), but many states have created sales tax exemptions simply to encourage or reward certain industries, including exemptions for newspapers, vending machines, technology, warehousing, and chemical sprays. Advocates can create a list of unjustified sales tax exemptions and target some or all of them for suspension or elimination.

■ **Sales Tax—Apply to some services.** The sales tax, which is the largest source of revenue for many states, usually applies only to the purchase of tangible personal property (e.g., clothing, housewares, appliances), and in some cases, to the installation or repair of property (e.g., plumbing or auto repair). However, most business, financial and professional services are exempt from the sales tax. States can expand revenue by extending the sales tax to cover specific categories of services, such as advertising, data processing, business consulting, engineering, or architectural services.

■ **Luxury Tax—Impose a special sales tax on luxury goods and services.** Sales taxes are regressive; they absorb a larger proportion of the income of lower-income taxpayers than of higher-income taxpayers. To counter this, states can single out "luxury" goods or services for a sales tax that is either equal to, or greater than, the normal sales tax rate. A surtax can apply to goods that are unusually expensive, for example, non-business purchases over $50,000. Or a tax can apply to athletic club, country club, or golf club memberships.

■ **Intangible Wealth Tax—Cover stocks, bonds, etc.** Following the lead of Florida, states can tax intangible wealth, such as stocks, bonds and money market accounts. For example, a one percent tax on personal and corporate intangible wealth, with a maximum exemption of $3,000 (excluding IRAs and other retirement accounts), would raise nearly $1 billion in the average state. A narrower version has been proposed in New Jersey. There, a one-fourth of one percent tax on intangible assets worth more than $2 million would affect only the richest one percent of taxpayers.

■ **Gasoline Tax—Increase the state tax.** Every state levies a gasoline tax in addition to the federal tax of 18.4 cents per gallon. Some states charge a flat rate per gallon while others tax the price, rather than the quantity, of gas sold. Some states charge as much as 29-31 cents per gallon (NY, RI, WI). 20 states have gas taxes below 20 cents per gallon: AL, AK, AZ, CA, FL, GA, HI, IL, IN, KY, MI, MS, MO, NH, NJ, NM, OK, SC, VA, and WY.

■ **Tax Enforcement—Hire tax investigators to collect more revenue.** Most states do a very poor job of enforcing tax law. As a result, hundreds of millions of dollars in revenue go uncollected. It has been estimated, for example, that Illinois could generate $160 million by hiring 100 additional tax investigators. Similarly, a report in Minnesota found that the state was losing $288 million in uncollected tax revenue. In 2001, Kansas invested $3 million to create 75 new tax collection positions. While the legislature projected that the additional collection efforts would yield $48 million, the state actually collected nearly $110 million in additional revenue.

■ **Medicaid Spending Cut—Obtain supplemental rebates for prescription drugs.** States are being overcharged for the prescription drugs they buy through state programs. On average, states pay 20-25 percent more for outpatient drugs in their Medicaid programs than the federal government pays for the exact same medicines. States can save money by negotiating supplemental rebates from drug manufacturers. Prior to 2001, only California authorized the use of preferred drug lists and negotiated supplemental rebates to lower prescription drug prices paid by the state Medicaid program. Since 2001, at least 26 states have initiated these policies (AL, CT, FL, GA, HI, IL, IN, KY, LA, ME, MD, MA, MI, MN, NM, NC, OH, SC, SD, TN, TX, UT, VT, VA, WA, and WV), saving over one billion dollars per year.

■ **Interest Payments Spending Cut—Refinance existing general obligation debt at lower interest rates.** Several states have saved millions of dollars by refinancing debt. States should re-evaluate state debt with an eye toward refinancing at today's lower interest rates.

■ **Corporate Subsidies Spending Cut—Delete or suspend subsidy and grant programs.** Many states offer subsidies, loan guarantees, grants, and other financial benefits to businesses under a variety of business development programs. States can save revenue by eliminating, suspending or freezing these subsidy programs.

■ **Corrections Department Spending Cut—Divert incarcerated non-violent drug offenders to drug treatment programs.** Over the last decade, a wave of laws intended to get tough on crime has resulted in the incarceration of over 125,000 non-violent drug offenders. While it costs states more than $26,000 per year to house an inmate, community corrections and drug treatment programs are substantially less expensive. Coupled with a moratorium on the construction of new prison cells, this policy could save states hundreds of millions of dollars.

If progressives don't offer a program to balance state budgets, the conservative program—laying off government workers and slashing social services—will prevail.

A budget is a statement of a government's fundamental values. It allocates resources among the programs and policies that are important to state residents. Progressives must demonstrate that their budget proposals reflect American values by apportioning taxes fairly and spending the funds wisely.

The portions of this policy summary dealing with corporate and estate taxes rely in large part on information from the Center on Budget and Policy Priorities.

Endnotes

[1] National Conference of State Legislators, "State Budget & Tax Actions 2003."

[2] Liz McNichol, "The State Fiscal Crisis Was Not Caused By Overspending," Center on Budget and Policy Priorities, May 2003.

[3] Nicholas Johnson, "Federal Tax Changes Likely To Cost States Billions Of Dollars In Coming Years," Center on Budget and Policy Priorities, June 2003.

[4] Michael Mazerov, "Many States Could Avoid An Unnecessary Revenue Loss During The Current Fiscal Crisis By Disallowing Business Operating Loss Carrybacks," Center on Budget and Policy Priorities, May 2003.

Balancing State Budgets

For more information...

Center for Policy Alternatives
1875 Connecticut Avenue NW, Suite 710
Washington, DC 20009
202-387-6030
www.stateaction.org

Center on Budget and Policy Priorities
820 First Street NE, Suite 510
Washington, DC 20002
202-408-1080
www.cbpp.org

Civil Marriage
Equality

The state has the same interest in promoting family stability for same-sex couples as it has in promoting traditional marriage between men and women.

Civil Marriage Equality

Summary

- State and federal laws routinely discriminate against same-sex couples.
- There is a fast-growing movement toward civil marriage and civil union equality.
- Civil marriage would build on America's tradition of moving civil rights forward and erasing the inequities of the past.
- Civil marriage, and to a lesser extent civil unions, protect couples.
- Civil marriage promotes stable, long-lasting relationships between same-sex partners.
- Civil marriage strengthens families and safeguards children.
- No religious institution would be required to perform a ceremony.
- Public support for civil marriage and civil unions is growing.
- States have a mixed record on providing benefits to domestic partners.

State and federal laws routinely discriminate against same-sex couples.

The U.S. General Accounting Office has listed more than 1,000 federal rights, protections and responsibilities automatically granted to married heterosexual couples but denied to same-sex couples.[1] States have similar laws that protect married partners but not same-sex partners, including:

- The right to visit a sick spouse in the hospital.
- The right to make decisions during a medical emergency.
- The right to leave work to care for an ill spouse.
- The right to access pensions, workers' compensation, and survivor benefits.
- The right to sue for wrongful death of a spouse.
- The right to inherit without a will.

There is a fast-growing movement toward civil marriage and civil union equality.

In November 2003, the Supreme Judicial Court of Massachusetts ruled that state law must allow same-sex couples to marry. The state constitution guarantees "the right to marry the person of one's choice" regardless of gender, the Court decided. In June 2003, an Ontario appeals court ruled that the Canadian constitution requires civil marriage equality for same-sex couples, which led to the legalization of same-sex marriage in Canada. In December 1999, the Vermont Supreme Court ruled that it was unconstitutional to deny marriage licenses to same-sex couples in that state, which led to the legalization of same-sex civil unions. More than ten nations, including Belgium, Denmark, Germany, Iceland, Netherlands, Portugal and Sweden, already allow same-sex couples to marry or enter into federally recognized domestic partnerships.

Civil marriage would build on America's tradition of moving civil rights forward and erasing the inequities of the past.

This is not the first time in our country that a group of people has been denied the freedom to marry. African American slaves were not permitted to marry. There was a time when Asian Americans were not permitted to marry in some Western states. And it was not until 1967 that the U.S. Supreme Court struck down Jim Crow state laws that made interracial marriage illegal. Clearly, Americans have the capacity to move beyond discrimination.

Civil marriage, and to a lesser extent civil unions, protect couples.

A state civil union law grants same-sex couples the rights of married couples, but only within that state. Civil marriages would likely be recognized across state lines under the U.S. Constitution's full faith and credit clause.

Civil marriage promotes stable, long-lasting relationships between same-sex partners.

Civil marriage is not just about benefits. Marriage also imposes responsibilities on the partners for each other's welfare and the welfare of their dependents. The state has the same interest in promoting family stability for same-sex couples as it has in promoting traditional marriage between men and women. Married couples are viewed and treated differently than single individuals by the state, by friends, family and the rest of society, and by each other. Setting aside the issue of discrimination, it is illogical for government to promote marriage for some but not for all.

Civil marriage strengthens families and safeguards children.

Children are more secure if they are raised in homes with two loving parents who have a legal relationship with them and can share the responsibility of parenthood. According to conservative estimates from the 2000 census, there are more than 1 million children being raised by same-sex couples in the United States.[2] Without the ability to establish a legal relationship to both parents, children of same-sex couples are left without important protections, such as survivor benefits. These children should not be penalized just because their parents are gay.

No religious institution would be required to perform a ceremony.

Just as no religious institution can be required by the government to marry an interfaith couple, no religious institution could be told to marry a same-sex couple. Right now, Reform Judaism, Unitarianism, and many United Church of Christ congregations and Quaker meetings do sanction same-sex unions. When the government refuses to honor marriages blessed by these religious groups, it consequently refuses to honor their religious freedom.

Public support for civil marriage and civil unions is growing.

An August 2003 poll jointly conducted by the Democratic polling firm Hart Research and the Republican firm American Viewpoint found that, by a margin of 50 to 47 percent, Americans support granting civil marriage licenses to gay and lesbian couples as long as religious institutions do not have to recognize or perform these marriages. In a September 2003 Gallup poll, only 35% of Americans said that same-sex couples "should not be allowed all the same legal rights as married couples in every state" when given three choices: support, opposition or "it doesn't matter." The concept of same-sex

marriage has steadily gained support in recent years, and that support is likely to increase. In 1996, only 27 percent supported same-sex marriage, compared to 50 percent today. When polls are broken down by age group, the younger the respondent, the stronger the support for same-sex marriage.

States have a mixed record on providing benefits to domestic partners.

In 2003, California enacted a law that provides registered domestic partners almost all of the state-conferred rights and responsibilities of spouses. In Hawaii, same-sex couples are able to formalize their relationships under the state's reciprocal beneficiary statute, which entitles registered same-sex couples to many rights available to married spouses, including those associated with survivorship, inheritance, property ownership, and insurance. Ten states (CA, CT, IA, ME, NM, NY, OR, RI, VT, WA) and the District of Columbia offer domestic partner benefits to the same-sex partners of public employees, as do several dozen cities and counties. Nonetheless, 37 states have passed laws that explicitly prohibit the recognition of marriage between same-sex couples. The 13 which have not passed such laws are CT, MD, MA, NH, NJ, NM, NY, OH, OR, RI, VT, WI and WY.

Federal law against same-sex marriage is unconstitutional.

In 1996, Congress passed an anti-gay marriage bill called the Defense of Marriage Act (DOMA). Legal scholars argue that DOMA flagrantly violates the "full faith and credit" clause of the U.S. Constitution. The issue has never been resolved in court.

This policy summary relies in large part on information from Human Rights Campaign, the National Center for Lesbian Rights, and the National Gay and Lesbian Task Force.

Endnotes

[1] U.S. General Accounting Office, "Tables of Laws in the United States Code Involving Marital Status, by Category," 1997.

[2] U.S. Census Bureau, "Married-Couple and Unmarried-Partner Households," 2003.

Civil Marriage Equality

For more information...

Center for Policy Alternatives
1875 Connecticut Avenue NW, Suite 710
Washington, DC 20009
202-387-6030
www.stateaction.org

National Gay and Lesbian Task Force
1325 Massachusetts Avenue NW, Suite 600
Washington, DC 20005
202-393-5177
www.ngltf.org

The Federation of Lesbian, Gay, Bisexual and Transgender Advocacy Organizations
1222 South Dale Mabry, Suite 652
Tampa, FL 33629
813-870-3735
www.federationlgbt.org

Human Rights Campaign
1640 Rhode Island Avenue NW
Washington, DC 20036
202-628-4160
www.hrc.org

Lambda Legal Defense and Education Fund
120 Wall Street, Suite 1500
New York, NY 10005
212-809-8585
www.lambdalegal.org

National Center for Lesbian Rights
870 Market Street, Suite 570
San Francisco, CA 94102
415-392-6257
www.nclrights.org

Civil Marriage Equality Act

SECTION 1. SHORT TITLE

This Act shall be called the "Civil Marriage Equality Act."

SECTION 2. FINDINGS AND PURPOSE

(A) FINDINGS—The legislature finds that:

1. The state has a strong interest in promoting marriage to encourage close, stable and lasting families, and to foster strong economic and social support systems among all family members.

2. Marriage brings with it numerous benefits, responsibilities and protections, both for spouses and for their children.

3. Without the protections, benefits and responsibilities associated with marriage, same-sex couples suffer many obstacles and hardships.

(B) PURPOSE—This law is enacted so that same-sex couples shall be eligible to marry in the same manner and with the same requirements as opposite-sex couples, and that same-sex marriages legally performed outside of the state shall be recognized in the same manner and with the same requirements as opposite-sex marriages performed outside of the state.

SECTION 3. CIVIL MARRIAGE EQUALITY

(A) In section XXX, after "The following marriages are prohibited:" delete "a marriage between persons of the same sex."

(B) In section XXX, paragraph XXX [any language that blocks civil marriage equality] is deleted.

(C) In section XXX, insert: "No provision of state or local law shall be construed to prohibit, or prevent the recognition of, marriages between persons of the same gender."

SECTION 4. EFFECTIVE DATE

This Act shall take effect on July 1, 2004

Civil Marriage Equality

Civil Union Equality Act

SECTION 1. SHORT TITLE

This Act shall be called the "Civil Union Equality Act."

SECTION 2. FINDINGS AND PURPOSE

(A) FINDINGS—The legislature finds that:

1. The state has a strong interest in promoting marriage to encourage close, stable and lasting families, and to foster strong economic and social support systems among all family members.

2. Marriage brings with it numerous benefits, responsibilities and protections, both for spouses and for their children.

3. Without the protections, benefits and responsibilities associated with marriage, same-sex couples suffer many obstacles and hardships.

4. While a system of civil unions does not bestow the status of marriage, it will significantly improve the legal protections afforded to same-sex couples.

(B) PURPOSE—This law is enacted to provide eligible same-sex couples the opportunity to obtain the benefits, protections, rights and responsibilities afforded to opposite-sex couples by marriage.

SECTION 3. CIVIL UNION EQUALITY

In section XXX, the following new paragraphs shall be inserted:

(A) ELIGIBILITY FOR CIVIL UNION—Two persons may form a civil union if they are of the same sex and otherwise meet the requirements for marriage set forth in section XXX [the section of state law applying to marriage].

(B) RIGHTS AND RESPONSIBILITIES WITHIN A CIVIL UNION

1. A civil union shall provide those joined in it with a legal status equivalent to marriage. All laws of the state, whether they derive from statute, administrative or court rule, policy, common law, or any other source of civil law, that are applicable to marriage shall also be applicable to civil unions.

2. Parties joined in a civil union shall have all the same benefits, protections, rights and responsibilities under law, whether they derive from statute, administrative or court rule, policy, common law, or any other source of civil law, as are granted to spouses in a marriage.

3. Parties joined in a civil union shall be included in any definition or use of the terms "spouse," "family," "immediate family," "dependent," "next of kin," "husband," "wife," or other terms that denote the spousal relationship, as those terms are used throughout state law.

4. The term marriage as it is used throughout state law, whether in statutes, administrative or court rule, policy, common law, or any other source of civil law, shall be read, interpreted, and understood to include marriage and civil union.

5. Parties to a civil union may modify the terms, conditions, or effects of their civil union in the same manner and to the same extent as married persons who execute a pre-nuptial agreement or other agreement recognized and enforceable under the law, setting forth particular understandings with respect to their union.

(C) ADMINISTRATION AND ENFORCEMENT

1. The [state registry of vital statistics] shall provide civil union license and certificate forms to all city and county clerks, and shall keep a record of all civil unions and the dissolution thereof.

2. The [family courts] shall have jurisdiction over all proceedings relating to the dissolution of civil unions. The dissolution of civil unions shall follow the same rules and procedures, and be subject to the same substantive rights and obligations, that are involved in the dissolution of marriage.

3. To the extent that state law adopts, refers to, or relies upon provisions of federal law, parties joined in civil unions shall be treated under the law of the state as if federal law recognized a civil union in the same manner as the law of the state.

4. This section shall be construed liberally in order to secure to eligible couples the option of a legal status with all the attributes, effects, benefits and protections of marriage.

SECTION 4. NONCONFORMING SECTIONS

In section XXX, paragraph XXX [any language that blocks civil union equality] is deleted.

SECTION 5. EFFECTIVE DATE

This Act shall take effect on July 1, 2004.

Contraceptive Equity

Health insurance companies are discriminating against women by denying them contraceptive coverage while routinely covering prescriptions for Viagra.

Contraceptive Equity

Summary:

- Millions of women are denied coverage for their contraceptive needs by health insurance and managed care organizations. It is largely for this reason that women pay 68 percent more in out-of-pocket medical expenses than men.
- The denial of contraceptive coverage constitutes sex discrimination.
- The same health plans that refuse payment for contraception routinely cover Viagra.
- Increased access to contraception decreases the need for abortions.
- Increased access to contraception improves women's and children's health.
- The public supports equitable coverage for contraception.
- The insurance industry falsely claims that requiring equitable coverage for contraception will drive up the cost of health care.
- Denial clauses hinder contraceptive equity.

Millions of women are denied coverage for their contraceptive needs by health insurance and managed care organizations.

More than one-third of employer-based health plans do not cover any oral contraceptives, and only 41 percent cover all types of reversible contraceptives.[1] This lack of insurance coverage for contraception harms women economically. Women of reproductive age spend 68 percent more than their male counterparts on out-of-pocket healthcare costs, with contraceptives and reproductive healthcare services accounting for much of the difference.

The denial of contraceptive coverage constitutes sex discrimination.

Over 97 percent of health insurance plans provide coverage for prescription drugs. Both the Equal Employment Opportunity Commission and a federal court have ruled that an employer's failure to cover prescription contraceptives, when it covers other preventive medicines and devices, constitutes sex discrimination in violation of federal law.

The same health plans that refuse payment for contraception routinely cover Viagra.

This insurance company practice that favors men and discriminates against women has been referred to as "redlining in the bedroom."

Increased access to contraception decreases the need for abortions.

Nearly half of all pregnancies in the United States are unintended, and approximately half of unintended pregnancies end in abortion.

Increased access to contraception improves women's and children's health.

Women with unintended pregnancies are less likely to obtain timely, adequate prenatal care, increasing the likelihood of low birth-weight babies and infant mortality. Effective family planning could reduce the incidence of low birth-weight by 12 percent and infant mortality by 10 percent.[2]

The public supports equitable coverage for contraception.

A nationwide poll conducted in 2001 by the NARAL Foundation found that 77 percent of Americans support legislation requiring health insurance companies to cover the cost of contraception. Similarly, a 1998 survey by the Kaiser Family Foundation found that 73 percent of Americans support insurance coverage of contraception even when participants are told that the coverage could increase premiums by $1-5 per month.[3]

Twenty-one states have enacted contraceptive equity.

Since 1998, 21 states have enacted comprehensive laws or regulations to address imbalances in private insurance coverage for contraception (AZ, CA, CT, DE, GA, HI, IL, IA, ME, MD, MA, MO, NV, NH, NM, NY, NC, RI, TX, VT, WA).

The insurance industry falsely claims that requiring equitable coverage for contraception will drive up the cost of health care.

The added cost for employers to provide coverage for the full range of reversible contraceptives is approximately $1.43 per employee, per month, according to a comprehensive analysis. The cost is significantly lower for health plans that currently cover some form of contraception.[4] At the same time, insurers generally pay the medical costs of unintended pregnancy, including ectopic pregnancy (average cost $4,994), spontaneous abortion ($1,038), and term pregnancy ($8,619). Therefore, covering contraceptives could save insurers a considerable sum.

Denial clauses hinder contraceptive equity.

Opponents of contraceptive equity sometimes propose denial clauses, also called "conscience" clauses, which permit employers and/or insurers who object to contraception to refuse to provide for its coverage. This leaves patients unable to obtain necessary care.

This policy brief relies in large part on information from NARAL Pro-Choice America.

Endnotes

[1] Kaiser Family Foundation, "HRET Employer Health Benefits: 2001 Annual Survey."

[2] Rachel Benson Gold, "The Need for Mandating Private Insurance Coverage of Contraception," *The Alan Guttmacher Report on Public Policy*, 1998.

[3] Kaiser Family Foundation, "Kaiser Family Foundation National Survey on Insurance Coverage of Contraceptives," 1998.

[4] Jacqueline Darroch, "Cost to Employer Health Plans of Covering Contraceptives, Summary, Methodology and Background," Alan Guttmacher Institute, 1998.

Contraceptive Equity

For more information...

Center for Policy Alternatives
1875 Connecticut Avenue NW, Suite 710
Washington, DC 20009
202-387-6030
www.stateaction.org

Alan Guttmacher Institute
1120 Connecticut Avenue NW, Suite 460
Washington, DC 20036
202-296-4012
www.agi-usa.org

NARAL Pro-Choice America
1156 15th Street NW, Suite 700
Washington, DC 20005
202-973-3000
www.prochoiceamerica.org

Planned Parenthood Federation of America
434 West 33rd Street
New York, NY 10001
212-541-7800
www.plannedparenthood.org

Reproductive Freedom Project
American Civil Liberties Union
125 Broad Street, 18th Floor
New York, NY 10004
212-549-2500
www.aclu.org

Center for Reproductive Rights
120 Wall Street
New York, NY 10005
917-637-3600
www.reproductiverights.org

Contraceptive Equity Act

Summary: The Equity in Prescription Insurance and Contraceptive Coverage Act prohibits health insurance plans that cover prescription drugs and devices from refusing coverage for contraceptives.

SECTION 1. SHORT TITLE

This Act may be cited as the "Equity in Prescription Insurance and Contraceptive Coverage Act."

SECTION 2. FINDINGS AND PURPOSE

(A) FINDINGS—The legislature finds that:

1. Insurance coverage of contraceptives is lacking. Three-fourths of women of childbearing age rely on some form of private employment-related insurance to defray their medical expenses. Yet nearly half of all typical large group insurance plans do not routinely cover any contraceptive method at all.
2. Nationally, 97 percent of large group insurance plans routinely cover prescription drugs, yet only 15 percent routinely cover all five primary reversible contraceptive methods: oral contraception, IUD insertion, diaphragm, Norplant insertion, and Depo-Provera injection.
3. In [STATE], [number or percentage] of insurance plans do not provide coverage for [the full range of/any] contraceptives.

(B) PURPOSE—This law is enacted to protect the health and safety of women of childbearing age and to remedy inequity in health insurance coverage.

SECTION 3. CONTRACEPTIVE EQUITY

(A) DEFINITIONS—In this section:

1. "Covered person"means a policy holder, subscriber, certificate holder, enrollee, or other individual who is participating in, or receiving coverage under, a health insurance plan.
2. "Health insurance plan" means any individual or group plan, policy, certificate, subscriber contract, or contract of insurance that is delivered, issued, renewed, modified, amended or extended by a health insurer.
3. "Health insurer" means a disability insurer, health care insurer, health maintenance organization, accident and sickness insurer, fraternal benefit society, nonprofit hospital service corporation, health service corporation, health care service plan, preferred provider organization or arrangement, self insured employer, or multiple employer welfare arrangement.
4. "Outpatient contraceptive services" means consultations, examinations, procedures and medical services provided on an outpatient basis and related to the use of contraceptive drugs and devices to prevent pregnancy.

(B) PARITY FOR CONTRACEPTIVES

1. Health insurance plans that provide benefits for prescription drugs or devices shall not exclude or restrict benefits to covered persons for any prescription contraceptive drug or device approved by the Food and Drug Administration. [Optional: Health care plans must allow enrollees to obtain at least a 90-day supply of oral contraceptives per refill.]
2. Health insurance plans that provide benefits for outpatient services provided by a health care professional shall not exclude or restrict outpatient contraceptive services for covered persons.

Contraceptive Equity

(C) EXTRAORDINARY SURCHARGES PROHIBITED

A health insurance plan is prohibited from:

1. Imposing deductibles, copayments, other cost-sharing mechanisms, or waiting periods for prescription contraceptive drugs or devices that are greater than deductibles, copayments, other cost-sharing mechanisms, or waiting periods for other covered prescription drugs or devices.

2. Imposing deductibles, copayments, other cost-sharing mechanisms, or waiting periods for outpatient contraceptive services that are greater than deductibles, copayments, other cost-sharing mechanisms, or waiting periods for other covered outpatient services.

(D) OTHER PROHIBITIONS

A health insurance plan is prohibited from:

1. Denying eligibility, continued eligibility, enrollment, or renewal of coverage to any individual because of their use or potential use of contraceptives.

2. Providing monetary payments or rebates to covered persons to encourage them to accept less than the minimum protections available under this section.

3. Penalizing, or otherwise reducing or limiting the reimbursement of a health care professional because such professional prescribed contraceptive drugs or devices, or provided contraceptive services.

4. Providing incentives, monetary or otherwise, to a health care professional to induce such professional to withhold contraceptive drugs, devices or services from covered persons.

(E) ENFORCEMENT

In addition to any remedies at common law, the [insurance commissioner] shall receive and review written complaints regarding compliance with this section. The [insurance commissioner] may use all investigatory tools available to verify compliance with this section. If the [insurance commissioner] determines that a health insurance plan is not in compliance with any section in this section, the [commissioner] shall:

1. Impose a fine of up to $10,000 per violation of this section. An additional $10,000 may be imposed for every 30 days that a health insurance plan is not in compliance; and

2. Suspend or revoke the certificate of authority or deny the health insurer's application for a certificate of authority.

SECTION 4. SEVERABILITY

If any provision, word, phrase or clause of this Act, or the application thereof, to any person, entity or circumstance should be held invalid, such invalidity shall not affect the remaining provisions, words, phrases or clauses of this act which can be given effect without the invalid provision, word, phrase, clause or application, and to this end, the provisions, words, phrases or clauses of this act are declared severable.

SECTION 5. EFFECTIVE DATE

This Act shall take effect on July 1, 2004. This Act shall apply to any health insurance plan delivered, issued, renewed, modified, amended or extended on or after the effective date.

*This model is based on legislation developed by **NARAL** Pro-Choice America.*

Corporate
Accountability

Every year, states and cities spend more than $50 billion on subsidies—mostly tax incentives—for businesses. But few states have mechanisms to monitor the cost-effectiveness of tax expenditures, much less hold businesses accountable for promises of job creation.

Corporate Accountability

Summary

- Every year, states and cities spend more than $50 billion on subsidies—mostly tax incentives—for businesses.
- In recent years, states have significantly expanded their use of tax expenditures.
- Few states have mechanisms to monitor the cost-effectiveness of tax expenditures, much less hold businesses accountable for promises of job creation.
- Tax breaks costing more than $100,000 per job created are not unusual.
- Even those jobs created from tax expenditures often fail to meet any standard of good jobs.
- It is just plain good government and economic sense to ensure that tax expenditures are spent wisely and well.
- States, cities and counties are beginning to demand accountability for tax expenditures.
- Corporate accountability legislation ensures an annual assessment of the cost effectiveness of tax incentive programs.

Every year, states and cities spend more than $50 billion on subsidies—mostly tax incentives—for businesses.

The subsidies take many forms: corporate income tax credits, property tax abatements, low-interest loans, enterprise zones, tax increment financing, training grants, land and site preparation, and infrastructure. In return, companies promise economic development, especially the creation of new jobs.

In recent years, states have significantly expanded their use of tax expenditures.

In 1977, only nine states gave tax credits to businesses for research and development; now 36 states do. Only 13 states made loans for machinery and equipment; now 43 do. Only 20 states provided tax-free revenue bond loans; now 44 do. Only 21 states granted corporate income tax exemptions; now 37 do.

Few states have mechanisms to monitor the cost-effectiveness of tax expenditures, much less hold businesses accountable for promises of job creation.

In most states, it is currently not possible to calculate the cost-effectiveness of tax incentives. Moreover, once granted, measures initiated in the name of economic development are seldom audited or sunsetted, especially tax breaks.

Tax breaks costing more than $100,000 per job created are not unusual.

In those states where tax expenditure costs are disclosed, dozens of deals have been discovered in which subsidies exceed $100,000 per job created.[1] The ratio of dollars in tax subsidies to the actual number of jobs retained or created as the result of tax expenditures is often enormous.

Even those jobs created from tax expenditures often fail to meet any standard of good jobs.

When companies locate in economically underdeveloped areas, wages and benefits are often well below the state's median earnings. Moreover, tax breaks intended to help blighted urban areas are frequently diverted to suburbs. Programs such as tax increment financing and enterprise zones, originally created to reverse inner-city decline, have been stretched or deregulated so that even affluent suburbs can use them, often simply to pirate jobs from other jurisdictions in the same metropolitan area.[2]

It is just plain good government and economic sense to ensure that tax expenditures are spent wisely and well.

Citizens rely upon elected officials to be fiscally responsible with taxpayer dollars. Tax breaks and subsidies should be at least as well-scrutinized as line items in the state budget. But they are not.

While lawmakers hold public schools strictly accountable based upon test scores, and judge social services using cost and quality of service indicators, few states apply the same accountability standards to incentives such as sales tax exemptions, tax abatements, tax credits, and industrial revenue bonds.

States, cities and counties are beginning to demand accountability for tax expenditures.

In 2003, Illinois enacted a landmark corporate accountability law that catalogues all state subsidies, mandates extensive disclosure in applications for economic assistance, requires annual progress reports from companies that receive assistance, and provides for the recapture of tax credits from corporations that do not meet their obligations. In addition, at least 37 states and more than 80 cities and counties have attached some job quality standards—such as "living wages," health care benefits, and full-time hours—to incentives such as tax abatements, revenue bonds, and investment tax credits.[3] Job quality standards promote fiscal responsibility, since they help to avoid the phenomenon of taxpayers subsidizing poverty-level jobs with additional outlays such as food stamps, Medicaid and the Earned Income Tax Credit.

Corporate accountability legislation ensures an annual assessment of the cost effectiveness of tax incentive programs.

Model legislation based upon "corporate accountability" laws enacted in Illinois, Minnesota and Maine provides comprehensive accountability standards. The legislation gives policymakers and the public information about specific deals and overall programs. This legislation:

■ Requires an analysis of every kind of state expenditure for economic development.

■ Imposes disclosure requirements for annual, company-specific reports on each incentive deal, as well as company-specific disclosure of state corpo-

rate income tax credits (with small-business exceptions), as part of a comprehensive report on each state program, including both appropriations and tax expenditures.

■ Caps incentives at $35,000 per job, a level derived from two federal agencies, the Department of Housing and Urban Development and the Small Business Administration.

■ Mandates a market-based system of wage floors pegged at 85 percent of the market, with an extra 10 percent allowance for small businesses.

This policy summary relies in large part on information from Good Jobs First.

Endnotes

[1] Council of State Governments biannual survey.

[2] Good Jobs First, "Straying from Good Intentions: How States are Weakening Enterprise Zone and Tax Increment Financing Programs," August 2003.

[3] Good Jobs First, "The Policy Shift to Good Jobs," 2000.

Corporate Accountability

For more information...

Center for Policy Alternatives
1875 Connecticut Avenue NW, Suite 710
Washington, DC 20009
202-387-6030
www.stateaction.org

AFL-CIO
815 16th Street NW
Washington, DC 20006
202-637-5000
www.aflcio.org

Corporation for Enterprise Development:
Business Incentives Reform Clearinghouse
777 North Capitol Street NE, Suite 800
Washington, DC 20002
202-408-9788
www.cfed.org/main/econDev/bi/main/default.htm

Good Jobs First
1311 L Street NW
Washington, DC 20005
202-737-4315
www.ctj.org/itep/gjf.htm

Corporate Accountability

Economic Development and Corporate Accountability Act

SECTION 1. SHORT TITLE

This Act shall be called the "Economic Development and Corporate Accountability Act."

SECTION 2. FINDINGS AND PURPOSE

(A) FINDINGS—The legislature finds:

1. Although the state and its local government units have granted numerous economic development subsidies over the last 25 years, the real wage levels and healthcare coverage of working families have declined.

2. When workers receive low wages and poor benefits, such jobs often impose hidden costs on the state, in the form of Medicaid, food stamps, earned income tax credits, and other forms of public assistance to the working poor and their families.

3. Citizen participation in economic development has been impeded by a lack of readily accessible information regarding expenditures and outcomes.

4. It is necessary to collect, analyze and make public information regarding those expenditures for economic development, and to enact certain safeguards for their use.

(B) PURPOSE—This law is enacted to improve the effectiveness of economic development expenditures and to ensure that such expenditures raise living standards for working families.

SECTION 3. ECONOMIC DEVELOPMENT AND CORPORATE ACCOUNTABILITY

After section XXX, the following new section XXX shall be inserted:

(A) DEFINITIONS—In this section:

1. "Corporate parent" means any person, association, corporation, joint venture, partnership, or other entity, that owns or controls 50 percent or more of a recipient corporation.

2. "Date of subsidy" means the date that a granting body provides the initial monetary value of a development subsidy to a recipient corporation. If the subsidy is for the installation of new equipment, such date shall be the date the corporation puts the equipment into service. If the subsidy is for improvements to property, such date shall be the date the improvements are finished, or the date the corporation occupies the property, whichever is earlier.

3. "Development subsidy" means any expenditure of public funds with a value of at least $25,000, for the purpose of stimulating economic development within the state, including but not limited to bonds, grants, loans, loan guarantees, enterprise zones, empowerment zones, tax increment financing, grants, fee waivers, land price subsidies, matching funds, tax abatements, tax exemptions, and tax credits.

4. "Full-time job" means a job in which an individual is employed by a recipient corporation for at least 35 hours per week.

Corporate Accountability

5. "Granting body" means any agency, board, office, public benefit corporation, or authority of the state or local government unit that provides a development subsidy.

6. "Local government unit" means an agency, board, commission, office, public benefit corporation, or public authority of a political subdivision of the state.

7. "Part-time job" means a job in which an individual is employed by a recipient corporation for less than 35 hours per week.

8. "Project site" means the site of a project for which any development subsidy is provided.

9. "Property-taxing entity" means any entity which levies taxes upon real or personal property.

10. "Recipient corporation" means any person, association, corporation, joint venture, partnership, or other entity that receives a development subsidy.

11. "Small business" means a corporation whose corporate parent, and all subsidiaries thereof, employed fewer than 20 full-time employees, or had total gross receipts of less than $1 million during the previous calendar year.

12. "State" means an agency, board, commission, office, public benefit corporation, or public benefit authority of the state.

13. "Subsidy value" means the face value of any and all development subsidies provided to a recipient corporation.

14. "Temporary job" means a job in which an individual is hired for a season, or for a limited period of time.

(B) UNIFIED ECONOMIC DEVELOPMENT BUDGET

The [Department of Revenue] shall submit an annual Unified Economic Development Budget to the legislature no later than three months after the end of the state's fiscal year. The report shall present all types of expenditures for economic development during the prior fiscal year, including but not limited to:

1. The amount of uncollected state tax revenues resulting from every corporate tax credit, abatement, exemption and reduction provided by the state or a local governmental unit including but not limited to gross receipts, income, sales, use, raw materials, excise, property, utility, and inventory taxes.

2. The name of each corporate taxpayer which claimed any tax credit, abatement, exemption or reduction with a value of $5,000 or more, together with the dollar amount received by each such corporation.

3. Any tax credit, abatement, exemption or reduction received by a corporation of less than $5,000 each shall not be itemized. The [Department of Revenue] shall report an aggregate dollar amount of such expenditures and the number of companies so aggregated for each tax expenditure.

4. All state appropriated expenditures for economic development, including line-item budgets for every state-funded entity concerned with economic development, including but not limited to [list appropriate state agencies].

Corporate Accountability

(C) UNIFIED REPORTING OF PROPERTY TAX REDUCTIONS AND ABATEMENTS

1. Each property-taxing entity shall annually submit a report to the [Department of Revenue] regarding any real property in the entity's jurisdiction that has received a property tax abatement or reduction during the fiscal year. The report shall contain information including, but not limited to: the name of the property owner; the address of the property; the start and end dates of the property tax reduction or abatement; the schedule of the tax reduction; each tax abatement, reduction and exemption for the property; and the amount of property tax revenue not paid to the taxing entity as a result of the reduction or abatement.

2. Each property-taxing entity shall also submit a report to the [Department of Revenue] setting forth the total property tax revenue not paid to such entity during the fiscal year as a result of all property tax reductions and abatements in the entity's jurisdiction.

3. The reports required under paragraphs (1) and (2) shall be prepared on two forms approved by the [Department of Revenue], and shall be submitted to the Department by the property-taxing entity no later than three months after the end of the fiscal year.

4. The [Department of Revenue] shall annually compile and publish all of the data contained in the reports required under paragraphs (1) and (2) in both written and electronic form, including publication on the Department's website.

5. If a property-taxing entity fails to submit required reports to the [Department of Revenue] within the prescribed time, the Department shall notify the [Comptroller], whereupon the [Comptroller] shall withhold further payments of any development subsidy to the delinquent entity until the entity files its reports with the Department.

(D) APPLICATION FOR ECONOMIC DEVELOPMENT SUBSIDIES

1. A development subsidy applicant shall complete an application for the subsidy on a form prepared by the [Department of Economic Development]. The information required on the application shall include the following:

    a. An application tracking number provided by the granting agency for the project.
    b. The name, street and mailing address, and phone number of the chief officer of the granting body provided by the granting agency.
    c. The name, street and mailing address, and phone number of the chief officer of the applicant's corporate parent.
    d. The name, street and mailing address, and phone number of the chief officer of the applicant.
    e. The street address of the project site.
    f. The three-digit North American Industry Classification System number of the project site.
    g. The total number of individuals employed by the applicant at the project site on the date of the application, broken down by full-time, part-time, and temporary positions;
    h. The total number of individuals employed in the state by the applicant's corporate parent, and all subsidiaries thereof, as of December 31 of the prior fiscal year, broken down by full-time, part-time and temporary positions.
    i. The development subsidy or subsidies being applied for with the granting body, and the value of such subsidy or subsidies.
    j. The number of new jobs to be created by the applicant at the project site, broken down by full-time, part-time, and temporary positions.

Corporate Accountability

k. The average hourly wage to be paid to all current and new employees at the project site, broken down by full-time, part-time, and temporary positions, and further broken down by wage groups as follows: $6.00 or less an hour, $6.01 to $7.00 an hour, $7.01 to $8.00 an hour, $8.01 to $9.00 an hour, $9.01 to $10.00 an hour, $10.01 to $11.00 an hour, $11.01 to $12.00 an hour, $12.01 to $13.00 an hour, $13.01 to $14.00 an hour, and $14.01 or more per hour.

l. For project sites located in a Metropolitan Statistical Area, as defined by the federal Office of Management and Budget, the average hourly wage paid to non-managerial employees in the State for the industries involved at the project, as established by the U.S. Bureau of Labor Statistics.

m. For project sites located outside of Metropolitan Statistical Areas, the average weekly wage paid to non-managerial employees in the county for industries involved at the project, as established by the U.S. Department of Commerce.

n. The type and amount of health care coverage to be provided by the applicant within ninety days of commencement of employment at the project site, including any costs to be borne by the employees.

o. A list of all development subsidies that the applicant is requesting, and the name of any other granting body from which such subsidies are sought.

p. A statement as to whether the development subsidy may reduce employment at any other site controlled by the applicant or its corporate parent, within or without of the state, resulting from automation, merger, acquisition, corporate restructuring, or other business activity.

q. A statement as to whether or not the project involves the relocation of work from another address and if so, the number of full-time, part-time and temporary jobs to be relocated, and the address from which they are to be relocated.

r. A certification by the chief officer of the applicant as to the accuracy of the application.

2. If the granting body shall approve the application, it shall send a copy to the [Department of Economic Development] within 15 days of such approval. If the application is not approved, the granting body shall retain the application in its records.

(E) ANNUAL REPORTS

1. Each granting body shall file a progress report with the [Department of Economic Development] for each project for which a development subsidy has been granted, no later than February 1 each year. The report shall include the following information:

a. The application tracking number.

b. The name, street and mailing addresses, phone number, and chief officer of the granting body.

c. The name, street and mailing addresses, phone number, and chief officer of the recipient corporation.

d. A summary of the number of jobs required, created and lost, broken down by full-time, part-time and temporary positions, and by wage groups as defined in (D)(1)(k).

e. The type and amount of healthcare coverage provided to the employees at the project site, including any costs borne by the employees.

f. The comparison of the total employment in the state by the recipient's corporate parent on the date of the application and the date of the report, broken down by full-time, part-time and temporary positions;

g. A statement as to whether the use of the development subsidy during the previous fiscal year reduced employment at any other site controlled by the recipient corporation or its corporate parent, within or outside of the state as a result of automation, merger, acquisition, corporate restructuring or other business activity.

h. A signed certification by the chief officer of the recipient corporation as to the accuracy of the progress report.

2. On all subsequent annual progress reports, the granting body shall indicate whether the recipient corporation is still in compliance with its job creation, wage, and benefit goals, and whether the corporate parent is still in compliance with its state employment requirement.

Corporate Accountability

3. Granting bodies and recipient corporations shall file annual progress reports for the duration of the subsidy, or not less than five years, whichever period is greater.

(F) TWO YEAR-REPORT

1. No later than 15 days after the second anniversary of the date of subsidy, the granting body shall file a two-year progress report with the [Department of Economic Development], and include the same information as required under section (E). The recipient corporation shall certify as to the accuracy of such report.

2. The granting body shall state in the two-year report whether the recipient corporation has achieved its job creation, wage, and benefit goals, and whether the corporate parent has maintained 90 percent of its employment in the state.

3. The [Department of Economic Development] shall compile and publish all data from the progress reports in both written and electronic form, including publication on the Department's website.

4. The granting body and the [Department of Economic Development] shall have access at all reasonable times to the project site and the records of the recipient corporation in order to monitor the project and to prepare progress reports.

5. A recipient corporation that fails to provide the granting body with the information or access required under this section shall be subject to a fine of not less than $500 per day to commence within 10 working days after the February 1 deadline, and of not less than $1,000 per day to commence 20 days after such deadline.

(G) SUBSIDY LIMIT AND JOB QUALITY STANDARDS

1. A granting body shall not award a development subsidy if the cost per job is greater than $35,000. Such cost shall be determined by dividing the amount of the subsidy by the number of full-time jobs required under the application approved by the granting body.

2. A granting body shall not grant a subsidy to an applicant unless the wages paid to employees at the project site are equal to or exceed 85 percent of the average wage as established under paragraphs (D)(1)(l) and (D)(1)(m), provided, however, that for small businesses, the average wage must equal or exceed 75 percent of the wages established thereunder. The computation of wages under this section shall only apply to a recipient corporation that provides the health care coverage as approved in its application by the granting body.

(H) RECAPTURE

1. A recipient corporation shall fulfill its job creation, wage, healthcare and other benefit requirements for the project site within two years of the date of subsidy. Such recipient shall maintain its wage and benefit goals as long as the subsidy is in effect, or five years, whichever is longer.

2. The corporate parent of a recipient corporation must maintain at least 90 percent of its employment in the state as long as the development subsidy is in effect, or not less than five years, whichever is longer.

Corporate Accountability

3. If the requirements under paragraphs (1) or (2) are not fulfilled, the granting body shall recapture the development subsidy from the recipient corporation as follows:

a. Upon a failure by the recipient corporation to create the required number of jobs, or to pay the required wages or benefits, the amount recaptured shall be based on the pro rata amount by which the unfulfilled jobs, wages or benefits bear to the total amount of the development subsidy.
b. Upon a failure of the corporate parent to maintain 90 percent of its employment in the State, the rate of recapture shall equal twice the percentage by which such employment is less than 90 percent.

4. The granting body shall provide notice and explanation to the recipient corporation of its intent to recapture the development subsidy and state the amount to be recaptured. The recipient corporation shall remit to the governing body such amount within 60 calendar days of the date of such notice.

5. If a recipient corporation defaults on a development subsidy in three consecutive calendar years, the granting body shall declare the subsidy null and void, and shall so notify the [Department of Economic Development] and the recipient corporation. The recipient corporation shall pay back to the granting body all remaining value of the development subsidy it has not previously repaid within 180 calendar days of the date of the notice of such default.

(I) PRIVATE ENFORCEMENT ACTION

If a granting body fails to enforce any provision of this section, any individual who paid personal income taxes to the state in the calendar year prior to the year in dispute, or any organization representing such taxpayers, shall be entitled to bring a civil action in state court to compel enforcement under this statute. The court shall award reasonable attorney's fees and costs to such prevailing taxpayer or organization.

(J) PUBLIC RECORD DISCLOSURE

All records required to be prepared or maintained under this section, including but not limited to applications, progress reports, recapture notices, and any other records or proceedings relating thereto, shall be subject to disclosure under the [state's open records act, cite appropriate section].

(K) NO REDUCTION IN WAGES

Nothing in this section shall be construed to require or authorize a recipient corporation to reduce wages established by any collective bargaining agreement or state or federal prevailing wage laws.

SECTION 4. SEVERABILITY

The provisions of this Act shall be severable, and if any phrase, clause, sentence, or provision is declared to be invalid or is preempted by federal law or regulation, the validity of the remainder of this Act shall not be affected.

SECTION 5. EFFECTIVE DATE

This act shall take effect on July 1, 2004.

Death Penalty -
Juveniles

The United States has the dubious distinction of being the world's leader in executing juvenile offenders. States should stop this practice, which violates widely accepted international human rights law.

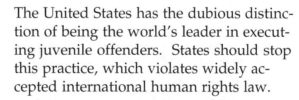

Death Penalty - Juveniles

Summary

- Since the death penalty was reinstated in 1976, 22 juvenile offenders have been executed, and 75 await execution on death row.
- Twenty-two states permit the execution of juvenile offenders, yet Texas has executed nearly two-thirds of all juvenile offenders put to death since 1977.
- There is a striking racial disparity in the application of capital punishment to juvenile offenders.
- The United States is the only industrialized country–and one of only three countries in the world–that continues to execute juvenile offenders.
- Juveniles who commit violent crimes are not fully competent, and should not be subject to capital punishment.
- The American public strongly opposes the execution of juveniles.
- States are acting to stop the execution of juveniles.

Since the death penalty was reinstated in 1976, 22 juvenile offenders have been executed, and 75 await execution on death row.

Every juvenile offender sentenced to death was adjudged in a state court. There is no death penalty for juvenile offenders under federal law.[1]

Twenty-two states permit the execution of juvenile offenders, yet Texas has executed nearly two-thirds of all juvenile offenders put to death since 1977.

More than one-third of all juvenile offenders on death row are in Texas prisons, and more than one third of those were convicted in a single county. Outside Texas, the execution of juvenile offenders is a rare practice.

There is a striking racial disparity in the application of the death penalty to juvenile offenders.

In the 20th century, nearly 75 percent of those executed for childhood offenses were African American. Since 1976, 60 percent of those sentenced to death for childhood offenses have been either African American or Latino, even though these racial groups make up only 12.7 percent and 11.2 percent of the juvenile population, respectively. Of the 75 juvenile offenders currently on death row, approximately two-thirds are persons of color.

The United States is the only industrialized country–and one of only three countries in the world–that continues to execute juvenile offenders.

The United States has the dubious distinction of being the world's leader in executing juvenile offenders. Executing juvenile offenders is legal in only five countries, including the United States, Iran and the Republic of Congo. While it remains legal in Saudi Arabia and Nigeria, these countries have not executed a juvenile offender in years. Over the past decade, three countries have abolished the juvenile death penalty altogether – Yemen in 1994, China in 1997, and Pakistan in 2000. Capital punishment for juvenile offenders violates widely accepted international human rights law.

Juveniles who commit violent crimes are not fully competent, and should not be subject to capital punishment.

Recent medical research demonstrates that the portion of the brain that governs an individual's impulse control and judgment does not fully develop until that person is between 18 and 22 years old. A study conducted by the Harvard University Medical Center shows that the frontal and pre-frontal lobes of the brain, which regulate impulse control and judgment, are the last to develop. According to the study, "the very brain system necessary for inhibition and goal-directed behavior comes 'on board' last, and is not fully operational until early adulthood (about 18-22 years)."[2]

The American public strongly opposes the execution of juveniles.

According to a May 2002 Gallup Poll, 69 percent of Americans oppose the execution of juvenile offenders.

States are acting to stop the execution of juveniles.

In 2002, Indiana enacted legislation barring the execution of juveniles. Montana enacted similar legislation in 1999. In addition, the Missouri Supreme Court ruled in 2003 that executing juvenile offenders is unconstitutional, and the Florida Supreme Court ruled in 1999 that the execution of a person who was 16 at the time of his crime is "cruel and unusual."

This policy summary relies in large part on information from the National Coalition to Abolish the Death Penalty.

Endnotes

[1] Death Penalty Information Center, Juveniles and the Death Penalty, July 2002.

[2] Dr. Ruben Gur, "Adolescent Brain Development and Legal Culpability," 2003.

Death Penalty - Juveniles

For more information...

Center for Policy Alternatives
1875 Connecticut Avenue NW, Suite 710
Washington, DC 20009
202-387-6030
www.stateaction.org

American Bar Association
541 N. Fairbanks Court
Chicago, IL 60611
312-988-5522
www.abanet.org/crimjust/juvjus/
juvdp.html

American Civil Liberties Union
125 Broad Street, 18th Floor
New York, NY 10004
212-549-2500
www.aclu.org

Amnesty International USA
Program to Abolish the Death Penalty
600 Pennsylvania Avenue SE, 5th Floor
Washington, DC 20003
202-544-0200
www.aiusa.org/abolish

Campaign for Criminal Justice Reform
1725 Eye Street NW, 4th Floor
Washington, DC 20006
202-638-5855
www.cjreform.org

Citizens United for Alternatives to the Death Penalty
PMB 297, 177 U.S. Hwy #1
Tequesta, FL 33469
800-973-6548
www.cuadp.org

Coalition for Juvenile Justice
2030 M Street NW, Suite 701
Washington, DC 20036
202-467-0864
www.juvjustice.org

Death Penalty Information Center
1320 18th Street NW, 5th Floor
Washington, DC 20036
202-293-6970
www.deathpenaltyinfo.org

Equal Justice USA/Moratorium Now!
P.O. Box 5206
Hyattsville, MD 20782
301-699-0042
www.quixote.org/ej

National Coalition to Abolish the Death Penalty
1436 U Street NW, Suite 104
Washington, DC 20009
888-286-2237
www.ncadp.org

Death Penalty - Juveniles

Juvenile Protection Act

SECTION 1. SHORT TITLE

This Act shall be called the "Juvenile Protection Act."

SECTION 2. ABOLITION OF THE DEATH PENALTY FOR JUVENILE OFFENDERS

After section XXX, the following new section XXX shall be inserted:

If the person was less than 18 years of age at the time the crime was committed, the maximum punishment shall be life imprisonment without possibility of parole.

SECTION 3. COMMUTATION OF DEATH SENTENCES FOR JUVENILE OFFENDERS

If a person has been sentenced to death for a crime that was committed when that person was less than 18 years of age, the sentence shall be commuted to life imprisonment without possibility of parole.

SECTION 4. EFFECTIVE DATE

This Act shall take effect on July 1, 2004.

Death Penalty Reform

Dozens of innocent people have been sentenced to death in recent years. States have options to address this injustice: reduce the risk that innocent persons may be executed by providing a DNA safeguard in capital cases, and/or suspend the operation of the death penalty while a commission studies its fairness.

Death Penalty Reform

Summary

- In recent years, dozens of innocent people have been sentenced to death. Between 1977 and 2003, more than 110 people were released from death rows in at least 25 states because of significant evidence of innocence.
- Since 1976, when the U.S. Supreme Court reinstated the death penalty, innocence and wrongful convictions have required the release of one person from death row for every seven executed.
- From 1900-91, at least 400 innocent people were placed on death row, and at least 23 of them were executed.
- Minority defendants are more frequently convicted in capital cases and are executed in disproportionate numbers.
- Two states have implemented death penalty moratoriums.
- In 2003, eight states enacted laws guaranteeing DNA testing.
- While the public has supported capital punishment in theory, Americans now object to it in practice.

In recent years, dozens of innocent people have been sentenced to death. Between 1977 and 2003, more than 110 people were released from death rows in at least 25 states because of significant evidence of innocence.[1]

For example:

■ In 2003, a jury took less than an hour to acquit John Thompson at his retrial for a New Orleans murder. Thompson was sentenced to death in 1985. Just five weeks before his scheduled execution, Thompson's attorney discovered blood analysis evidence that had been withheld by prosecutors, which ultimately led to the retrial and acquittal.

■ In 2003, Florida death row inmate Rudolph Holton was released from prison after spending 16 years on death row. His release followed DNA tests that contradicted a prosecution witness, and a circuit court ruling that the state had withheld evidence that pointed to another perpetrator.

■ In 2002, Ray Krone was released from death row by the state of Arizona after DNA tests confirmed his innocence.

■ In 2001, charges were dropped against Charles Irvin Fain, a Vietnam veteran who spent over 18 years on Idaho's death row. He was released after new forensic tests contradicted an expert's testimony at trial that hairs found on the victim's body were Fain's.

■ In 2000, Virginia Governor James Gilmore pardoned Earl Washington after DNA testing found no trace of him at the scene of the murder for which he was convicted. "We came breathtakingly close to executing a man who wasn't guilty of the crime," said State Senator Janet Howell.

Since 1976, when the U.S. Supreme Court reinstated the death penalty, innocence and wrongful convictions have required the release of one person from death row for every seven executed.

The releases were not due to a system that works; rather, many of the released proved their innocence only thanks to unpaid lawyers and activists.

At least 23 innocent people were executed in the United States during the 20th century.

There were more than 400 known cases of wrongful conviction for capital offenses in the U.S. between 1900 and 1991, according to Amnesty International. Most of the convictions were upheld on appeal, and evidence proving defendants' innocence emerged years after sentencing. But at least 23 individuals were executed before exonerating evidence surfaced.

Minority defendants are more frequently convicted in capital cases and are executed in disproportionate numbers.

A study by two of the country's foremost researchers on race and capital punishment, law professor David Baldus and statistician George Woodworth, revealed that the odds of receiving a death sentence are nearly four times higher if the defendant is black. These results were obtained after analyzing and controlling for case differences, such as the severity of the crime and the background of the defendant.

Two states have implemented death penalty moratoriums.

Illinois Governor George Ryan paved the way for much of the reform work in the states. When he implemented the first statewide moratorium on executions in January 2000, after Illinois had executed 12 men and freed 13 innocent men from death row since reinstating the death penalty in 1976. In 2002, Maryland Governor Parris Glendening followed suit, implementing a moratorium so that a study could be conducted on the fairness of sentencing practices with a specific focus on racial disparities. Despite the study's conclusion that Maryland's death penalty system is clouded by racial and geographic bias, Glendening's successor lifted the moratorium, and executions may resume in 2004.

In 2003, eight states enacted laws to guarantee DNA testing.

Implementing a variety of procedures, CO, CT, GA, IL, MT, NV, NM and OH acted in 2003 to allow some inmates access to DNA testing in order to establish their innocence. AR, FL, MD, PA, TX and VA enacted similar laws in 2001-02.

The Innocence Protection Act would reduce the risk that innocent persons are executed.

It would provide a safeguard in capital punishment cases by:

■ Allowing prisoners on death row to request DNA testing of evidence in the government's possession.

■ Ensuring that wrongfully convicted persons have an opportunity to establish their innocence through DNA testing, and requiring the preservation of DNA evidence.

The Death Penalty Moratorium Act would suspend executions while a commission studies the system's fairness.

Specifically, it would:

■ Appoint a commission to study all aspects of the state's death penalty. The commission would make a preliminary report within one year, and a final report within two years.

■ Place a moratorium on executions until the commission reports its findings and the legislature responds to them.

While the public has supported capital punishment in theory, Americans now object to it in practice.

■ Americans believe innocent people have been executed. A May 2003 Gallup poll found that 73 percent of Americans believe that an innocent person has been executed within the past five years. Only 22 percent believe no wrongful execution has happened.

■ Americans strongly support a suspension of the death penalty. A March 2001 Hart Research poll found that 72 percent of the public favored "a suspension of the death penalty until questions about its fairness can be studied." Only 20 percent opposed.

■ The same poll reported that 91 percent agreed states should "give convicted persons on death row the opportunity to have DNA tests conducted in order to prove their innocence." Only two percent disagreed. Americans overwhelmingly believe death row inmates should have the right to use DNA testing to prove their innocence.

Endnotes

[1] Death Penalty Information Center, "Innocence and the Death Penalty," 2003.

Death Penalty Reform

For more information...

Center for Policy Alternatives
1875 Connecticut Avenue NW, Suite 710
Washington, DC 20009
202-387-6030
www.stateaction.org

American Bar Association
541 N. Fairbanks Court
Chicago, IL 60611
312-988-5522
www.abanet.org

American Civil Liberties Union
125 Broad Street, 18th Floor
New York, NY 10004
212-549-2500
www.aclu.org

Amnesty International USA
Program to Abolish the Death Penalty
600 Pennsylvania Avenue SE, 5th Floor
Washington, DC 20003
202-544-0200
www.amnestyusa.org/abolish

Campaign for Criminal Justice Reform
1725 Eye Street NW, 4th Floor
Washington, DC 20006
202-638-5855
www.cjreform.org

Citizens United for Alternatives to the Death Penalty
PMB 297, 177 U.S. Hwy #1
Tequesta, FL 33469
800-973-6548
www.cuadp.org

Death Penalty Focus
870 Market Street, Suite 859
San Francisco, CA 94102
888-2-Abolish (888-222-6547)
415-243-0143
www.deathpenalty.org

Death Penalty Information Center
1320 18th Street NW, 5th Floor
Washington, DC 20036
202-293-6970
www.deathpenaltyinfo.org

Equal Justice USA/Moratorium Now!
P.O. Box 5206
Hyattsville, MD 20782
301-699-0042
www.quixote.org/ej

Human Rights Watch
350 Fifth Avenue, 34th Floor
New York, NY 10118
212-290-4700
www.hrw.org

Murder Victims' Families for Reconciliation
2161 Massachusetts Avenue
Cambridge, MA 02140
617-868-0007
www.mvfr.org

National Coalition to Abolish the Death Penalty
920 Pennsylvania Avenue SE
Washington, DC 20003
888-286-2237
www.ncadp.org

Southern Center for Human Rights
83 Poplar Street NW
Atlanta, GA 30303
404-688-1202
www.schr.org

Death Penalty Reform

Innocence Protection Act

SECTION 1. SHORT TITLE

This Act shall be called the "Innocence Protection Act."

SECTION 2. FINDINGS AND PURPOSE

(A) FINDINGS - The legislature finds that:

1. Over the past decade, deoxyribonucleic acid testing (referred to in this section as "DNA testing") has emerged as the most reliable forensic technique for identifying criminals when biological materials are left at a crime scene.

2. Because of its scientific precision, DNA testing can, in some cases, conclusively establish the guilt or innocence of a criminal defendant. In other cases, DNA testing may not conclusively establish guilt or innocence, but may have significant probative value to a judge or jury.

3. While DNA testing is increasingly commonplace in pretrial investigations today, it was not widely available in cases tried prior to 1994. Moreover, new forensic DNA testing procedures have made it possible to obtain results from minute samples that could not previously be tested, and to obtain more informative and accurate results than earlier forms of forensic DNA testing could produce. Consequently, convicted inmates have been exonerated by new DNA tests after earlier tests had failed to produce definitive results.

4. Since DNA testing is often feasible on relevant biological material that is decades old, it can, in some circumstances, prove that a conviction that predated the development of DNA testing was based upon incorrect factual findings. Uniquely, DNA evidence showing innocence, produced decades after a conviction, provides a more reliable basis for establishing a correct verdict than any evidence proffered at the original trial. DNA testing, therefore, can and has resulted in the post-conviction exoneration of innocent Americans.

5. In the past decade, there have been more than 100 post-conviction exonerations in the United States and Canada based upon DNA testing. At least 11 individuals sentenced to death have been exonerated through post-conviction DNA testing, some of whom came within days of being executed.

6. The advent of DNA testing raises serious concerns regarding the prevalence of wrongful convictions, especially wrongful convictions arising out of mistaken eyewitness identification testimony. According to a 1996 Department of Justice study titled "Convicted by Juries, Exonerated by Science: Case Studies of Post-Conviction DNA Exonerations," in approximately 20-30 percent of the cases referred for DNA testing, the results excluded the primary suspect. Without DNA testing, many of these individuals might have been wrongfully convicted.

7. If biological material is not subjected to DNA testing in appropriate cases, a significant risk exists that persuasive evidence of innocence will not be detected and, accordingly, that innocent persons will be unconstitutionally incarcerated or executed.

8. There is also a compelling need to ensure the preservation of biological material for post-conviction DNA testing. Since 1992, the Innocence Project at the Benjamin N. Cardozo School of Law has studied inmates' claims that DNA testing could prove them innocent. In over 70 percent of those cases in which DNA testing could have been dispositive if the biological material were available, the material had been destroyed or lost. In two-thirds of the cases in which the evidence was found, and DNA testing conducted, the results have exonerated the inmate.

9. In at least 14 cases, post-conviction DNA testing that exonerated a wrongly convicted person also provided evidence leading to the apprehension of the actual perpetrator, thereby enhancing public safety. This would not have been possible if the biological evidence had been destroyed.

(B) PURPOSE - This law is enacted by the legislature to ensure the availability of DNA testing in appropriate cases and ensure that wrongfully convicted persons have an opportunity to establish their innocence

Death Penalty Reform

through DNA testing, by requiring the preservation of DNA evidence.

SECTION 3. DNA TESTING
After section XXX, the following new section XXX shall be inserted:

(A) APPLICATION - Notwithstanding any other provision of law, a person in custody pursuant to the judgment of a court of this state may, at any time after conviction, apply to the court that entered the judgment for forensic DNA testing of:
1. Biological material related to the investigation or prosecution that resulted in the judgment.
2. Biological material in the actual or constructive possession of the state.
3. Biological material not previously subjected to DNA testing, or which can be subjected to retesting with new DNA techniques that provide a reasonable likelihood of more accurate and probative results.

(B) NOTICE TO GOVERNMENT
1. The court shall notify the state of an application made under subsection (A) and shall afford the state an opportunity to respond.
2. Upon receiving notice of an application for DNA testing, the state shall ensure that any remaining biological material secured in connection with the case is preserved pending the completion of proceedings under this section.
3. The court shall order DNA testing upon a determination that an applicant's testing may produce noncumulative, exculpatory evidence relevant to the applicant's claim of wrongful conviction or sentence.

(C) COST - The cost of DNA testing ordered under subsection (B)(3) shall be borne by the state or the applicant, as the court may order in the interests of justice, if it is shown that the applicant is not indigent and possesses the means to pay.

(D) COUNSEL - The court may at any time appoint counsel for an indigent applicant.

(E) POST-TESTING PROCEDURES
1. If the results of DNA testing conducted under this section are unfavorable to the applicant, the court shall:
    a. Dismiss the application.
    b. In the case of an applicant who is not indigent, the court may assess the applicant for the cost of such testing.
2. If the results of DNA testing conducted under this section are favorable to the applicant, the court shall:
    a. Order a hearing, notwithstanding any provision of law that would bar such a hearing.
    b. Enter any order that serves the interests of justice, including orders vacating and setting aside the judgment, discharging the applicant if the applicant is in custody, resentencing the applicant, or granting a new trial.

(F) RULE OF CONSTRUCTION - Nothing in this section shall be construed to limit the circumstances under which a person may obtain DNA testing or other post-conviction relief under any other provision of law.

(G) PRESERVATION OF BIOLOGICAL MATERIAL - Notwithstanding any other provision of law, the state shall preserve any biological material secured in connection with a criminal case for such period of time as any person remains incarcerated in connection with that case.

SECTION 4. EFFECTIVE DATE—This act shall take effect on July 1, 2004.

Death Penalty Moratorium Act

SECTION 1. SHORT TITLE

This Act shall be called the "Death Penalty Moratorium Act."

SECTION 2. FINDINGS AND PURPOSE

(A) FINDINGS - The legislature finds that:
1. The administration of the death penalty should be consistent with the state's fundamental principles of justice, equality and due process.
2. The fairness of the administration of the death penalty, however, has recently come under serious scrutiny, specifically raising questions of racial disparity [details specific to your state here].

(B) PURPOSE - This law is enacted by the legislature to ensure fairness in the operation of the state's death penalty and guarantee that innocent persons are not put to death.

SECTION 3. DEATH PENALTY MORATORIUM

After section XXX, the following new section XXX shall be inserted:
The state shall not carry out any sentence of death imposed under state law until the legislature considers the final findings and recommendations of the Commission on the Death Penalty in the report submitted under section 4, and enacts legislation repealing this section and implementing or rejecting the guidelines and procedures recommended by the Commission.

SECTION 4. COMMISSION ON THE DEATH PENALTY

(A) ESTABLISHMENT- There is established a commission to be known as the Commission on the Death Penalty (in this title referred to as the "Commission").

(B) MEMBERSHIP
1. Members of the Commission shall be appointed by the Governor in consultation with the President of the Senate and the Speaker of the House.
2. The Commission shall be composed of 15 members, of whom-
    a. Three members shall be state prosecutors.
    b. Three members shall be attorneys experienced in capital defense.
    c. Two members shall be current or former state judges.
    d. Two members shall be current or former state law enforcement officials.
    e. Five members shall be individuals from the public or private sector who have knowledge or expertise, whether by experience or training, in matters to be studied by the Commission, which may include:
        (i) Officers or employees of the state or local governments.
        (ii) Members of academia, nonprofit organizations, the religious community, or business.
        (iii) Other interested individuals.
3. In appointing the members of the Commission, the Governor shall, to the maximum extent practicable, ensure that the membership of the Commission is fairly balanced with respect to the opinions of the members of the Commission regarding support for or opposition to the use of the death penalty.
4. The appointments of the initial members of the Commission shall be made not later than 30 days after the date of enactment of this Act.

Death Penalty Reform

5. The Governor shall designate one member appointed under subsection (B)(1) to serve as the Chair of the Commission.

6. Members shall be appointed for the life of the Commission. Any vacancy in the Commission shall not affect its powers, but shall be filled in the same manner as the original appointment.

7. Not later than 30 days after all initial members of the Commission have been appointed, the Commission shall hold its first meeting.

8. The Commission shall meet at the call of the Chair.

9. A majority of the members of the Commission shall constitute a quorum for conducting business, but a lesser number of members may hold hearings.

(C) RULES AND PROCEDURES - The Commission shall adopt rules and procedures to govern its proceedings.

SECTION 5. DUTIES OF THE COMMISSION

(A) IN GENERAL - The Commission shall conduct a thorough study of all matters relating to the administration of the death penalty at the state level to determine whether it comports with constitutional principles and requirements of fairness, justice, equality and due process.

(B) MATTERS STUDIED - The matters studied by the Commission shall include the following:

1. Racial disparities in capital charging, prosecuting and sentencing decisions.

2. Disproportionality in capital charging, prosecuting and sentencing decisions based on, or in correlation to, the geographic location and income status of defendant, or any other factor resulting in such disproportionality.

3. Adequacy of representation of capital defendants, including consideration of the American Bar Association "Guidelines for the Appointment and Performance of Counsel in Death Penalty Cases" (adopted February 1989) and Association policies intended to encourage competency of counsel in capital cases (adopted February 1979, February 1988, February 1990, and August 1996).

4. Whether innocent persons have been sentenced to death, and the reasons the wrongful convictions have occurred.

5. Procedures to ensure that persons sentenced to death have access to forensic evidence and modern testing of such evidence, including DNA testing, when such testing could result in new evidence of innocence.

6. Any other law or procedure to ensure that death penalty cases are administered fairly and impartially, in accordance with the state Constitution.

(C) REPORT

1. Not later than one year after the date of enactment of this Act, the Commission shall submit a preliminary report to the Governor and the legislature containing a preliminary statement of findings and conclusions.

2. Not later than two years after the date of enactment of this Act, the Commission shall submit a report to the Governor and the legislature containing a detailed statement of its findings and conclusions, together with its recommendations for legislative and administrative actions.

SECTION 6. EFFECTIVE DATE—This Act shall take effect on July 1, 2004.

Earned Income
Tax Credit

The Earned Income Tax Credit (EITC) is the most effective anti-poverty program in America, helping more working parents and children move out of poverty than any other government assistance program.

Earned Income Tax Credit

Summary

- **Nearly one in six American children live in poverty.**
- **The worsening economy will increase rates of poverty among American families.**
- **The federal Earned Income Tax Credit (EITC) was created in 1975 to provide tax relief to low-income workers and is now the most effective anti-poverty program in America.**
- **Most of the federal EITC's benefits are targeted toward families with children.**
- **The EITC has only recently gained momentum at the state level.**
- **State EITCs are good policy, administratively efficient, non-bureaucratic, and enjoy bipartisan support.**
- **State EITCs enhance economic security and promote economic opportunity for low-income working families.**

Nearly one in six American children live in poverty.

While welfare reform has been hailed as a success, former welfare recipients and other low-income Americans often earn wages at or below the poverty level at their new jobs—not nearly enough to support a family. In the current economic downturn, the financial position of low-income families will only worsen.

The federal Earned Income Tax Credit (EITC) was created in 1975 to support low-income workers.

The program was expanded in 1986, 1990, 1993 and most recently in 2001, and has now become a central part of federal efforts to fight poverty and move Americans from welfare to work. Only wage-earners qualify for this program, and the value of the tax credit depends on a worker's income and family size. Workers who earn around the minimum wage benefit the most from EITCs.

Most of the federal EITC's benefits are targeted toward families with children.

In tax year 2003, qualifying families with two or more children could receive up to $4,204 and families with one child up to $2,547. Workers with no dependent children are only eligible to receive a maximum of $382 from the federal EITC.

The federal program is a "refundable" credit. That means that if a credit exceeds a family's total income tax liability, the difference is paid to the family as a refund.

If a family doesn't earn enough to owe income tax, it receives a check based on its annual household income. Twelve states and the District of Columbia offer a refundable credit that is a percentage of the federal EITC, while four states have less effective "non-refundable" EITC statutes. In those states, the credit can erase tax liability, but the poorest wage earners, those with incomes too low to owe any state income taxes, receive no state benefit at all.

The EITC has only recently gained momentum at the state level.

Of the 16 states and the District of Columbia which currently have an EITC, eleven states and DC adopted or substantially increased EITCs since 2000. In 2003, Illinois made its EITC both refundable and permanent.

State EITCs are both good policy and good politics:

■ EITCs address economic crisis.

In an economic downturn, low and moderate-income families are the most likely to be hit with layoffs or reductions in work hours. A state EITC provides tax relief to Americans who are most in need.

■ EITCs are proven to reduce poverty.

The federal EITC helps more working parents and children move out of poverty than any other government program. According to Census Bureau data, the federal EITC lifts 4.7 million people out of poverty annually, including more than 2.7 million children. Adding a state EITC helps offset the high costs of health care, child care, housing, and other necessities of life.

■ **EITCs complement welfare reform.**

At its maximum, the federal EITC pays working poor families 40 cents for every dollar earned. State EITCs, combined with federal credits, increase the incentive for individuals to move from welfare to work.

■ **EITCs are finely targeted and effective in reaching the working poor and near-poor.**

The program puts extra dollars directly into the pockets of people who need help the most—those who are working for poverty-level wages. According to one estimate, 85 percent of those eligible for the credit apply for it.

■ **EITCs are administratively simple, efficient and non-bureaucratic.**

Because it is a fairly straightforward tax credit, the EITC is simple to administer. Nearly all of the funds spent on EITC programs go to workers who need the money, rather than government administration costs.

■ **EITCs garner bipartisan support.**

The federal EITC was enacted during the presidency of Gerald Ford and expanded under the Reagan, Clinton and both Bush administrations. Similarly, state EITC programs have been created by governments led by both Democrats and Republicans, and supported by both business groups and social service advocates.

State EITCs enhance economic security and promote economic opportunity for low-income working families.

Emerging research shows that many EITC recipients use their EITC refunds not only to meet day-to-day expenses but also to make the kind of investments that enhance economic security and promote economic opportunity—paying off debt, investing in education, and obtaining decent housing. States are increasingly recognizing the important effects EITCs can have on low-wage workers.

STATE EARNED INCOME TAX CREDITS BASED ON THE FEDERAL EITC

State	Percentage of the Federal EITC
Refundable Credits:	
Colorado	10% (suspended for 2003)
District of Columbia	25%
Illinois	5%
Indiana	6%
Kansas	15%
Maryland*	18% in 2003, 20% thereafter
Massachusetts	15%
Minnesota	Varies with earnings, averages 33%
New Jersey	20% if income is under $20,000
New York	30%
Oklahoma	5%
Vermont	32%
Wisconsin	4% - one child, 14% - two children, 43% - three children
Non-Refundable Credits:	
Iowa	6.5%
Maine	5%
Oregon	5%
Rhode Island**	25%

* Maryland also offers a non-refundable EITC set at 50 percent of the credit. Taxpayers may claim either the refundable credit or the non-refundable credit, but not both.
** A very small portion of the Rhode Island EITC was made refundable effective in 2003.

Source: Center on Budget and Policy Priorities.

This policy summary relies in large part on information from the Center on Budget and Policy Priorities.

Earned Income Tax Credit

For more information...

Center for Policy Alternatives
1875 Connecticut Avenue NW, Suite 710
Washington, DC 20009
202-387-6030
www.stateaction.org

Center on Budget and Policy Priorities
820 First Street NE, Suite 510
Washington, DC 20002
202-408-1080
www.cbpp.org

Economic Policy Institute
1660 L Street NW, Suite 1200
Washington, DC 20036
202-775-8810
www.epinet.org

Internal Revenue Service
1111 Constitution Avenue NW
Washington, DC 20224
202-622-2000
www.irs.gov/individuals/article/0,,id=96456,00.html

Making Wages Work
The Welfare Information Network
1401 New York Avenue NW, Suite 800
Washington, DC 20005
202-587-1000
www.makingwageswork.org

National Council of La Raza
1111 19th Street NW, Suite 1000
Washington, DC 20036
202-785-1670
www.nclr.org

The Urban Institute
2100 M Street NW
Washington DC 20037
202-833-7200
www.urbaninstitute.org

Earned Income Tax Credit

Earned Income Tax Credit Act

Summary: The Earned Income Tax Credit Act would provide low-income workers with a refundable state tax credit based on the federal Earned Income Tax Credit.

SECTION 1. SHORT TITLE

This Act shall be called the "[STATE] Earned Income Tax Credit Act."

SECTION 2. EARNED INCOME TAX CREDIT

Section XXX of the Code is hereby amended by adding the following new section:

EARNED INCOME TAX CREDIT

1. A taxpayer shall be allowed a tax credit equal to 20 percent of the earned income credit allowed under section 32 of the federal Internal Revenue Code, as amended and in effect for the current taxable year.

2. The credit under this subsection shall be allowed against the taxes imposed by this chapter for the taxable year, reduced by other credits permitted by this section. If the credit exceeds the tax as so reduced, the [TAX COMMISSIONER] shall treat such excess as an overpayment, and shall pay the taxpayer, without interest, the amount of such excess.

3. In the case of a husband and wife who file their state tax returns separately, the credit allowed may be applied against the tax of either, or divided between them, as they elect.

4. The [TAX COMMISSIONER] shall make efforts every year to alert taxpayers who may be eligible to receive the credit. In making a determination as to whether a taxpayer may be eligible for such a credit, the [TAX COMMISSIONER] shall use appropriate and available data, including, but not limited to, data available from the U.S. Department of Treasury, the Internal Revenue Service, and state income tax returns from preceding tax years.

5. The [TAX COMMISSIONER] shall prepare an annual report containing statistical information regarding the credits granted for the prior calendar year, including the total amount of revenue expended on the earned income tax credit, the number of credits claimed, and the average value of credits granted to taxpayers whose earned income falls within various income ranges.

SECTION 3. EFFECTIVE DATE

This Act shall take effect for taxable years beginning on or after January 1, 2005.

Education -
Mandatory Testing

The federal No Child Left Behind Act of 2001 aims to dramatically increase the use and importance of standardized tests. However, standardized tests are poor yardsticks to measure student achievement.

Education - Mandatory Testing

Summary

- The federal No Child Left Behind Act of 2001 aims to dramatically increase the use and importance of standardized tests.
- In fact, standardized tests are poor yardsticks to measure student achievement.
- An emphasis on standardized testing encourages teaching to the test, skews school programs and priorities, and drives quality teachers out of the profession.
- Since standardized test scores can fluctuate rapidly, they are virtually useless for comparing a school's progress from one year to the next.
- The Comprehensive School Assessment Act reduces the state's reliance on standardized testing.
- The School Testing Right to Know Act highlights the primary causes of low student achievement.

The federal No Child Left Behind Act of 2001 aims to dramatically increase the use and importance of standardized tests.

President Bush's No Child Left Behind Act of 2001, also known as the Elementary and Secondary Education Act, requires annual "assessments" of all students in grades 3-8 in reading and math, beginning in the 2005-06 school year. Periodic science assessments will be added in 2007-08. These assessments will be used to measure each school's Adequate Yearly Progress toward the goal of making every public school student "proficient" in these subjects within 12 years. Schools that fail to make the required progress are declared "low performing" and are subject to sanctions.

In fact, standardized tests are poor yardsticks to measure student achievement.

Standardized tests reward the ability to quickly answer superficial questions that do not require critical thinking or genuine analysis. They do not measure the ability to write; to understand math, scientific methods, or reasoning; or to grasp social science concepts. They cannot adequately measure thinking skills or assess what students can do when presented with real-world tasks.

An emphasis on standardized testing encourages teaching to the test.

The higher the stakes, the more schools focus instruction on standardized tests. Because they are under the most pressure to increase test scores, schools in low-income neighborhoods are most actively teaching to the test, dumbing down both curriculum and instruction. Entire subjects are dropped, and skills that cannot be measured with standardized tests, such as writing research papers or conducting laboratory experiments, are neglected. Instruction starts to look like the tests. For example, reading is reduced to short passages followed by multiple-choice questions, a kind of "reading" that neither exists in the real world nor improves actual comprehension skills, which are key to successful literacy. Writing becomes a series of lessons to master the "five-paragraph essay," a form useless outside of standardized tests. The major consequence of teaching to the test is that students are, in fact, left behind—they are not taught the knowledge and skills required to be successful in life.

An emphasis on standardized testing skews school programs and priorities.

Under pressure to increase test scores, schools reach for quick fixes. Incessant drills and practice tests waste valuable classroom time that should be devoted to increasing students' real knowledge and skills. Library budgets are spent on test prep materials. Teachers are converted to test-taking coaches, giving tips like "what to do with only one minute left," and professional development is reduced to training teachers to be better test coaches.

An emphasis on standardized testing drives quality teachers out of the profession and turns off bright students.

Good teachers and bright students are often discouraged, even disgusted, by an overemphasis on testing. Many excellent teachers leave the profession. It is absurd to believe that the "best and brightest" will want to become teachers when teaching is reduced to test prep.

Since standardized test scores can fluctuate rapidly, they are virtually useless for comparing a school's progress from one year to the next.

Even at the very best schools, standardized test scores never consistently rise every year. They fluctuate from year to year based on any number of factors, including student turnover, new teachers, or even a bad flu season. An in-depth study of test scores in North Carolina elementary schools found, for example, that 70 percent of the year-to-year change in average test scores was caused by external factors, rather than actual change in student performance.[1] At the same time, a growing number of research studies have shown that, because of statistical margins of error based on the number of children tested at a given school, the scores used to judge schools are often inaccurate. This means that some satisfactory schools are punished for inaccurate bad scores while some unsatisfactory schools are rewarded for inaccurate good scores. Furthermore, a student's mastery of content and skills can only be accurately measured through testing if the assessment is closely aligned with state and district content standards, which is not always the case. The result is that students are tested on material that is not in the curriculum. This is all the more reason why any accountability program must use multiple measures of student learning, and not just rely on one standardized test.

The Comprehensive School Assessment Act reduces the state's reliance on standardized testing.

The No Child Left Behind Act does not specifically mandate annual statewide standardized tests. It requires "yearly student academic assessments."[2] A number of states are seeking to satisfy the requirements of federal law without resorting to standardized tests. The Comprehensive School Assessment Act, based on a model written by parents and educators in Massachusetts, holds the state Board of Education responsible for defining the core body of knowledge and skills that students should acquire. It also directs local school boards to create assessment systems that meet the needs of their student populations and provide fair and comprehensive assessments of student learning. Each assessment system must be approved by the state education authorities and be consistent with uniform statewide standards.

The School Testing Right to Know Act highlights the primary causes of low student achievement.

Despite overwhelming evidence to the contrary, President Bush's No Child Left Behind Act is based on the assumption that student achievement is primarily the result of the instruction children receive in their current school. This premise focuses the blame for low-performing schools on teachers and school administrators, and distracts attention from the major causes of low student achievement: the special challenges faced by low-income students and a lack of resources available to meet those challenges. The School Testing Right to Know Act requires that whenever a government entity releases standardized test scores, it must simultaneously release school-specific data on key factors that affect test scores, including the percentage of students who qualify for free or reduced-price meals, per-pupil expenditures, and average class size. With this information, both policymakers and the public will have a more accurate idea of what real problems need to be addressed so that our schoolchildren can succeed.

This policy summary relies in large part on information from the National Center for Fair & Open Testing (FairTest).

Endnotes

[1] Tom Kane and Douglas Staiger, "Volatility in School Test Scores," 2001.

[2] 20 U.S.C. Sec. 6311(a)(3).

Education - Mandatory Testing

For more information...

Center for Policy Alternatives
1875 Connecticut Avenue NW, Suite 710
Washington, DC 20009
202-387-6030
www.stateaction.org

The National Center for Fair & Open Testing (FairTest)
342 Broadway
Cambridge, MA 02139
617-864-4810
www.fairtest.org

American Federation of Teachers
555 New Jersey Avenue NW
Washington, DC 20001
202-879-4400
www.aft.org

National Education Association
1201 16th Street NW
Washington, DC 20036
202-833-4000
www.nea.org

Public Education Network
601 Thirteenth Street NW, Suite 900
Washington, DC 20005
202-628-7460
www.publiceducation.org

Education - Mandatory Testing

School Testing Right to Know Act

SECTION 1. SHORT TITLE

This Act shall be called the "School Testing Right to Know Act."

SECTION 2. FINDINGS AND PURPOSE

(A) FINDINGS – The legislature finds that:

1. The federal No Child Left Behind Act aims to dramatically increase the use and importance of primary and secondary school standardized tests.

2. However, standardized test scores do not accurately assess the causes of low student achievement. Instead, they distract attention from the major causes of low academic performance: poverty and the lack of resources available to meet low-income students' needs.

3. When standardized test scores are released to the public, policymakers, parents and taxpayers have the right to know all relevant data relating to these scores.

(B) PURPOSE – This law is enacted to provide policymakers and the public with accurate information with which to make future decisions about the direction of education policy in this state.

SECTION 3. SCHOOL TESTING RIGHT TO KNOW

After section XXX, the following new section XXX shall be inserted:

No agency of the state, or any governmental entity within the state, shall release any school-by-school or district-by-district listing of primary or secondary school standardized test scores to the public without simultaneously listing the following information for the same schools or districts:

1. Percentage of students who qualify for free or reduced-price meals.

2. Student mobility rate, that is, a measure of students who enter or leave a school during the school year.

3. Per-student expenditure by school, not including district-wide administrative costs.

4. Average class size.

5. For students who enter a school after grade 3, the percentage whose skills are assessed at below basic upon entering the school.

6. Percentage of students who qualify for special education services.

SECTION 4. EFFECTIVE DATE

This Act shall take effect on July 1, 2004.

Education - Mandatory Testing

Comprehensive School Assessment Act

SECTION 1. SHORT TITLE

This Act shall be called the "Comprehensive School Assessment Act."

SECTION 2. FINDINGS AND PURPOSE

(A) FINDINGS – The legislature finds that:

1. The federal No Child Left Behind Act requires "yearly student academic assessments" in public school grades 3-8 beginning in the 2005-06 school year. The Act does not specifically mandate annual statewide standardized tests.

2. An emphasis on standardized testing results in teaching to the test, it skews school programs and priorities, and it discourages quality teachers, sometimes driving them out of the profession. As a result, it will inhibit, rather than support, high-quality learning, and may well cause more students to be left behind.

3. The best, most accurate school assessment system is one that is locally created and operated following established guidelines for the development and use of multiple assessment measures.

(B) PURPOSE – This law is enacted to meet the requirements of federal law while providing [STATE] schools and schoolchildren with the highest quality assessment system.

SECTION 3. COMPREHENSIVE SCHOOL ASSESSMENT

After section XXX, the following new section XXX shall be inserted:

(A) COMPREHENSIVE ASSESSMENTS BASED ON STATEWIDE STANDARDS

1. The state [Board of Education] shall adopt statewide academic standards embodied in curriculum frameworks in the areas of English, mathematics, science and technology, history and social science, foreign languages, and the arts. Such standards shall delineate essential knowledge and skills, that, taken as a whole will not require more than [one half/two-thirds] of typical instructional time to enable students to meet, thereby allowing time and opportunity for individual student interests and school or district standards designed to meet special interests (e.g., an arts school) or local interests (e.g., agricultural science). State standards and frameworks for each subject area shall be approved by the relevant professional body of educators.

2. Each school district shall develop and adopt a system for assessing on an annual basis the extent to which the district, and every public school within the district, succeeded in improving or failed to improve student performance. Student performance shall be measured as the acquisition of the skills, competencies and knowledge called for by the statewide academic standards and curriculum frameworks, as well as local school and district standards and expectations, and the assessment of student progress toward areas of their own particular interest.

3. Each assessment system shall be designed to fairly and comprehensively measure outcomes and results regarding student performance, including complex and higher order thinking and application, and extended

Education - Mandatory Testing

student work, and to improve the effectiveness of curriculum and instruction. In its design and application, each assessment system shall employ a variety of assessment instruments, including classroom-based and teacher-made assessments, using either comprehensive or statistically valid sampling. Each school or district shall include in its plan a description of how it will use assessment information to improve teaching and guide professional development, and how information will be summarized for public reporting purposes.

4. Instruments used as part of the assessment system shall be criterion referenced, assessing whether students are meeting the statewide academic standards. Such instruments shall include work samples, projects, and portfolios based on regular student classroom work to facilitate authentic and direct gauges of student performance.

5. The state [Board of Education] shall provide technical assistance to schools and school districts to design and implement the evaluation systems required by this section, including the development of models for local evaluation systems.

(B) STATE APPROVAL OF ASSESSMENT SYSTEMS

Every school district shall submit a written description of its proposed assessment system to the state [Board of Education] for review and approval prior to implementation. Each assessment system shall include data on student achievement based on state standards that can be compared from district to district and reported in a uniform manner on forms designed by the state [Board of Education]. The state [Board of Education] shall not approve an assessment system unless it meets or exceeds the requirements of Section 1111(a)(3) of the federal No Child Left Behind Act of 2001, 20 U.S.C. Sec. 6311(a)(3).

(C) PUBLIC REPORTING OF ASSESSMENT RESULTS

Each school district shall annually report to the public how its students performed under the assessment system established by the district. The report shall be in a format approved by the state [Board of Education], and shall break down the data by school, race, gender, special education, or transitional bilingual education status and such other categories as are required by the state [Board of Education], provided that data will not allow identification of individual students.

SECTION 4. EFFECTIVE DATE

This Act shall take effect on July 1, 2004.

Education -
Safe Schools

Harassment, intimidation and bullying impede both a student's ability to learn and a school's ability to educate its students in a safe environment.

Education - Safe Schools

Summary

- A safe and civil environment in school is necessary in order for students to learn and achieve high academic standards.
- At least 10 percent of students are bullied at school.
- More than 80 percent of lesbian, gay, bisexual and transgender (GLBT) students report being verbally or physically harassed because of their sexual orientation or gender identification.
- Students experiencing harassment are more likely to skip school out of fear.
- Harassment impairs student achievement, educational attainment, and ultimately earning potential.
- An overwhelming majority of parents support policies to remedy the harassment and discrimination faced by GLBT youth in schools.
- The Safe Schools Act can protect students from harassment and discrimination.
- Thirteen states now offer protections for GLBT students.

A safe and civil environment in school is necessary in order for students to learn and achieve high academic standards.

Harassment, intimidation and bullying, like other disruptive or violent behaviors, impede both a student's ability to learn and a school's ability to educate its students in a safe environment.

At least 10 percent of students are bullied at school.

In a study of 15,686 students, 10 percent reported being bullied, and half of those students reported being bullied on a weekly basis.[1] These numbers don't take into account the students who do not report incidents of harassment, intimidation or bullying because of embarrassment or fear. This pervasive problem is often inadequately addressed or completely ignored by teachers, principals and administrators who are not equipped with the information or training to address the problem.

More than 80 percent of gay, lesbian, bisexual and transgender (GLBT) students report being verbally or physically harassed because of their sexual orientation or gender identification.

Compared to other students, GLBT youth are at increased risk of being targeted for harassment and discrimination in schools. A 2001 survey of GLBT students found that 83 percent experienced verbal harassment and 42 percent experienced physical harassment over the course of a year.[2]

Students who experience harassment are more likely to skip school out of fear.

The climate of fear created by harassment and discrimination often results in increased rates of absenteeism and decreased academic performance. Each day, about 160,000 American students skip school because they're afraid of bullies, according to the National Association of School Psychologists. As many as seven percent of America's eighth-graders stay home at least once a month because of bullies.[3] A recent survey found that over 30 percent of GLBT students had missed at least one entire day of school in the prior month because they felt unsafe.[4] Absences and concerns about personal safety can impact students' performance on standardized tests, affecting both individual educational achievement and school funding.

Harassment impairs student achievement, educational attainment, and ultimately earning potential.

Obviously, students who skip school to avoid harassment miss instruction, putting them at a disadvantage. But even when students stay in school, they are less able to learn while subject to bullying and harassment. Educational attainment significantly affects financial success. For example, the 2000 median earnings for women aged 25 and older who held a high school diploma and worked full-time was $23,700, yet women with some high school experience but no diploma had a median income of only $17,200. Similarly, men with a high school diploma earned $32,500, while those with some high school but no diploma had median earnings of only $24,400.[5]

An overwhelming majority of parents support adopting policies to remedy the harassment and discrimination faced by GLBT youth in schools.

Eighty percent of parents favor expanding existing anti-harassment and anti-discrimination policies to include GLBT students.[6] The same majority support teacher sensitivity training that includes instructions for dealing with anti-gay harassment in schools. Nearly two-thirds also support including information about transgender people in such sensitivity training.

The Safe Schools Act can protect students, including GLBT individuals, from harassment and discrimination.

States can protect students and avoid potential liability suits by adopting and implementing laws that:

■ Prohibit discrimination and harassment on the basis of *actual or perceived* characteristics, including race, color, religion, mental, physical or sensory disability, national origin, sexual orientation, and gender identity or expression.

■ Establish clear procedures for responding to complaints under this policy.

■ Provide necessary training to staff and teachers to implement policies.

Thirteen states now offer protections for GLBT students.

Eight states (CA, CT, MA, MN, NJ, VT, WA and WI) have laws prohibiting harassment and discrimination on the basis of sexual orientation. Of these, California, Minnesota and New Jersey also include gender identity in their coverage. Five states (AK, FL, PA, RI and UT) have regulations, policies or ethical codes that prohibit harassment and/or discrimination on the basis of sexual orientation.

This policy summary relies in large part on information from the Gay, Lesbian, Straight Education Network, Human Rights Campaign, and the National Center for Lesbian Rights.

Endnotes

[1] Journal of the American Medical Association, "Bullying Behaviors Among U.S. Youth: Prevalence and Association with Psychosocial Adjustment," April 25, 2001.

[2] GLSEN National School Climate Survey, 2001.

[3] Dan Olweus, "Bullying at School: What We Know and What We Can Do," 1993.

[4] GLSEN National School Climate Survey, 2001.

[5] U.S. Census Bureau, "America at the Dawn of a New Century: Population Profile of the United States," 2000.

[6] "A Focus on the American Parent: A Nationwide Survey of Parents of 5-18 Year Olds," conducted for GLSEN, Lake Snell Perry & Associates, December 2001.

Education - Safe Schools

For more information...

Center for Policy Alternatives
1875 Connecticut Avenue NW, Suite 710
Washington, DC 20009
202-387-6030
www.stateaction.org

American Federation of Teachers
555 New Jersey Avenue NW
Washington, DC 20001
202-879-4400
www.aft.org

Gay, Lesbian, Straight Education Network
121 West 27th Street, Suite 804
New York, NY 10001
212-727-0135
www.glsen.org

Human Rights Campaign
1640 Rhode Island Avenue NW
Washington, DC 20036
202-628-4160
www.hrc.org

National Center for Lesbian Rights
870 Market Street, Suite 570
San Francisco, CA 94102
415-392-6257
www.nclrights.org

National Education Association
1201 16th Street NW
Washington, DC 20036
202-833-4000
www.nea.org

Education - Safe Schools

Safe Schools Act

SECTION 1. SHORT TITLE

This Act shall be called the "Safe Schools Act."

SECTION 2. FINDINGS AND PURPOSE

(A) FINDINGS – The legislature finds that:

1. A safe and civil environment in school is necessary in order for students to learn and achieve high academic standards.

2. Harassment, intimidation and bullying, like other disruptive or violent behaviors, impede both a student's ability to learn and a school's ability to educate its students in a safe environment.

3. Since students learn by example, school administrators, faculty, staff, and volunteers should be commended for demonstrating appropriate behavior, treating others with civility and respect, and refusing to tolerate harassment, intimidation and bullying.

(B) PURPOSE – This law is enacted to protect the health and welfare, and improve the learning environment for [STATE] schoolchildren.

SECTION 3. SAFE SCHOOLS

After section XXX, the following new section XXX shall be inserted:

(A) DEFINITIONS – In this section:

"Harassment, intimidation or bullying" means any gesture or written, verbal or physical act that is reasonably perceived as being motivated by any actual or perceived characteristic, such as race, color, religion, ancestry, national origin, gender, sexual orientation, gender identity and expression, or a mental, physical or sensory disability that takes place on school property, at any school-sponsored function, or on a school bus, and that:

    a. A reasonable person should know, under the circumstances, will have the effect of harming a student or damaging a student's property, or placing a student in reasonable fear of harm to his or her person or damage to his or her property; or

    b. Has the effect of insulting or demeaning any student or group of students in such a way as to cause substantial disruption in, or substantial interference with, the orderly operation of the school.

(B) NO HARASSMENT, INTIMIDATION OR BULLYING

1. No person shall engage in harassment, intimidation or bullying.

2. No person shall engage in reprisal, retaliation or false accusation against a victim, witness or one with reliable information about an act of harassment, intimidation or bullying.

Education - Safe Schools

3. A school employee, student or volunteer who has witnessed, or has reliable information that a student has been subject to, harassment, intimidation or bullying shall report the incident to the appropriate school official.

(C) ADOPTION OF ANTI-HARASSMENT SCHOOL POLICIES

1. Before September 1, 2005, each local school district shall adopt a policy prohibiting harassment, intimidation or bullying on school property, at a school-sponsored function, or on a school bus. The school district shall involve parents and guardians, school employees, volunteers, students, administrators, and community representatives in the process of adopting the policy.

2. A local school district shall have control over the content of the policy, except that the policy shall contain, at a minimum, the following components:

    a. A statement prohibiting harassment, intimidation or bullying of a student.

    b. A definition of harassment, intimidation or bullying no less inclusive than that set forth in this section.

    c. A description of the type of behavior expected from each student.

    d. Consequences and appropriate remedial action for a person who commits an act of harassment, intimidation or bullying.

    e. A procedure for reporting an act of harassment, intimidation or bullying, including a provision that permits a person to report an act of harassment, intimidation or bullying anonymously. However, this shall not be construed to permit formal disciplinary action solely on the basis of an anonymous report.

    f. A procedure for prompt investigation of reports of serious violations and complaints, identifying either the principal or the principal's designee as the person responsible for the investigation.

    g. The range of ways in which a school will respond once an incident of harassment, intimidation or bullying is confirmed.

    h. A statement that prohibits reprisal or retaliation against any person who reports an act of harassment, intimidation or bullying, and the consequence and appropriate remedial action for a person who engages in reprisal or retaliation.

    i. Consequences and appropriate remedial action for a person found to have falsely accused another.

    j. A statement of how the policy is to be publicized, including notice that the policy applies to participation in school-sponsored functions.

3. To assist local school districts in developing policies for the prevention of harassment, intimidation or bullying, the state Board of Education shall develop model policies applicable to grades kindergarten through 12. These model policies shall be issued no later than December 1, 2004.

4. Notice of a local school district's policy shall appear in any school district publication that sets forth the comprehensive rules, procedures and standards of conduct for schools within the school district, and in any student handbook.

Education - Safe Schools

5. Information regarding a local school district policy against harassment, intimidation or bullying shall be incorporated into a school's employee training program.

6. Schools and school districts are encouraged to establish bullying prevention programs, and other initiatives involving school staff, students, administrators, volunteers, parents, law enforcement, and community members.

7. To the extent funds are appropriated for these purposes, a local school district shall:

a. Provide training on the school district's harassment, intimidation or bullying policies to school employees and volunteers who have significant contact with students.

b. Develop a process for discussing the district's harassment, intimidation or bullying policy with students.

(D) CIVIL LIABILITY

1. This section shall not be interpreted to prevent a victim from seeking redress under any other available law, either civil or criminal. This section does not create or alter any tort liability.

2. A school employee or volunteer who promptly reports an incident of harassment, intimidation or bullying to the appropriate school official designated by the local school district's policy, and who makes this report in compliance with the procedures in the district's policy, is immune from a cause of action for damages arising from any failure to remedy the reported incident.

SECTION 4. EFFECTIVE DATE

This Act shall take effect on July 1, 2004.

Education - SAGE

Compared head-to-head against school vouchers, the SAGE approach is far more effective at boosting student achievement in schools serving low-income communities.

Education - SAGE

Summary

- The Student Achievement Guarantee in Education (SAGE) program has been proven to boost student achievement in schools serving low-income communities.
- SAGE is a statewide Wisconsin program that reduces the student-teacher ratio to 15 students per teacher in grades K-3.
- SAGE is successful because it does more than lower class size—it mandates comprehensive reform.
- Participating school districts are required to strengthen academic curricula, implement professional development programs and accountability measures for staff, and keep school buildings open longer hours to accommodate before and after-school programs.
- Annual evaluations show SAGE students outperform students from comparable schools.
- Compared head-to-head against school vouchers, SAGE is far more effective in improving student achievement.

The Student Achievement Guarantee in Education (SAGE) program has been proven to boost student achievement in schools serving low-income communities.

Established in 1995, SAGE is a statewide Wisconsin program that reduces the student-teacher ratio to 15 students for every teacher in kindergarten through third grade, and implements a package of school-based reforms.

SAGE is successful because it does more than lower class size—it mandates comprehensive reform.

Under SAGE, participating school districts sign contracts with the state that require:

■ A rigorous academic curriculum designed to improve student achievement.

■ An extension of school hours to accommodate before and after-school enrichment programs.

■ Collaboration with community organizations to make educational, recreational and social service programs available in the school.

■ Orientation programs for all newly-hired professional staff to facilitate their transition into the school district.

■ Each teacher and administrator to submit to the school board a professional development plan that focuses on how he or she will help improve student academic achievement.

■ An evaluation process for professional staff members that identifies individual strengths and weaknesses, clearly describes areas in need of improvement, provides opportunities to learn and improve, and systematically documents performance in accordance with the plan.

■ Dismissal of professional staff members whose failure to learn and improve has been documented over a two-year period.

The School of Education at the University of Wisconsin-Milwaukee has conducted rigorous evaluations of SAGE.

These annual evaluations measure the academic achievement of the SAGE schools against comparison schools. Students are tested in reading, language arts, and math.[1]

Annual evaluations show SAGE students outperform students from comparable schools.

In the 2000-01 school year for example, African-American third-graders in SAGE schools scored higher than African-American students in comparable schools. In fact, SAGE students outperformed comparable students on every subject tested, including language arts, math and reading. Further, comparing third-grade test scores to first grade pre-test scores, SAGE students showed significantly greater improvement than their counterparts.

Compared head-to-head against school vouchers, SAGE easily comes out on top.

Milwaukee began its voucher program in 1990, and SAGE was enacted in 1995. A multi-year study by the University of Wisconsin-Madison revealed that SAGE students showed improved test scores, while Milwaukee voucher students performed no better than comparable Milwaukee Public Schools students in any year of the program to date.

Reducing classroom size improves the quality of teaching.

Based on a study of teaching practices, reducing class size results in: fewer discipline problems and therefore more instructional time; more individualization of instruction to students; more frequent hands-on activities; and greater teacher satisfaction with their jobs.[2]

Reducing classroom size in early grades is proven to have significant long-term educational benefits.

The Student/Teacher Ratio (STAR) Project, the most significant long-term study on the benefits of reducing class size in early education, involved more than 3,000 K-3 students in select rural, suburban, urban and inner-city Tennessee schools from 1985-89. This $12 million study revealed that students in small classes consistently scored higher on achievement and basic skills tests. And inner-city, predominantly minority children in small classes outscored their counterparts in larger classes. This success continued through high school.

Endnotes

[1] Data from these evaluations from 1996 through 2001 are presented in "Class Size Reduction in Wisconsin: A Fresh look at the Data," Education Policy Studies Laboratory, Arizona State University, September 2003, www.asu.edu/educ/epsl/SAGE.

[2] "SAGE Advice: Research on Teaching in Reduced-Size Classes," Education Policy Studies Laboratory, Arizona State University, January 2003.

Education - SAGE

For more information...

Center for Policy Alternatives
1875 Connecticut Avenue NW, Suite 710
Washington, DC 20009
202-387-6030
www.stateaction.org

National Education Association
1201 16th Street NW
Washington, DC 20036
202-833-4000
www.nea.org

American Federation of Teachers
555 New Jersey Avenue NW
Washington, DC 20001
202-879-4400
www.aft.org

Education Policy Studies Laboratory
Arizona State University
P.O. Box 872411
Tempe, AZ 85287
480-965-1886
edpolicylab.org

Wisconsin Department of Public Instruction
P.O. Box 7841
Madison, WI 53707
608-266-2489
www.dpi.state.wi.us/dpi/oea/sage

Student Achievement Guarantee in Education (SAGE) Act

SECTION 1. SHORT TITLE

This Act shall be called the "[STATE] Student Achievement Guarantee in Education Act."

SECTION 2. STUDENT ACHIEVEMENT GUARANTEE IN EDUCATION (SAGE)

After section XXX, the following new section XXX shall be inserted:

(A) DEFINITIONS—in this section:

1. "Class size" means the number of pupils assigned to a regular classroom teacher on the 3rd Friday of September.

2. "Low income" means the measure of low income that is used by the school district under 20 USC 2723.

3. "Department" means the [State Department of Education].

(B) ELIGIBILITY

1. The school board of any school district in which a school in the previous school year had an enrollment of at least 50 percent [could use a lower percentage] low-income students is eligible to participate in the program.

2. If, in any year, eligible school districts apply for more achievement guarantee contracts than are possible within the budget appropriated for this purpose, the Department shall determine which school board to contract with based on the number of low-income pupils in kindergarten and grade one enrolled in the schools, and on the balance of rural and urban school districts currently participating in the program.

3. A selected school district shall enter into an achievement guarantee contract on behalf of up to 10 schools [could use a lower number or phase in over time].

(C) CONTRACT REQUIREMENTS

An achievement guarantee contract shall require the school board to do all of the following in each participating school:

1. Class size—Reduce each class size to 15 in the following manner:

    a. In the first year of participation, in at least kindergarten and grade one.
    b. In the second year of participation, in at least kindergarten and grades one and two.
    c. In the third year of participation, in at least kindergarten and grades one, two and three.

2. Education and human services—

    a. Keep school buildings open to accommodate before school and after-school enrichment programs.
    b. Collaborate with community organizations to make educational and recreational opportunities, as well as a variety of community and social services, available in the school to all school district residents.

Education - SAGE

3. Curriculum—

   a. Provide a rigorous academic curriculum designed to improve pupil academic achievement.
   b. In consultation with the Department, and with the participation of the school's professional staff and school district residents, review the school's current curriculum to determine how well it promotes pupil academic achievement.
   c. If necessary, outline any changes to the curriculum to improve pupil academic achievement.

4. Staff development and accountability—

   a. Develop a one-year program for all newly hired professional staff that helps them make the transition from their previous employment or school to their current employment.
   b. Provide time for employees to collaborate and plan.
   c. Require that each teacher and administrator submit to the school board a professional development plan that focuses on how he or she will help improve student academic achievement. The plan shall include a method by which the staff member will receive evaluations on the success of his or her efforts from a variety of sources.
   d. Regularly review staff development plans to determine whether they are effective in helping to improve pupil academic achievement.
   e. Establish an evaluation process for professional staff that does all of the following:
      (1) Identifies individual strengths and weaknesses.
      (2) Clearly describes areas in need of improvement.
      (3) Includes a support plan that provides opportunities to learn and improve.
      (4) Systematically documents performance in accordance with the plan.
      (5) Allows professional staff members to comment on and contribute to revisions in the evaluation process.
      (6) Provides for the dismissal of professional staff members whose failure to learn and improve has been documented over a two-year period.

(D) IMPLEMENTATION OF STUDENT ACHIEVEMENT—Each achievement guarantee contract shall include all of the following:

1. A description of how each school will implement each of the elements under subsection (C), including any alternative class configurations for specific educational activities that may be used to meet the class size requirements.

2. A description of the method that the school district will use to evaluate the academic achievement of the students enrolled in the school.

3. A description of each school's performance objectives for the academic achievement of the students enrolled in the school and the means that will be used to evaluate success in attaining the objectives. Performance objectives shall include all of the following:

   a. Where applicable, improvement in scores of tests administered to students under [applicable state law].
   b. The attainment of any educational goals adopted by the school board.
   c. Professional development objectives.

4. A description of the methods by which the school involves students, parents or guardians of students, and other school district residents in decisions affecting the school.

5. A description of any statute or rule that is waived under [state law] if the waiver is related to the contract.

6. A description of the means by which the Department will monitor compliance with the terms of the contract.

(E) ANNUAL REVIEW AND NONCOMPLIANCE

1. At the end of each school year, the Department may terminate a contract if a school board has failed to fully implement the provisions under subsection (C).

2. Annually, by June 30, a committee consisting of the [state superintendent, the chairpersons of the education committees in the senate and house] and the individual chiefly responsible for the evaluation under subsection (H) shall review the progress made by each participating school. The committee may recommend that the Department terminate a contract if the committee determines that the school board has violated the contract or if the school has made insufficient progress toward achieving its performance objectives. The Department may terminate the contract if it agrees with the committee's recommendation.

(F) STATE AID

1. From appropriations specifically designated for this purpose, the Department shall pay to each participating school district $2,000 multiplied by the number of low-income students enrolled in grades K-3 in each participating school covered by achievement guarantee contracts.

2. The Department shall cease payments under this section to any school district if the school board withdraws from the contract before it expires.

(G) RULES

The Department shall promulgate rules to implement and administer the payment of state aid under this section.

(H) EVALUATION

The Department shall arrange for an annual independent evaluation of the program under this section.

SECTION 3. EFFECTIVE DATE—This Act shall take effect on July 1, 2004.

Education - School Vouchers

No reputable study has demonstrated that school vouchers improve student performance. Instead, they rob public schools of needed funding, and only a small percentage of students participate.

Education - School Vouchers

Summary

- The U.S. Supreme Court's 2002 decision upholding the constitutionality of school vouchers has re-ignited voucher battles in the state legislatures.
- School vouchers are public subsidies that help parents pay tuition at a private or religious school, or even for home schooling in some proposals.
- No credible study has demonstrated that vouchers improve student performance.
- Vouchers do not provide "school choice," because private school admissions offices retain the choice of which students to admit or reject.
- Vouchers do not pay the full cost of many private schools.
- Private schools that accept vouchers are not held to the same standards of accountability as public schools.
- Americans want public money to be used for public schools instead of for private school vouchers.
- Despite the U.S. Supreme Court Ruling, school vouchers continue to violate most state constitutions.

The U.S. Supreme Court's 2002 decision upholding the constitutionality of school vouchers has re-ignited voucher battles in the state legislatures.

In 2003, legislation to create or expand vouchers was defeated in 12 states (AR, CA, CT, FL, LA, MN, MS, OH, OK, TX, VA and WI). Colorado adopted a voucher program that targets 11 school districts and could cover about 20,000 students by 2007. However, public school advocates have filed suit to block the program, pointing out that the Colorado Constitution explicitly prohibits the use of public funds for religious schools.

School vouchers are public subsidies that help parents pay tuition at a private or religious school, or even for home schooling in some proposals.

So far, taxpayer-funded voucher programs are operating only in Milwaukee, Cleveland, and Florida. Vouchers range in value, but are consistently much less than tuition at elite private schools (which may cost $10,000-20,000 a year).

■ In Cleveland, over 5,000 students use vouchers, each worth no more than $2,250. Only one in five of those students attended a Cleveland public school the year before receiving a voucher. The cost to the state of Ohio was more than $10 million in 2001-02. These funds were diverted from a portion of the state budget dedicated to disadvantaged public school students.

■ In Milwaukee, where the program has been operating since 1999, more than 11,000 low-income students use vouchers worth $5,783 to attend about 100 private schools, most of which are religious. The program diverted approximately $60 million from public schools in 2001-02.

■ Florida has two voucher programs. The so-called "A+" program targets schools that have been graded "F" by the state for two years within any four-year period. Approximately 600 students are enrolled in this program, at an annual cost to the state of $2.1 million. The McKay program offers vouchers to students with disabilities who are dissatisfied with their public schools. The value of the voucher is based on the child's disability, but averages more than $5,000. With almost 9,000 students, this program costs the state more than $50 million annually.

No credible study has demonstrated that vouchers improve student performance.

The official study of Cleveland's voucher program found no achievement gains for voucher students compared to students in the public schools in the first year of the program. In the second year, voucher students scored slightly better than public school students in science and language, but not in math, reading or social studies. The most recent results do not reveal any significant impact on student achievement; in fact, voucher students performed slightly worse in math, reading and overall achievement.[1] Likewise, Milwaukee's official evaluation found that voucher students did not outperform public school students.[2] A controversial study of privately-funded vouchers in New York City, Washington, DC, and Dayton, Ohio claimed a 6.3 percent gain in test scores by African-American students,[3] but one of the companies hired to gather the research publicly rebutted that conclusion. Reanalysis of the data confirmed that the claims are insupportable, and that vouchers had no statistically significant impact on student achievement.

Vouchers do not provide "school choice," because private school admissions offices retain the choice of which students to admit or reject.

Students are often unable or ineligible to attend many private schools that accept vouchers because of long waiting lists and restrictive admissions standards based on academic performance, religion, sex, disability and other factors.

Vouchers do not pay the full cost of many private schools.

Vouchers will not cover the full cost of the more expensive and elite private schools, which decline to participate in programs that require them to accept the voucher as complete tuition payment. Moreover, the cost of private education is much more than tuition. Parents must also pay for transportation, uniforms, books and other expenses. Many, if not most, low- and middle-income parents are unable to afford these costs, so their kids cannot attend private school.

Private schools that accept vouchers are not held to the same standards of accountability as public schools.

Voucher proposals rarely demand accountability for the quality of education students receive, and, according to a U.S. Department of Education report, many private schools would not participate in a voucher program if it required them to make changes in admissions, student testing, curriculum, or religious training.[4] The federal No Child Left Behind law does not apply to private schools.

Americans want public money to be used for public schools instead of for private school vouchers.

The 2003 Phi Delta Kappa/Gallup poll found that the number of Americans who support the diversion of public funds for private school tuition fell to 38 percent.[5] A meta-analysis of polling data confirmed that vouchers are the least popular of all proposals to improve education, garnering less than half as much support as tutoring and remedial support for students or professional development for teachers.[6] In the most important gauge of public opinion, voters have consistently rejected school voucher initiatives. In 2000, California and Michigan voters turned back voucher proposals by two-to-one margins. Since 1972, all eight attempts to create state voucher programs by referendum have failed.

Despite the U.S. Supreme Court ruling, school vouchers continue to violate most state constitutions.

Nearly every state constitution (all but LA, ME and NC) contains a provision that limits state support of religious institutions. Thirty-six state constitutions include language that expressly forbids the transfer of money to religious schools. So the constitutionality of vouchers remains in serious question.

This policy brief relies in large part on information from the National Education Association.

Endnotes

[1] Kim Metcalf et al., "Evaluation of the Cleveland Scholarship and Tutoring Program, Summary Report 1998-2001," Indiana University, 2003.

[2] John Witte et al., "Fifth Year Report: Milwaukee Parental Choice Program," University of Wisconsin, 1995.

[3] Howell, Wolf, Peterson, and Campbell, "Test-score effects of school vouchers in Dayton, Ohio; New York City; and Washington, D.C.: Evidence from randomized field trials," September 2000.

[4] Muraskin et al., "Barriers, Benefits, and Costs of Using Private Schools to Alleviate Overcrowding in Public Schools: Preliminary Report," 1997.

[5] http://www.pdkintl.org/kappan/k0309pol.pdf.

[6] Meg Bostrom, "Fulfilling the Promise of No Child Left Behind: A MetaAnalysis of Attitudes Toward Public Education," Public Knowledge LLC, April 2003.

Education - School Vouchers

For more information...

Center for Policy Alternatives
1875 Connecticut Avenue NW, Suite 710
Washington, DC 20009
202-387-6030
www.stateaction.org

American Federation of Teachers
555 New Jersey Avenue NW
Washington, DC 20001
202-879-4400
www.aft.org

Americans United for Separation of Church and State
518 C Street NE
Washington, DC 20002
202-466-3234
www.au.org

National Association for the Advancement of Colored People
4805 Mt. Hope Drive
Baltimore, MD 21215
410-521-4939
www.naacp.org

National Education Association
1201 16th Street NW
Washington, DC 20036
202-833-4000
www.nea.org

People for the American Way
2000 M Street NW, Suite 400
Washington, DC 20036
202-467-4999
www.pfaw.org

Balanced Student Assessment Act

The Balanced Student Assessment Act is intended to be offered in the context of a debate over school vouchers, either as a freestanding bill or as an amendment to a voucher bill.

SECTION 1. SHORT TITLE

This Act shall be called the "Balanced Student Assessment Act."

SECTION 2. FINDINGS AND PURPOSE

(A) FINDINGS—The legislature finds that:

1. The federal No Child Left Behind Act of 2001 requires public schools to perform annual assessments of their students' academic achievement.

2. Under the No Child Left Behind Act, these assessments are "the primary means of determining the yearly performance of the State and of each local educational agency and school in the State in enabling all children to meet the State's challenging student academic achievement standards."

3. Private schools that accept state funding should be measured by the same "challenging student academic achievement standards" as the public schools.

(B) PURPOSE—This law is enacted to require private schools that accept public funding to participate in the same annual assessments of their students' academic achievement as are required of public schools, in order to provide standards, accountability and balance in evaluating the relative merit of state funding for private schools.

SECTION 3. BALANCED STUDENT ASSESSMENTS

After section XXX, the following new section XXX shall be inserted:

(A) DEFINITIONS—In this section:

1. "Private school" means a primary or secondary school [accredited by the state] that is not part of a city or county public school system.

2. "Secretary" means the Secretary of the Department of [Education], or the Secretary's designee(s).

(B) ASSESSMENTS REQUIRED—In order to be eligible to receive any state funds pursuant to [list appropriate sections], a private school must:

1. Assess the academic achievement of all its students, using the same assessments required of public schools in the same district pursuant to section 1111(b)(3)(A) of the federal No Child Left Behind Act of 2001 (Public Law 107-110).

2. Provide the results of those assessments to the Secretary [of Education].

Education - School Vouchers

3. Disclose any identifiable personal information about the assessments only to the parents of the students to whom the information relates.

(C) ANNUAL EVALUATION

Based on the assessments of academic achievement, the Secretary shall conduct an annual school-by-school evaluation of student achievement for private schools which receive any state funds pursuant to this section, including a comparison of the achievement of the private school's students to demographically similar public school students.

SECTION 4. EFFECTIVE DATE

This Act shall take effect on July 1, 2004.

Electronic
Recording of Interrogations

Electronic recording of interrogations protects the innocent and provides the best evidence against the guilty.

Electronic Recording of Interrogations

Summary

- Every year, hundreds of innocent Americans are convicted of crimes because of false confessions.
- Many more innocent Americans are imprisoned and later released because of false confessions.
- There are many reasons why the innocent "confess," ranging from coercion to mental illness.
- Electronic recording of interrogations protects the innocent and provides the best evidence against the guilty.
- Three states—Alaska, Illinois and Minnesota—and many cities and counties now require electronic recording of interrogations.
- Jurisdictions that use electronic recording have proven its value.
- The costs of electronic recording are more than offset by the savings.

Every year, hundreds of innocent Americans are convicted of crimes because of false confessions.

Of the 111 people sentenced to death and then exonerated since 1976, 27 of them—nearly one in four—had made false confessions. It is estimated that at least 300 innocent people are convicted of major crimes each year as a result of false confessions.[1] For example:

■ Jerry Frank Townsend, a mentally retarded man, confessed in 1979 to six murders and a rape, serving 22 years in a Florida prison. After he died of cancer on death row, DNA tests exonerated him.

■ In 1985, Ronald Jones confessed to a murder in Illinois after police beat him and threatened further abuse. He spent 14 years in prison, eight of them on death row, before being exonerated by DNA evidence.

■ In 1988, Christopher Ochoa confessed to a rape-murder in Texas after police falsely claimed they had overwhelming evidence against him and that he could only avoid the death penalty if he confessed. He was later definitively cleared.

■ In 1993, police induced Gary Gauger to speculate that he could have murdered his parents during an alcoholic blackout. While Gauger waited on death row, federal agents learned that the murders were actually committed by a Wisconsin motorcycle gang.

Many more innocent Americans are imprisoned and later released because of false confessions.

It is impossible to count how many times people are charged based on false confessions and subsequently released after exonerating evidence comes to light. A *Washington Post* investigation into one jurisdiction—Prince George's County, Maryland—described four egregious cases where homicide detectives coerced confessions which were later proven false and charges were dropped before any trial.[2] Similarly, the *Chicago Tribune* conducted a study that found 247 instances in which the defendants' self-incriminating statements were thrown out by a court or found insufficiently convincing by a jury.[3]

There are many reasons why the innocent "confess," ranging from coercion to mental illness.

While physical abuse by police still occurs,[4] interrogators don't have to use force to elicit confessions from the mentally retarded, mentally ill, juveniles, and even some poorly educated suspects. Suspects struggling with alcohol or drug problems are especially susceptible to psychologically powerful interrogation tactics. Sleep deprivation can lead to confusion, temporary psychosis, and even hallucinations. After 28 hours in an interrogation room, Keith Longtin began to believe police suggestions that he had a split personality and the "other self" had murdered his wife. He spent the next eight months in jail until DNA evidence fingered the real killer.[5]

Electronic recording of interrogations protects the innocent and provides the best evidence against the guilty.

Electronic recording prevents overt misconduct, settles disputes about what was actually said, and provides the context for any suspect's statement to police. It eliminates uncertainty and demonstrates truth.

Three states—Alaska, Illinois and Minnesota— and many cities and counties now require electronic recording of interrogations.

In 2003, Illinois became the first state to enact legislation requiring electronic recording. That law, which takes effect in 2005, applies to homicide cases and major juvenile offenses. Two other states have employed the practice for years. The Minnesota Supreme Court ruled in 1984 that custodial interrogations must be recorded "to ensure the fair and equitable presentation of evidence at trial."[6] In 1985, the Alaska Supreme Court held that an unexcused failure to record custodial interrogations violated the suspect's right to due process under the state constitution.[7] Other major jurisdictions that require electronic recording include Austin, Denver, San Diego County, Broward County, and Portland, Maine.

Jurisdictions that use electronic recording have proven its value.

A study of recorded interrogations for the U.S. Department of Justice found that jurisdictions with taping policies experience significant improvement in the quality of their police interrogations. Ninety-seven percent of police departments that have ever videotaped suspects' statements found the practice useful, the study found.[8] Judges say it streamlines the process, and prosecutors and police argue that it helps them disprove phony claims of misconduct. In jurisdictions that tape custodial interrogations, motions by the defense to suppress a confession have gone down, and guilty pleas are up.

The costs of electronic recording are more than offset by the savings.

The only real argument against electronic recording is that cameras are costly. But today such technology, especially when purchased in bulk, is not very expensive. At the same time, electronic recording saves tax money by reducing multi-million dollar awards in false arrest and police misconduct lawsuits, lowering the number of time-consuming evidence suppression hearings, and encouraging more plea agreements before trial. It also helps prevent crimes by keeping police focused on the guilty rather than the innocent. For example, in the case of Keith Longtin, cited above, the real killer sexually assaulted seven more women while Longtin languished in jail.

This policy brief relies in large part on information from the Campaign for Criminal Justice Reform.

Endnotes

[1] Richard P. Conti, "The Psychology of False Confessions," *The Journal of Credibility Assessment and Witness Psychology*, Vol. 2, No. 1, 1999.

[2] April Witt, "Allegations of Abuses Mar Murder Cases," *Washington Post*, June 3, 2001.

[3] Ken Armstrong, Steve Mills, and Maurice Possley, "Coercive and illegal tactics torpedo scores of Cook County murder cases," *Chicago Tribune*, December 16, 2001.

[4] For example, U.S. District Judge Milton Shadur wrote in 1999: "It is now common knowledge that in the early- to mid-1980s, Chicago Police Cmdr. Jon Burge and many of the officers working under him regularly engaged in the physical abuse and torture of prisoners to extract confessions." *Chicago Tribune* editorial, April 21, 2002.

[5] April Witt, "Allegations of Abuses Mar Murder Cases," *Washington Post*, June 3, 2001.

[6] Minnesota v. Scales, 518 N.W.2d 587 (Minn. 1984).

[7] Stephan v. State, 711 P.2d 1156 (Alaska 1985).

[8] William Geller, "Police Videotaping of Suspect Interrogations and Confessions," Report to the National Institute of Justice, 1992.

Electronic Recording of Interrogations

For more information...

Center for Policy Alternatives

1875 Connecticut Avenue NW, Suite 710
Washington, DC 20009
202-387-6030
www.stateaction.org

Campaign for Criminal Justice Reform

1725 Eye Street NW, 4th Floor
Washington, DC 20006
202-638-5855
www.cjreform.org

Innocence Project

Benjamin N. Cardozo School of Law
55 5th Avenue, 11th Floor
New York, NY 10003
212-790-0200
www.innocenceproject.org

National Association of Criminal Defense Lawyers

1150 18th Street NW, Suite 950
Washington, DC 20036
202-872-8600
www.nacdl.org

Electronic Recording of Interrogations

Electronic Recording of Interrogations Act

SECTION 1. SHORT TITLE

This Act shall be called the "Electronic Recording of Interrogations Act."

SECTION 2. FINDINGS AND PURPOSE

(A) FINDINGS—The legislature finds that:

1. Every year, many people are jailed because of false confessions during custodial interrogations.

2. Interrogators don't have to use force to elicit confessions from the mentally retarded, mentally ill, juveniles, and even some poorly educated suspects.

3. Electronic recording of interrogations protects the innocent and provides the best evidence against the guilty.

(B) PURPOSE—The purpose of this Act is to require the creation of an electronic record of an entire custodial interrogation in order to eliminate disputes in court as to what actually occurred during the interrogation, thereby improving prosecution of the guilty while affording protection to the innocent.

SECTION 3. ELECTRONIC RECORDING OF INTERROGATIONS

After section XXX, the following new section XXX shall be inserted:

(A) DEFINITIONS – In this section:

1. "Electronic recording" means a motion picture, audiotape, videotape or digital recording.

2. "Custodial interrogation" means any interrogation which is conducted in a place of detention and during which a reasonable person in the subject's position would consider himself or herself to be in custody.

3. "Place of detention" means a police station, correctional facility, holding facility for prisoners, or other government facility where persons are held in detention in connection with criminal charges which have been or may be filed against them.

(B) ELECTRONIC RECORDING OF INTERROGATIONS REQUIRED

1. During the prosecution of a class [insert as appropriate] felony, an oral, written or sign language statement of a defendant made during a custodial interrogation shall be presumed inadmissible as evidence against a defendant in a criminal proceeding unless an electronic recording is made of the custodial interrogation in its entirety and the recording is substantially accurate and not intentionally altered.

2. If the court finds that the defendant was subjected to a custodial interrogation in violation of paragraph 1, then any statements made by the defendant following that custodial interrogation, even if otherwise in compliance with this section, are also presumed inadmissible.

Electronic Recording of Interrogations

3. The State may rebut a presumption of inadmissibility through clear and convincing evidence that the statement was both voluntary and reliable, and law enforcement officers had good cause for failing to electronically record the entire interrogation. Examples of good cause include:

a. the interrogation took place in a location other than a police station, correctional facility, or holding facility for prisoners and where the requisite recording equipment was not readily available;
b. the accused refused to have his/her interrogation electronically recorded, and the refusal itself was electronically recorded; or
c. the failure to electronically record an entire interrogation was the result of equipment failure and obtaining replacement equipment was not feasible.

4. Nothing in this section precludes the admission of:

a. a statement made by the accused in open court at his or her trial, before a grand jury, or at a preliminary hearing;
b. a spontaneous statement that is not made in response to a question;
c. a statement made after questioning that is routinely asked during the processing of the arrest of the suspect;
d. a statement made during a custodial interrogation that is conducted out-of-state;
e. a statement obtained by a federal law enforcement officer in a federal place of detention;
f. a statement given at a time when the interrogators are unaware that a class [insert as appropriate] felony has in fact occurred; or
g. a statement, otherwise inadmissible under this section, that is used only for impeachment and not as substantive evidence.

5. The State shall not destroy or alter any electronic recording made of a custodial interrogation until such time as the defendant's conviction for any offense relating to the interrogation is final and all direct and habeas corpus appeals are exhausted, or the prosecution of that offense is barred by law.

SECTION 4. GRANTS FOR ELECTRONIC RECORDING EQUIPMENT

From appropriations made for that purpose, the Secretary of [Public Safety] shall make grants to local law enforcement agencies for the purchase of equipment for electronic recording of interrogations. The Secretary shall promulgate rules to implement this paragraph.

SECTION 5. TRAINING OF LAW ENFORCEMENT OFFICERS

From appropriations made for that purpose, the Secretary of [Public Safety] shall initiate, administer, and conduct training programs for law enforcement officers and recruits on the methods and technical aspects of electronic recording of interrogations.

SECTION 6. EFFECTIVE DATE

Sections 4 and 5 of this Act shall take effect on July 1, 2004. Section 3 of this Act shall take effect on July 1, 2005.

Emergency Contraception -

Collaborative Practice

Greater use of emergency contraception would reduce the number of unintended pregnancies and abortions. Collaborative drug therapy—the practice of dispensing drugs directly from pharmacists—is a viable approach for states to increase access to emergency contraception.

Emergency Contraception - Collaborative Practice

Summary

- Emergency contraception has been available for more than 25 years—it is safe and effective.
- Emergency contraception does not induce abortion.
- Despite its effectiveness, a large percentage of women do not know that emergency contraception is available.
- Greater use of emergency contraception would reduce the number of unintended pregnancies and abortions.
- Even when women are aware of emergency contraception, it can be difficult to obtain in a timely manner because the pills require a prescription.
- Collaborative drug therapy—the practice of dispensing drugs directly from pharmacists—is a viable approach to increasing access to emergency contraception.
- The public and pharmacists both support increased access to emergency contraception through collaborative practice.
- Currently Alaska, California, Hawaii, New Mexico, and Washington allow pharmacists to dispense emergency contraceptives without a prescription.

Emergency contraception has been available for more than 25 years—it is safe and effective.

Emergency contraception has been available for more than 25 years, and has been proven safe—so safe that emergency contraceptives are available without a prescription in many industrialized nations. Two types of emergency contraception options exist: special doses of regular birth control pills, commonly known as "morning after pills," and use of a copper-T intrauterine device (IUD). If taken within 120 hours after intercourse, the commonly used emergency contraceptive pills substantially reduce the risk of pregnancy. Copper-bearing IUDs have an even higher success rate.

Emergency contraception does not induce abortion.

Emergency contraception inhibits ovulation, fertilization or implantation before a pregnancy occurs. Mifeprex, commonly called RU-486 or the "abortion pill," is not an emergency contraceptive.

Despite its effectiveness, a large percentage of women do not know that emergency contraception is available.

In a recent nationwide survey, fully one-third of women aged 18-44 said they did not know there is something a woman can do to prevent pregnancy after unprotected sex.[1] And because many women confuse it with Mifeprex, it is likely that substantially more than one-third do not know enough about emergency contraception to request it.[2] Further, women who may need emergency contraception the most know the least. A survey in New York City found that 95 percent of inner-city youth aged 14-18 had never heard of emergency contraception.[3]

Greater use of emergency contraception would reduce the number of unintended pregnancies and abortions.

Increased use of emergency contraception could reduce the number of unintended pregnancies by half, thereby greatly reducing recourse to abortion.[4]

Most medical professionals and facilities underutilize or misuse emergency contraception.

While nearly all OB/GYN doctors believe emergency contraception is safe and effective, only 31 percent prescribe emergency contraception more than five times per year. Only 20 percent of OB/GYNs discuss emergency contraception with their patients most or all of the time as part of routine contraceptive counseling.[5] One survey found that 37 percent of New York City pharmacists knew nothing or provided only incorrect information about emergency contraception.[6]

Even when women are aware of emergency contraception, it can be difficult to obtain in a timely manner because the pills require a prescription.

Because emergency contraceptive pills are more effective within 120 hours of unprotected sex—and most effective within the first 12 hours—barriers to obtaining a prescription pose a serious threat to women's reproductive health. Currently, women have difficulty obtaining emergency contraceptives in a timely manner because they must first make an appointment with a physician to get a prescription. Women in rural areas may have to travel great distances to reach the nearest doctor or clinic, making a prescription within 120 hours of unprotected sex difficult to obtain.

Collaborative drug therapy—the practice of dispensing drugs directly from pharmacists—is a viable approach to increasing access to emergency contraception.

Collaborative drug therapy authorizes pharmacists to dispense specified prescription drugs without requiring patients to consult a doctor. In 1999, the state of Washington completed a successful two-year pilot project that tested collaborative practice for emergency contraception, providing pills to nearly 12,000 women.

The public and pharmacists both support increased access to emergency contraception through collaborative practice.

A January 2000 Peter Hart Research poll in New Jersey and Oregon found strong support for access to emergency contraception: 62 percent of voters in New Jersey, and 64 percent in Oregon. Additionally, pharmacists in these states support adding emergency contraceptives to the list of drugs prescribed under collaborative drug therapy programs: 56 percent in New Jersey, and 67 percent in Oregon.

Currently Alaska, California, Hawaii, New Mexico, and Washington allow pharmacists to dispense emergency contraceptives without a prescription.

In 2003, New Mexico issued a regulation and Hawaii enacted a law allowing pharmacists to dispense emergency contraception without a doctor's prescription.

This policy summary relies in large part on information from NARAL Pro-Choice America.

Endnotes

[1] Kaiser Family Foundation and SELF Magazine, "A National Survey of Women about Their Sexual Health," 2003.

[2] See e.g., Kaiser Family Foundation and Lifetime Television, "Vital Signs Index No. 2: Emergency Contraception," 2000.

[3] "Adolescents Unaware of Emergency Contraception, According to Survey," Kaiser Daily Reproductive Health Report, November 19, 2003.

[4] Cynthia Dailard, "Increased Awareness Needed to Reach Full Potential of Emergency Contraception," *The Guttmacher Report on Public Policy*, Vol. 4, No. 3, June 2001.

[5] Kaiser Family Foundation, "Women's Health Care Providers' Experiences with Emergency Contraception," Survey Snapshot, November 2000.

[6] Tammy Draut, "Emergency Contraception: Do Pharmacists Know About This Important Method to Prevent Pregnancy?," Planned Parenthood of New York City, 1999.

Emergency Contraception - Collaborative Practice

For more information...

Center for Policy Alternatives
1875 Connecticut Avenue NW, Suite 710
Washington, DC 20009
202-387-6030
www.stateaction.org

Alan Guttmacher Institute
120 Wall Street, 21st Floor
New York, NY 10005
212-248-1111
www.agi-usa.org

Henry J. Kaiser Family Foundation
2400 Sand Hill Road
Menlo Park, CA 94025
650-854-9400
www.kff.org

NARAL Pro-Choice America
1156 15th Street NW, Suite 700
Washington, DC 20005
202-973-3000
www.naral.org

Planned Parenthood Federation of America
434 West 33rd Street
New York, NY 10001
212-541-7800
www.plannedparenthood.org

Reproductive Health Technologies Project
1300 19th Street NW, 2nd Floor
Washington, DC 20036
202-557-3417
www.rhtp.org

Emergency Contraception - Collaborative Practice

Collaborative Practice for Emergency Contraception Act

Summary: The Collaborative Practice for Emergency Contraception Act would authorize pharmacists to initiate emergency contraception drug therapy in accordance with standardized protocols developed by the pharmacist and an authorized prescriber acting within his or her scope of practice.

SECTION 1. SHORT TITLE

This Act shall be called the "Collaborative Practice for Emergency Contraception Act."

SECTION 2. COLLABORATIVE PRACTICE

After section XXX, the following new section XXX shall be inserted:

COLLABORATIVE PRACTICE FOR EMERGENCY CONTRACEPTION

1. Notwithstanding any other provision of law, a pharmacist may initiate emergency contraception drug therapy in accordance with standardized procedures or protocols developed by the pharmacist and an authorized prescriber who is acting within his or her scope of practice.

2. Prior to performing any procedure authorized under this section, a pharmacist shall successfully complete emergency contraception drug therapy education and training in accordance with continuing education requirements established by the [State Board of Pharmacy]. A pharmacist who has had sufficiently recent education and training in emergency contraception may be exempted from this requirement.

3. For each emergency contraception drug therapy initiated pursuant to this section, the pharmacist shall provide each recipient of the emergency contraceptive drugs with a standardized fact sheet that includes: the indications for the use of the drug, the appropriate method for using the drug, information on the importance of follow-up health care, and healthcare referral information. The [Secretary of Health] shall develop this fact sheet in consultation with the American College of Obstetricians and Gynecologists and other relevant healthcare organizations. The provisions of this section do not preclude the use of existing publications developed by nationally recognized medical organizations.

4. Nothing in this section shall affect the requirements of existing law relating to maintaining the confidentiality of medical records.

SECTION 3. EFFECTIVE DATE

This Act shall take effect on July 1, 2004.

This model is based on legislation developed by NARAL Pro-Choice America.

Emergency Contraception

for Sexual Assault Victims

The American College of Emergency Physicians and the American College of Obstetricians and Gynecologists agree that emergency contraception should be offered to all victims of sexual assault. Yet many hospitals fail to provide emergency contraception.

Emergency Contraception for Sexual Assault Victims

Summary

- Every year, approximately 300,000 women are raped and about 25,000 become pregnant as the result of a sexual assault.
- Emergency contraception provides women with a safe and effective method to prevent unintended pregnancies soon after intercourse.
- Despite its benefits, a large percentage of women do not know that emergency contraception is available.
- Most hospitals do not provide emergency contraception—even to victims of sexual assault.
- The public supports increased availability of emergency contraception.
- In 2003, New Mexico, New York and Oregon enacted laws to provide access to emergency contraception for sexual assault victims.

Every year, approximately 300,000 women are raped and about 25,000 women become pregnant as the result of a sexual assault.[1]

About one in six American women will be raped at some point in their lives. Adding to the trauma of the assault, each year about 25,000 women who are raped will become pregnant by an attacker. As with other unintended pregnancies, about half of the pregnancies resulting from rape end in abortion.[2]

Emergency contraception provides women with a method to prevent unintended pregnancies soon after intercourse.

Among the types of emergency contraception currently available are special doses of regular birth control pills, commonly known as "morning after pills," and the use of a copper-T intrauterine device (IUD). Unlike Mifeprex, commonly called the "abortion pill," emergency contraception does not induce abortion. Instead, it inhibits ovulation, fertilization or implantation *before* a pregnancy occurs.

Emergency contraception is safe and effective.

Emergency contraceptive options have been available for more than 25 years, and emergency contraceptive pills can be used safely by most women, even those who cannot use oral contraceptives for the long term. If taken within 120 hours after intercourse, emergency contraceptive pills substantially reduce the risk of pregnancy. Copper-bearing IUDs used as emergency contraception have an even higher success rate.

Despite its benefits, a large percentage of women do not know that emergency contraception is available.

In a recent nationwide survey, fully one-third of women aged 18-44 said they did not know there is something a woman can do to prevent pregnancy after unprotected sex.[3] And because many women confuse it with Mifeprex, it is likely that substantially more than one-third do not know enough about emergency contraception to request it.[4] Further, women who may need emergency contraception the most know the least. A survey in New York City found that 95 percent of inner-city youth aged 14-18 had never heard of emergency contraception.[5]

Most hospitals do not provide emergency contraception—even to victims of sexual assault.

According to seven years of data from the Centers for Disease Control, less than half of all women who visited an emergency room after a sexual assault, and were not otherwise protected from pregnancy, received emergency contraception.[6] In a recent investigation, 66 percent of Catholic hospital emergency rooms did not provide emergency contraception to rape victims—despite the fact that the church does not prohibit its use.[7]

The American College of Emergency Physicians and the American College of Obstetricians and Gynecologists agree that emergency contraception should be offered to all victims of sexual assault.[8]

In fact, a California court ruled that a hospital could be held liable for failing to give a sexual assault victim information about, and access to, emergency contraception.[9]

The public supports increased availability of emergency contraception.

According to a national survey, over 80 percent of Americans believe that hospitals should not be allowed to deny emergency contraception to rape victims.[10] A January 2000 Peter Hart Research poll of New Jersey and Oregon voters found strong support for access to emergency contraception—62 percent in New Jersey and 64 percent in Oregon. Additionally, voters overwhelmingly oppose so-called "conscience clauses" that permit pharmacists to refuse to fill prescriptions—79 percent in New Jersey and 69 percent in Oregon.

In 2003, New Mexico, New York and Oregon enacted laws to provide access to emergency contraception for sexual assault victims.

The New Mexico and New York laws require hospital emergency rooms to provide sexual assault victims with both information about and access to emergency contraception. Oregon's statute establishes a Sexual Assault Victim's Emergency Medical Response Fund, which will pay the costs of emergency contraception to the extent monies are available. California, Illinois and Washington also have laws that facilitate the availability of emergency contraception to women who have been sexually assaulted.

This policy summary relies in large part on information from NARAL Pro-Choice America.

Endnotes

[1] Felicia Stewart and James Trussell, "Prevention of Pregnancy Resulting from Rape: A Neglected Preventive Health Measure," *American Journal of Preventive Medicine*, Vol. 19, No. 4, November 2000.

[2] Stanley Henshaw, "Unintended Pregnancy in the United States," *Family Planning Perspectives*, Vol. 30, No. 1, January-February 1998.

[3] Kaiser Family Foundation and SELF Magazine, "A National Survey of Women About Their Sexual Health," 2003.

[4] See e.g., Kaiser Family Foundation and Lifetime Television, "Vital Sign Index No. 2: Emergency Contraception," 2000.

[5] "Adolescents Unaware of Emergency Contraception, According to Survey," Kaiser Daily Reproductive Health Report, November 19, 2003.

[6] Annettee Amey and David Bishel, "Measuring the Quality of Medical Care for Women Who Experience Sexual Assault With Data from the National Hospital Ambulatory Medical Care Survey," *Annals of Emergency Medicine*, June 2002.

[7] Catholics for a Free Choice, "The Impact on Emergency Contraception," 2002. See http://www.cath4choice.org/indexhealth.htm.

[8] American College of Emergency Physicians Policy Statements, "Management of the Patient with the Complaint of Sexual Assault," October 2002; American College of Obstetricians and Gynecologists, "Violence Against Women, Acute Care of Sexual Assault Victims."

[9] *Brownfield v. Daniel Freeman Marina Hospital*, 208 Cal.App.3d 405 (Ct.App. 1989).

[10] American Civil Liberties Union Reproductive Freedom Project, "Religious and Reproductive Rights," 2002.

Emergency Contraception for Sexual Assault Victims

For more information...

Center for Policy Alternatives
1875 Connecticut Avenue NW, Suite 710
Washington, DC 20009
202-387-6030
www.stateaction.org

Alan Guttmacher Institute
1120 Connecticut Avenue NW, Suite 460
Washington, DC 20036
202-296-4012
www.agi-usa.org

Catholics for a Free Choice
1436 U Street NW, Suite 301
Washington, DC 20009
202-986-6093
www.cath4choice.org/indexhealth.htm

Center for Reproductive Law and Policy
120 Wall Street
New York, NY 10005
917-637-3600
www.crlp.org

Feminist Majority Foundation
1600 Wilson Boulevard, Suite 801
Arlington, VA 22209
703-522-2214
www.feminist.org

NARAL Pro-Choice America
1156 15th Street NW, Suite 700
Washington, DC 20005
202-973-3000
www.naral.org

Planned Parenthood Federation of America
434 West 33rd Street
New York, NY 10001
212-541-7800
www.plannedparenthood.org

Emergency Contraception for Sexual Assault Victims

Emergency Contraception for Sexual Assault Victims Act

SECTION 1. SHORT TITLE

This Act shall be called the "Emergency Contraception for Sexual Assault Victims Act."

SECTION 2. FINDINGS—The legislature finds that:

1. Each year, approximately 300,000 women are raped in the United States, and in [most recent year], [number] women were raped in [state].

2. Each year, approximately 25,000 women become pregnant as a result of rape and approximately 50 percent of these pregnancies end in abortion.

3. An estimated 22,000 of these pregnancies—88 percent—could be prevented if sexual assault victims had timely access to emergency contraception.

4. Approved for use by the Food and Drug Administration, emergency contraception prevents pregnancy after sexual intercourse.

5. Emergency contraception cannot and does not cause abortion.

6. While standards of emergency care established by the American Medical Association require that sexual assault victims be counseled about their risk of pregnancy and offered emergency contraception, most hospitals fail to provide emergency contraception to rape victims.

SECTION 3. EMERGENCY CONTRACEPTION FOR SEXUAL ASSAULT VICTIMS

After section XXX, the following new section XXX shall be inserted:

(A) DEFINITIONS—in this section:

1. "Emergency contraception" means any drug or device approved by the U.S. Food and Drug Administration that prevents pregnancy after sexual intercourse.

2. "Emergency care to sexual assault victims" means medical examinations, procedures, and services provided by a healthcare facility to a sexual assault victim following an alleged rape.

3. "Healthcare facility" means a hospital, emergency care facility, health clinic, or other healthcare center.

4. "Rape" means [as defined by state statute].

5. "Sexual assault victim" means a female who alleges or is alleged to have been raped.

Emergency Contraception for Sexual Assault Victims

(B) EMERGENCY CARE TO SEXUAL ASSAULT VICTIMS—It shall be the standard of care for healthcare facilities that provide emergency care to sexual assault victims to:

1. Provide each sexual assault victim with medically and factually accurate and unbiased written and oral information about emergency contraception.

2. Verbally inform each sexual assault victim of her option to be provided emergency contraception at the healthcare facility.

3. Provide emergency contraception immediately at the healthcare facility to each sexual assault victim who requests it. If the emergency contraception is in the form of pills, the provision must include the initial dose, which the sexual assault victim can take at the hospital, as well as any follow-up doses for the sexual assault victim to self-administer later.

(C) TRAINING—Every healthcare facility shall ensure that each person who provides care to sexual assault victims has medically and factually accurate and unbiased information about emergency contraception.

(D) PATIENT INFORMATION MATERIALS—The [Department of Health] shall develop and produce informational materials about emergency contraception for distribution in all emergency health facilities in the state. The informational materials must, in a medically and factually accurate and unbiased manner, describe the use, safety, efficacy and availability of emergency contraception, and the fact that it does not cause abortion.

(D) ENFORCEMENT—In addition to any remedies at common law, the [Department of Health] shall respond to complaints and shall periodically determine whether healthcare facilities are complying with this section. The [Department of Health] may use all investigative tools available to verify compliance with this section. If the [Department of Health] determines that a healthcare facility is not in compliance, the Department shall:

1. Impose a fine of $5,000 per sexual assault victim denied medically and factually accurate and unbiased information about emergency contraception, or who is not offered or provided emergency contraception.

2. Impose a fine of $5,000 for failure to comply with subsection C of this section. For every 30 days that the healthcare facility is not in compliance with subsection C, an additional fine of $5,000 shall be imposed.

3. After two violations, suspend or revoke the certificate of authority or deny the healthcare facility's application for certificate of authority.

SECTION 4. SEVERABILITY— If any provision, word, phrase or clause of this Act, or the application thereof, to any person, entity or circumstance should be held invalid, such invalidity shall not affect the remaining provisions, words, phrases or clauses of this Act which can be given effect without the invalid provision, word, phrase, clause or application, and to this end, the provisions, words, phrases or clauses of this Act are declared severable.

SECTION 5. EFFECTIVE DATE—This Act shall take effect on July 1, 2004.

*This model is based on legislation developed by **NARAL Pro-Choice America**.*

Energy Efficiency
Standards

If energy consumption is not reduced, states can expect power outages and blackouts, as well as increased energy prices.

Energy Efficiency Standards

Summary

- Energy consumption in the United States continues to grow unabated.
- If energy consumption is not reduced, many states can expect power outages and blackouts, as well as increased energy prices.
- Energy efficiency standards for large appliances and equipment, enacted by Congress in 1987 and 1992, have proven successful.
- Many household and commercial electrical products are unnecessarily wasteful because they are not subject to minimum energy efficiency standards.
- Implementing efficiency standards protects public health and the environment, and saves money for states and consumers.
- States can enact legislation that sets energy efficiency standards for small appliances.

Energy consumption in the United States continues to grow unabated.

During the 20th century, the amount of energy used in the United States doubled approximately every 20 years.[1] According to the U.S. Department of Energy, total energy consumption is projected to increase from 97 to 130 quadrillion British thermal units between 2001 and 2020.[2] If energy consumption is not reduced, states can expect power outages and blackouts, as well as increased energy prices.

Energy efficiency standards for large appliances and equipment, enacted by Congress in 1987 and 1992, have proven successful.

According to an analysis by the U.S. Department of Energy, federal efficiency standards reduced total U.S. electricity use by 2.5 percent in 2000. Reduced demand tends to lower prices for consumers.[3]

Many household and commercial electrical products are unnecessarily wasteful because they are not subject to minimum energy efficiency standards.

Common products such as torch lamps and ceiling fans continue to rely on outdated technology to govern their use of energy. While energy efficient versions of these and other products are available, insufficient incentives exist to create a robust market for them.

Efficiency standards save states and consumers money.

States can reduce their energy demands by up to five percent by implementing efficiency standards for 10 household and commercial products.[4] While efficiency standards have led to a modest increase in the price of regulated consumer goods, the savings reflected on lower energy bills are worth more than three times the additional costs.[5] Between 1990 and 2000, efficiency standards have saved consumers approximately $50 billion on their energy bills.[6]

Implementing efficiency standards protects public health and the environment.

Energy production and use account for nearly 80 percent of air pollution and emissions that contribute to smog, acid rain, respiratory problems, and other human and environmental hazards. For example, the energy needed to heat and light an average home produces twice the amount of greenhouse gases as the average car.[7] By lowering energy consumption, efficiency standards mean fewer power plants and lower emissions. This, in turn, means less smog, fewer asthma attacks, and reduced carbon dioxide emissions—the chief cause of climate change.

Businesses can benefit from new efficiency standards.

New jobs are created when businesses expand to meet the increased demand for energy-saving products. For example, the Maytag Corporation increased its workforce by 2,400 at one Illinois factory, and upgraded existing factories in AR, IN, MI and SC to comply with new refrigerator energy standards that went into effect in July 2001. In addition, standards encourage manufacturers to invest in energy efficient technologies, stimulating technological innovation in the marketplace.[8]

Energy efficiency standards can help safeguard national security.

The United States currently imports over half its oil, and the U.S. Department of Energy projects that U.S. reliance on imported oil will increase to two-thirds of consumption early this century. By reducing overall energy consumption, America's energy security becomes less dependent on foreign fossil fuels, and therefore less vulnerable to both price fluctuations and supply shortages.

States can enact legislation that sets energy efficiency standards for small appliances.

The Energy Efficiency Standards Small Appliances Act is based on California regulations instituted in 2000, which raise the efficiency standards for certain appliances and lighting fixtures sold in the state.

This policy summary relies in large part on information provided by the State Environmental Resource Center.

Endnotes

[1] Alliance to Save Energy, "Wasting Energy at Home?" February 22, 2002.

[2] Department of Energy: Energy Information Administration, "Annual Energy Outlook 2003 With Projections to 2025," January 9, 2003.

[3] American Council for an Energy Efficient Economy, "Appliance and Equipment Standards: One of America's Most Effective Energy-Saving Policies," 2002.

[4] Appliance Standards Awareness Project, "Why Standards?" 1999-2000.

[5] Ibid.

[6] "Appliance and Equipment Standards: One of America's Most Effective Energy-Saving Policies."

[7] "Change a Habit," *Grist Magazine,* January 17, 2002.

[8] Natalie Hildt, "Appliance and Equipment Efficiency Standards: New Opportunities for States," Appliance Standards Awareness Project, December 2001.

Energy Efficiency Standards

For more information...

Center for Policy Alternatives
1875 Connecticut Avenue NW, Suite 710
Washington, DC 20009
202-387-6030
www.stateaction.org

State Environmental Resource Center
106 East Doty Street, Suite 200
Madison, Wisconsin 53703
608-252-9800
www.serconline.org

American Council for an Energy Efficient Economy
1001 Connecticut Avenue NW, Suite 801
Washington, DC 20036
202-429-8873
www.aceee.org

Appliance Standards Awareness Project
20 Belgrade Avenue, Suite 1
Boston, MA 02131
617-363-9101
www.asap.org

Consortium for Energy Efficiency
One State Street, Suite 1400
Boston, MA 02109
617-589-3949
www.cee1.org/home/html

U.S. Department of Energy
1000 Independence Avenue SW
Washington, DC 20585
1-800-342-5363
www.energy.gov/efficiency

Energy Efficiency Standards

Energy Efficiency Standards Act

Summary: The Energy Efficiency Standards Act, based on Massachusetts and Connecticut statutes and California regulations, sets specific energy efficiency standards on selected products similar to Energy Star, the Federal Energy Management Program, and Consortium for Energy Efficiency specifications. This model legislation only covers products for which standards can be easily determined.

SECTION 1. SHORT TITLE

This Act shall be called the "Energy Efficiency Standards Act."

SECTION 2. ENERGY EFFICIENCY STANDARDS

After section XXX, the following new section XXX shall be inserted:

(A) DEFINITIONS – In this section:

1. "Ceiling fan" means a non-portable device that is suspended from a ceiling for circulating air via the rotation of fan blades.
2. "Ceiling fan light kit" means equipment designed to provide light from a ceiling fan which can be integral, such that the equipment is hardwired to the ceiling fan, or attachable, such that at the time of sale the equipment is not physically attached to the ceiling fan, but may be included inside the ceiling fan package at the time of sale or sold separately for subsequent attachment to the fan.
3. "Commercial clothes washer" means a soft mount horizontal- or vertical-axis clothes washer that has a clothes container compartment no greater than 3.5 cubic feet in the case of a horizontal-axis product or no greater than 4.0 cubic feet in the case of a vertical-axis product, and is designed for use by more than one household, such as in multi-family housing, apartments, or coin laundries.
4. "Commercial refrigerators and freezers" means refrigerators, freezers, or refrigerator-freezers designed for use by commercial or institutional facilities for the purpose of storing food products, ice, or other perishable items at specified temperatures that incorporate most components involved in the vapor-compression cycle and the refrigerated compartment in a single package, and may be configured with either solid or transparent doors as a reach-in cabinet, pass-through cabinet, roll-in cabinet, or roll-through cabinet. This term does not include products with 85 cubic feet or more of internal volume, walk-in refrigerators or freezers, or consumer products that are federally regulated pursuant to 42 U.S. Code section 6291 and subsequent sections.
5. "Digital cable television box" means a device that acts as a tuner for cable television programming and converts digital signals received from a cable service provider to a signal usable by a television set.
6. "Digital television converter box" means a device that receives and decodes digital broadcast signals for display by an analog television set, and is not a digital cable television box or wireless television receiver.
7. "Illuminated exit sign" means an internally-illuminated sign that is designed to be permanently fixed in place to identify an exit and consists of an electrically powered integral light source that illuminates the legend "EXIT" and any directional indicators and provides contrast between the legend, any directional indicators, and the background.
8. "Large packaged air-conditioning equipment" means packaged air-conditioning equipment having 240,000 Btu/hour or more of cooling capacity that is built as a package and shipped as a whole to end-user sites.
9. "Low voltage dry-type distribution transformer" means a distribution transformer that has an input voltage of 600 volts or less, is air-cooled, does not use oil as a coolant, and is rated for operation at a frequency of 60 Hertz. The term "low voltage dry-type transformer" does not include transformers with multiple voltage taps, with the highest voltage tap equaling at least 20 percent more than the lowest

Energy Efficiency Standards

voltage tap, or transformers, such as those commonly known as drive transformers, rectifier transformers, auto-transformers, Uninterruptible Power System transformers, impedance transformers, harmonic transformers, regulating transformers, sealed and non-ventilating transformers, machine tool transformers, welding transformers, grounding transformers, or testing transformers, that are designed to be used in a special purpose application and are unlikely to be used in general purpose applications.

10. "Multi-function device" means a physically integrated electronic device that has the core function of a digital cable television box and one or more additional functionalities, such as Internet access, personal digital recording, or video game operation.

11. "Pass-through cabinet" means a commercial refrigerator or freezer with hinged or sliding doors on both the front and rear of the unit.

12. "Reach-in cabinet" means a commercial refrigerator or freezer with hinged or sliding doors or lids, but does not include roll-in or roll-through cabinets or pass-through cabinets.

13. "Roll-in cabinet" means a commercial refrigerator or freezer with hinged or sliding doors that allow wheeled racks of product to be rolled into the unit.

14. "Roll-through cabinet" means a commercial refrigerator or freezer with hinged or sliding doors on two sides of the cabinet that allow wheeled racks of product to be rolled through the unit.

15. "Secretary" means the Secretary of the Department of [Consumer Protection].

16. "Set-top box" means a digital cable television box, wireless television receiver, or digital television converter box.

17. "Torchiere" means a portable electric lamp with a reflective bowl that directs light upward onto a ceiling so as to produce indirect illumination on the surfaces below.

18. "Traffic signal module" means a standard 8-inch (200mm) or 12-inch (300mm) traffic signal indication, consisting of a light source, a lens, and all other parts necessary for operation.

19. "Transformer" means a device consisting of two or more coils of insulated wire and that is designed to transfer alternating current by electromagnetic induction from one coil to another to change the original voltage or current value.

20. "Unit heater" means a self-contained, vented fan-type commercial space heater that uses natural gas, propane or fuel oil that is designed to be installed without ducts, within a heated space except that such term does not include any products covered by federal standards established pursuant to 42 U.S. Code section 6291 and subsequent sections or any product that is a direct vent, forced flue heater with a sealed combustion burner.

21. "Wireless television receiver" means a device used in conjunction with a dish antenna to receive satellite or other wireless television programming and that converts signals from a dish antenna for use by a television set.

(B) ENERGY EFFICIENCY STANDARDS ESTABLISHED

1. Not later than January 1, 2005, the Secretary, in consultation with [heads of other appropriate agencies] shall adopt regulations stablishing minimum efficiency standards for the following types of new products. For each product, minimum efficiency standards shall be no less strict than the following:

a. Ceiling fans and ceiling fan light kits shall meet the Tier 1 criteria of Version 1.1 of the product specification contained in the "Energy Star Program Requirements for Residential Ceiling Fans" prescribed by the U.S. Environmental Protection Agency.

b. Commercial clothes washers shall meet the requirements shown in Table P-3 of section 1605.3 of the California Code of Regulations, Title 20: Division 2, Chapter 4, Article 4: Appliance Efficiency Regulations that took effect on November 27, 2002.

c. Commercial refrigerators and freezers shall meet the August 1, 2004 requirements shown in Table A-6 of section 1605.3 of the California Code of Regulations, Title 20: Division 2, Chapter 4, Article 4: Appliance Efficiency Regulations that took effect on November 27, 2002.

d. Illuminated exit signs shall meet the Version 2.0 Energy Star Program performance requirements for illuminated exit signs prescribed by the U.S. Environmental Protection Agency.

Energy Efficiency Standards

e. Large packaged air-conditioning equipment shall meet the Tier 2 efficiency levels of the "Minimum Equipment Efficiencies for Unitary Commercial Air Conditioners" or "Minimum Equipment Efficiencies for Heat Pumps," as appropriate, developed by the Consortium for Energy Efficiency, Boston, MA, as in effect on January 1, 2002.

f. Low voltage dry-type distribution transformers shall meet the Class 1 efficiency levels for distribution transformers specified in Table 4-2 of the "Guide for Determining Energy Efficiency for Distribution Transformers" published by the National Electrical Manufacturers Association (NEMA Standard TP-1-2002).

g. Set-top boxes other than multi-function devices shall meet the Tier 1 criteria of the product specification of the U.S. Environmental Protection Agency's "Energy Star Program Requirements for Set-top Boxes" that took effect on January 1, 2001.

h. Torchieres shall consume not more than 190 watts and shall not be capable of operating with lamps that total more than 190 watts.

i. Red and green traffic signal modules shall meet the product specification of the "Energy Star Program Requirements for Traffic Signals" developed by the U.S. Environmental Protection Agency that took effect in February 2001 and shall be installed with compatible, electrically-connected signal control interface devices and conflict monitoring systems. The Commissioner, in consultation with the (Secretary of Transportation), may exempt specific traffic signals from this requirement upon a determination that installing compliant signals would not be cost-effective on a life-cycle cost basis.

j. Unit heaters shall be equipped with an intermittent ignition device and shall have either power venting or an automatic flue damper.

2. On or after January 1, 2006, no new commercial refrigerator or freezer, illuminated exit sign, large packaged air conditioning equipment, low voltage dry-type distribution transformer, torchiere, traffic signal module, or unit heater may be sold or offered for sale in the state unless the efficiency of the new product meets or exceeds the efficiency standards. On or after January 1, 2007, no new ceiling fan, ceiling fan light kit, commercial clothes washer, or set-top box may be sold or offered for sale in the state unless the efficiency of the new product meets or exceeds the efficiency standards.

3. On or after January 1, 2007, no new commercial refrigerator or freezer, illuminated exit sign, large packaged air conditioning equipment, low voltage dry-type distribution transformer, torchiere, traffic signal module, or unit heater may be installed in the state unless the efficiency of the new product meets or exceeds the efficiency standards. On or after January 1, 2008, no new ceiling fan, ceiling fan light kit, commercial clothes washer, or set-top box may be installed in the state unless the efficiency of the new product meets or exceeds the efficiency standards.

(C) REGULATORY AUTHORITY

1. The Secretary may establish increased efficiency standards on the products listed in Section (B)(1). The Secretary may also establish standards for products not specifically listed in Section (B)(1). In considering such new or amended standards, the Secretary, in consultation with the [heads of other appropriate departments], shall set efficiency standards upon a determination that increased efficiency standards would serve to promote energy conservation in the state and would be cost-effective for consumers who purchase and use such products. However, no new or increased efficiency standards shall become effective within one year following the adoption of any amended regulations providing for such increased efficiency standards. The Secretary may apply for a waiver of federal preemption in accordance with federal procedures for those products regulated by the federal government. The Secretary may adopt such further regulations as are necessary to implement the provisions of this section.

2. The Secretary, in consultation with [heads of other appropriate departments], shall adopt procedures for testing the energy efficiency of the new products covered by this section if such procedures are not provided for in the [state building code]. The Secretary shall use U.S. Department of Energy approved test methods, or in the absence of such test methods, other appropriate nationally recognized test methods. The

Energy Efficiency Standards

manufacturers of such products shall cause samples of such appliances to be tested in accordance with the test procedures adopted pursuant to this section or those specified in the [state building code].

3. Manufacturers of new products covered by this section shall certify to the Secretary that such products are in compliance with the provisions of this section. The Secretary shall promulgate regulations governing the certification of such products, and may propose to work in coordination with the certification programs of other states with similar standards.

4. The Secretary may test products covered by this section using an accredited testing facility. If tested products are found to be not in compliance with the minimum efficiency standards, the Secretary shall:
a. Charge the manufacturer of such product for the cost of product purchase and testing.
b. Provide information to the public on products found to be not in compliance with the standards.

5. The Secretary may cause periodic inspections to be made of distributors or retailers of new products covered by this section in order to determine compliance with the provisions of this section. The Secretary shall also work with the [head of building code administration] to coordinate inspections for new products that are also covered by the [state building code].

(D) EXEMPTIONS

The provisions of this section do not apply to:

1. New products manufactured in the state and sold outside the state.

2. New products manufactured outside the state and sold at wholesale inside the state for final retail sale and installation outside the state.

3. Products installed in mobile manufactured homes at the time of construction.

4. Products designed expressly for installation and use in recreational vehicles.

(E) ENFORCEMENT

1. The Secretary shall investigate complaints received concerning violations of this section and shall report the results of such investigations to the Attorney General. The Attorney General may institute proceedings to enforce the provisions of this section.

2. Any manufacturer, distributor or retailer who violates any provision of this section shall be issued a warning by the Secretary for any first violation. Repeat violations shall be subject to a civil penalty of not more than $250. Each violation of this section shall constitute a separate offense, and each day that such violation continues shall constitute a separate offense.

SECTION 3. SEVERABILITY

The provisions of this Act shall be severable, and if any phrase, clause, sentence, or provision is declared to be invalid or is preempted by federal law or regulation, the validity of the remainder of this Act shall not be affected.

SECTION 4. EFFECTIVE DATE

This Act shall take effect on July 1, 2004.

Equal
Pay

In America, people's wages should be based on the value of their work. But for many women and people of color, that American promise remains unfulfilled, and families are paying the price.

Equal Pay

Summary

- Millions of women and people of color continue to suffer wage discrimination.
- This inequity particularly affects women of color, with African-American women earning 68¢ and Latinas earning only 56¢ for every dollar paid to white male workers.
- The gender wage gap alone results in an average annual loss of more than $4,000 per American family.
- Existing laws are hard to enforce and do not address the problem of occupations that are undervalued because they are dominated by women or people of color.
- States can enact legislation that strengthens enforcement of existing laws and creates a means to identify and address the causes of unequal pay.
- Equal pay will not bust the budgets of businesses or governments.
- Equal pay is good business and can boost the economy.

Millions of women and people of color continue to suffer wage discrimination.

Today, according to the U.S. Census Bureau, women working full-time throughout the year earn 77¢ for every dollar earned by men.[1] African-American women earn 68¢ and Latinas earn 56¢ for every dollar paid to white male workers. Men of color also experience wage discrimination, with African-American men earning 75¢ and Latinos earning only 64¢ for every dollar paid to their white male counterparts.[2]

The gender wage gap alone results in an average annual loss of more than $4,000 per American family.[3]

If married women were paid the same as men doing comparable work, family incomes would rise and family poverty rates would fall. If single working mothers earned as much as men doing comparable work, their family poverty rates would be cut in half.[4] Moreover, lower lifetime earnings translate into less savings and lower pensions during retirement. Reductions in poverty rates would also reduce the need for government expenditures on assistance programs like the Earned Income Tax Credit and food stamps.

The wage gap is the result of both discrimination and the concentration of women and people of color in a narrow range of jobs that are undervalued and underpaid.

Although the wage gap can be partially explained by differences in education, experience and/or time in the workforce, a significant portion cannot be attributed to any of these factors and is the result of discrimination. In recent years, Home Depot and Publix Supermarkets each agreed to pay more than $80 million to settle lawsuits based on sex discrimination. In 2000, Coca-Cola settled a wage discrimination lawsuit brought by African-American workers for more than $190 million. Further, more than half of all women workers hold sales, clerical, service or caregiving jobs (child care, elder care, and nursing). These professions, held mainly by women, pay less than equivalent jobs held by men.

Existing laws are hard to enforce and do not address the problem of occupations that are undervalued because they are dominated by women or people of color.

Federal and state equal pay laws have been in effect for decades, yet wage discrimination continues. Not only are these laws poorly enforced, but they do not apply to the problem of unequal pay for *equivalent* work in *different* jobs.

States can enact legislation that strengthens enforcement of existing laws and creates a means to identify and address the causes of unequal pay.

One option, the Equal Pay Remedies and Enforcement Act, enhances existing laws and establishes a multi-sector Equal Pay Commission to study and make recommendations about the extent, causes and consequences of wage disparities. The Commission provides the research needed to craft state-specific policies.

States can also enact legislation requiring equal pay for equivalent jobs.

Another option, the Fair Pay Act, prohibits pay differentials between women and men and between minority and non-minority workers in jobs that are equal or that, though dissimilar, are nevertheless equivalent in their overall composite of skills, effort, responsibility and working conditions. Exceptions are made for differentials based on bona fide seniority, merit or other non-discriminatory factors.

States have led the way in closing the wage gap for over two decades.

States began taking action on equal pay in 1982, when Minnesota first implemented equal pay for all public sector employees. States continue to be the source of innovative solutions for solving the wage gap. In 2003, Illinois enacted a law that prohibits wage discrimination on the basis of gender; New Mexico and Utah passed bills requiring pay equity studies; and the West Wirginia legislature created an equal pay commission.

It is possible to compare different jobs within an organization to determine equivalent work.

For several decades American employers have used job evaluation studies to set pay and rank for different jobs within a company, often taking into consideration factors such as skill, effort, responsibility and working conditions. In fact, two out of three workers are employed by businesses that use some form of job evaluation. The federal government's job evaluation system, covering nearly 2 million employees, has been in use for over 70 years.

Equal pay will not bust the budgets of businesses or governments.

Pay adjustments tend to be modest and are phased in over a period of years. In Minnesota, where equal pay legislation was implemented for public sector employees over a four-year period, the cost was only 3.7 percent of the state's payroll budget. In the state of Washington, equal pay for state employees was achieved at a cost of 2.6 percent of personnel costs, implemented over an eight-year period.

Equal pay is good business and can boost the economy.

One survey found that businesses cited the elimination of wage discrimination between different jobs as "good business," and that equal pay is consistent with remaining competitive.[5] Furthermore, raising wages for women and people of color increases their purchasing power, which strengthens the economy. As working families continue to face economic hardship resulting from the recession, it is critical that women and people of color receive fair wages.

Endnotes

[1] Using 2002 annual earnings from the U.S. Census Bureau (Current Population Reports).

[2] U.S. Bureau of Labor Statistics (Current Population Survey).

[3] AFL-CIO & Institute for Women's Policy Research, "Equal Pay for Working Families: National and State Data on the Pay Gap and its Costs," 1999.

[4] Ibid.

[5] National Committee on Pay Equity, "Questions and Answers on Pay Equity," 2000.

Equal Pay

For more information...

Center for Policy Alternatives
1875 Connecticut Avenue NW, Suite 710
Washington, DC 20009
202-387-6030
www.stateaction.org

AFL-CIO
815 16th Street NW
Washington, DC 20006
202-637-5000
www.aflcio.org/women

American Federation of State, County and Municipal Employees
1625 L Street NW
Washington, DC 20036
202-429-1000
www.afscme.org

Business and Professional Women
1900 M Street NW, Suite 310
Washington, DC 20036
202-293-1100
www.bpwusa.org

9to5, National Association of Working Women
231 W. Wisconsin Avenue, Suite 900
Milwaukee, WI 53203
414-274-09251
www.9to5.org

Institute for Women's Policy Research
1707 L Street NW, Suite 750
Washington, DC 20036
202-785-5100
www.iwpr.org

Women's Bureau
U.S. Department of Labor
200 Constitution Avenue NW
Room No. S-3002
Washington, DC 20210
800-827-5335
www.dol.gov/wb/welcome.html

Women's Institute for Secure Retirement
1920 N Street NW, Suite 300
Washington, DC 20036
202-393-5452
www.wiser.heinz.org

National Education Association
1201 16th Street NW
Washington, DC 20036
202-833-4000
www.nea.org

Equal Pay Remedies and Enforcement Act

SECTION 1. SHORT TITLE

This Act shall be called the "Equal Pay Remedies and Enforcement Act."

SECTION 2. FINDINGS AND PURPOSE

(A) FINDINGS—The legislature finds that:

1. Despite federal and state laws banning discrimination in employment and pay in both the private and public sectors, wage differentials persist between women and men, and between minorities and non-minorities in the same jobs, and in jobs that are not the same but that require equivalent composites of skill, effort, responsibility and working conditions.

2. Wage discrimination not only harms individual women and people of color, it depresses living standards, contributes to higher poverty rates among female-headed and minority households, prevents the maximum utilization of available labor resources, causes labor disputes that burden commerce, and violates the state's expressed policy against discrimination.

3. Many people work in occupations that are dominated by individuals of their own sex, race and/or national origin, and discrimination in hiring, job assignment, and promotion has played a role in establishing and maintaining segregated workforces.

4. Current remedies imposed on employers who practice discrimination in pay between men and women, and between minorities and non-minorities, have proven to be only partially effective in eliminating such wage disparities.

5. Understanding the full extent and causes of wage disparities between men and women, and between minorities and non-minorities in the private and public sectors, would enable the state to take more effective measures to reduce disparities and to eliminate discrimination in wage-setting.

(B) PURPOSE—This law is enacted to protect the health and welfare of individual residents and improve the overall labor environment by correcting and deterring discriminatory wage practices based on sex, race, and/or national origin; developing reliable data about the extent of such wage discrimination; and providing greater understanding about its causes.

SECTION 3. ENHANCED PENALTIES

After section XXX [citation to remedial section of the state equal pay law], the following new paragraphs shall be inserted:

(A) Any employer who violates section(s) [citation to section(s) prohibiting wage discrimination] shall additionally be liable for such compensatory and punitive damages as may be appropriate.

(B) Any employer found liable by virtue of a final judgment under this Act for any monetary damages provided thereunder shall pay to the state a civil penalty equal to 10 percent of the amount of damages owed. Such civil penalty shall be used by the state solely for the purpose of carrying out its responsibilities

Equal Pay

for the administration and/or enforcement of this section, the Equal Pay Commission, and the enforcement of [insert name(s) of other state employment discrimination laws].

SECTION 4. EQUAL PAY COMMISSION

(A) Within 90 days after the effective date of this Act, the [Secretary of Labor] shall appoint a Commission of nine members, to be known as the "Equal Pay Commission."

(B) Membership of the Commission shall be as follows:

1. Two representatives of businesses in the state, who are appointed from among individuals nominated by state business organizations and business trade associations.

2. Two representatives of labor organizations, who have been nominated by a state labor federation chartered by a federation of national or international unions, that admits local unions as members, and exists primarily to carry on educational, legislative and coordinating activities.

3. Two representatives of organizations whose objectives include the elimination of pay disparities between men and women and/or minorities and non-minorities, and who have undertaken advocacy, educational or legislative initiatives in pursuit of that objective.

4. Three individuals, drawn from higher education or research institutions, who have experience and expertise in the collection and analysis of data concerning such pay disparities and whose research has already been used in efforts to promote the elimination of those disparities.

(C) The Commission shall make a full and complete study of:

1. The extent of wage disparities, in both the public and private sector, between men and women, and between minorities and non-minorities.

2. Those factors which cause, or which tend to cause, such disparities, including segregation of women and men, and of minorities and non-minorities across and within occupations; payment of lower wages for occupations traditionally dominated by women and/or minorities; child-rearing responsibilities; and education and training.

3. The consequences of such disparities on the economy and on affected families.

4. Actions, including proposed legislation, that are likely to lead to the elimination and prevention of such disparities.

(D) The Commission shall, no later than 12 months after its members are appointed, make its report to the [Secretary of Labor], who shall in turn transmit it to the Governor.

(E) The Commission's report shall include the results of its study as well as recommendations, legislative and otherwise, for the elimination and prevention of disparities in wages between men and women, and between minorities and non-minorities.

SECTION 5. EFFECTIVE DATE - This Act shall take effect on July 1, 2004.

Fair Pay Act

SECTION 1. SHORT TITLE

This Act shall be called the "Fair Pay Act."

SECTION 2. FINDINGS AND PURPOSE

(A) FINDINGS – The legislature finds that:

1. Despite federal and state laws banning discrimination in pay in both the public and private sectors, wage differentials persist between women and men and between minorities and non-minorities in the same jobs, and in jobs that are dissimilar but require equivalent composites of skill, effort, responsibility and working conditions.

2. The existence of such wage differentials depresses wages and living standards; reduces family incomes and contributes to higher poverty rates experienced by female-headed and minority households; prevents the maximum utilization of available labor resources; tends to cause labor disputes, thereby burdening and obstructing commerce; constitutes an unfair method of competition; and [insert a state specific finding, e.g., "constitutes an unfair labor practice under state law or violates the state's public policy against discrimination."]

3. Discrimination in wage-setting practices has played a role in depressing wages of women and minorities.

4. Many individuals work in occupations that are dominated by members of the same sex, race, and/or national origin, and discrimination in hiring, job assignment, and promotion has played a role in establishing and maintaining segregated workforces.

5. Eliminating discrimination in compensation based on sex, race and/or national origin would have many positive effects, including providing a solution to problems in the economy created by discriminatory wage differentials; reducing the number of working women and people of color earning low wages, thereby lowering their incidence of poverty during normal working years and in retirement; and promoting stable families by raising family incomes.

(B) PURPOSE – It is the purpose of this Act to correct, and as rapidly as practicable to eliminate, discriminatory wage practices based on sex, race and/or national origin.

SECTION 3. FAIR PAY

After section XXX, the following new section XXX shall be inserted:

(A) DEFINITIONS – In this section:

1. "Employer" means [cite existing definition in state employment law].

2. "Employee" includes any permanent employee, whether working full-time or part-time, and any temporary employee who has worked for a period of at least three months. "Employee" shall not include any individual employed by his/her parents, spouse or child.

Equal Pay

3. "Equivalent jobs" means jobs or occupations that are equal within the meaning of the Equal Pay Act of 1963, 29 U.S.C. 206(d), or jobs or occupations that are dissimilar but whose requirements are equivalent, when viewed as a composite of skill, effort, responsibility and working conditions.

4. "Person" means an individual, partnership, association, corporation or other legal entity, including the state and all of its political agencies and subdivisions.

5. "Labor organization" means any organization that exists for the purpose, in whole or in part, of collective bargaining, or of dealing with employers concerning grievances, terms or conditions of employment, or of other mutual aid or protection in connection with employment.

6. "Market rates" means the rates that employers within a prescribed geographic area actually pay, or are reported to pay for specific jobs, as determined by formal or informal surveys, wage studies, or other means.

7. "Wages and wage rates" shall include all compensation in any form that an employer provides to employees in payment for work done or services rendered, including, but not limited to, base pay, bonuses, commissions, awards, tips, or various forms of non-monetary compensation if provided in lieu of, or in addition to, monetary compensation, and that have economic value to an employee.

(B) PROHIBITION AGAINST DISCRIMINATION IN WAGES

1. It shall be an unlawful employment practice in violation of this chapter for an employer to discriminate between employees on the basis of sex, race and/or national origin by:

a. Paying wages to employees at a rate less than the rate paid to employees of the opposite sex or of a different race or national origin for work in equivalent jobs; and/or
b. Paying wages to employees in a job that is dominated by employees of a particular sex, race or national origin at a rate less than the rate at which such employer pays to employees in another job that is dominated by employees of the opposite sex or of a different race or national origin, for work on equivalent jobs.

2. Notwithstanding paragraph 1 above, it shall not be an unlawful employment practice for an employer to pay different wage rates to employees, where such payments are made pursuant to:

a. A bona fide seniority or merit system;
b. A system that measures earnings by quantity or quality of production; or
c. Any bona fide factor other than sex, race or national origin, provided, however, that wage differentials based on varying market rates for equivalent jobs or the differing economic benefits to the employer of equivalent jobs shall not be considered differentials based on bona fide factors other than sex, race or national origin.

3. An employer who is paying wages in violation of this section shall not, in order to comply with the provisions of this section, reduce the wages of any employee.

4. No labor organization or its agents representing employees of an employer having employees subject to any provision of this chapter shall cause or attempt to cause such an employer to discriminate against an employee in violation of paragraph 1 of this section.

5. The [State Department of Labor or other appropriate agency] shall promulgate regulations specifying the criteria for determining whether a job is dominated by employees of a particular sex, race, or national origin. Criteria shall include, but not be limited to, factors such as whether the job has ever been formally classified

as or traditionally considered to be a "male" or "female" or "white" or "minority" job; whether there is a history of discrimination against women and/or people of color with regard to wages, assignments or access to jobs, or other terms and conditions of employment; and the demographic composition of the workforce in equivalent jobs (e.g., numbers or percentages of women, men, white persons, and people of color). The regulations shall not include a list of jobs.

(C) OTHER PROHIBITED ACTS

It shall be an unlawful employment practice in violation of this chapter for an employer:

1. To take adverse actions or otherwise discriminate against any individual because such individual has opposed any act or practice made unlawful by this section; has sought to enforce rights protected under this section; or has testified, assisted or participated in any manner in an investigation, hearing or other proceeding to enforce this section; or

2. To discharge, or in any other manner discriminate against, coerce, intimidate, threaten, or interfere with any employee or any other person because an employee inquired about, disclosed, compared, or otherwise discussed an employee's wages, or because an employee exercised, aided or encouraged any other person to exercise any right granted or protected by this section.

(D) WAGE DISCLOSURE, RECORDKEEPING AND REPORTING REQUIREMENTS

1. Upon commencement of an individual's employment and at least annually thereafter, every employer subject to this section shall provide to each employee a written statement sufficient to inform the employee of his or her job title, wage rate, and how the wage is calculated. This notice shall be supplemented whenever an employee is promoted or reassigned to a different position with the employer, provided however, that the employer is not required to issue supplemental notifications for temporary reassignments that are no greater than three months in duration.

2. Every employer subject to this section shall make and preserve records that document the wages paid to employees and that document and support the method, system, calculations and other bases used to establish, adjust and determine the wage rates paid to said employer's employees. Every employer subject to this section shall preserve records and make reports from the records as shall be prescribed by regulation by the [State Department of Labor or other appropriate agency].

3. The regulations promulgated under this section relating to the form of reports required by paragraph 2 shall provide for protection of the confidentiality of employees, and shall expressly require that reports shall not include the names or other identifying information from which readers could discern the identities of employees. The regulations may also identify circumstances that warrant a prohibition on disclosure of reports or information identifying the employer.

4. The [State Department of Labor] may use the information and data it collects pursuant to paragraph 2 for statistical and research purposes, and may compile and publish such studies, analyses, reports and surveys based on the information and data, as it considers appropriate.

(E) ENFORCEMENT

1. This section may be enforced by a private cause of action under [appropriate section of state law].

Equal Pay

2. This section shall be enforced by [appropriate state agency], which shall promulgate such regulations as are necessary to implement and administer compliance. Regulations shall include procedures to receive, investigate and attempt to resolve complaints; and bring actions in any court of competent jurisdiction to recover appropriate relief for aggrieved employees.

3. In any action under this section in which an employee prevails:

   a. The employee shall be awarded monetary relief, including back pay in an amount equal to the difference between the employee's actual earnings and what the employee would have earned but for the employer's unlawful practices, and an additional amount in punitive damages, as appropriate.
   b. The employer shall be enjoined from continuing to discriminate against employees and the employer may be ordered to take such additional affirmative steps as are necessary, including reinstatement or reclassification of affected workers, to ensure an end to unlawful discrimination.
   c. The employer shall pay a reasonable attorney's fee, reasonable expert witness fees, and other costs of the action.

(F) STATUTE OF LIMITATIONS

An action may be brought under this section not later than two years after the date of the last event constituting the alleged violation for which the action is brought.

SECTION 4. SEVERABILITY

The provisions of this Act shall be severable, and if any phrase, clause, sentence or provision is declared to be invalid or is preempted by federal law or regulation, the validity of the remainder of this Act shall not be affected.

SECTION 5. EFFECTIVE DATE

This Act shall take effect on July 1, 2004.

Estate Tax
Decoupling

Unless legislatures act to "decouple" from the 2001 federal estate tax law amendments, states will lose billions of dollars.

Estate Tax Decoupling

Summary

- Unless legislatures act, states will lose billions of dollars in tax revenues because of a change in federal estate tax law.
- In order to preserve critical tax revenues, states need to "decouple" from the 2001 federal estate tax law amendments.
- With severe state budget shortfalls, 2004 is a bad year to lose estate tax revenues.
- A loss of revenue from estate taxes will jeopardize spending on a range of crucial state programs, such as health, transportation and education.
- This is the wrong time to provide additional tax breaks to the rich.
- Eighteen states and the District of Columbia are currently decoupled from the federal estate tax.

Unless legislatures act, states will lose billions of dollars in tax revenues because of a change in federal estate tax law.

In 2001, Congress enacted a sweeping tax reduction law that includes a phaseout of the federal estate tax, culminating in a full repeal in 2010. On a much faster track, the law repeals the federal estate tax credit over the next three years. Most estate taxes in the states are linked to this federal credit, and if not unlinked, states would collectively lose $13 billion in revenues by 2007.

In order to preserve critical tax revenues, states need to "decouple" from the 2001 federal estate tax law amendments.

Decoupling means protecting state taxes by linking the state tax code to the federal law as it existed prior to the 2001 amendments. In the short term, decoupling would maintain the level of estate tax revenues received in prior years. In the long run, decoupling would prevent the total elimination of estate taxes in 2010. Nearly every state has linked its estate tax law to the federal code, so repeal of the federal tax would have the effect of repealing state estate taxes.

With severe state budget shortfalls, 2004 is a bad year to lose estate tax revenues.

States have been struggling with unprecedented budget deficits, and the bulk of their problems come from reduced revenues. With states scrambling to balance their budgets, it makes no sense to let a federal policy, enacted during completely different economic times, dictate a state's ability to serve its people.

A loss of revenue from estate taxes will jeopardize spending on a range of crucial state programs, such as health, transportation and education.

When public services are cut, low-income families suffer first. In addition, when programs are cut during hard economic times it means less consumer spending, further damaging small businesses and exacerbating the weak economy.

This is the wrong time to provide additional tax breaks to the rich.

Estate taxes are designed to impact only the wealthiest Americans. The federal estate tax, for example, is paid on behalf of approximately two percent of those who die each year. Allowing the repeal of estate taxes has the effect of enriching heirs of millionaires and billionaires while hurting families who struggle to make ends meet.

Eighteen states and the District of Columbia are currently decoupled from the federal estate tax.

Of these, 12 states (IL, ME, MD, MA, MN, NE, NJ, NC, PA, RI, VT, WI) enacted legislation to decouple from the federal changes. Six other states (KA, NY, OH, OR, VA, WA) and the District of Columbia have laws that do not automatically change with federal law—they remain decoupled without taking further legislative action.[1]

This policy summary relies in large part on information from the Center on Budget and Policy Priorities.

RETAINED REVENUES IF STATES FULLY DECOUPLE FROM FEDERAL ESTATE TAX
Cumulative Total for 2003-07 (in millions)

Alabama	$213.3
Alaska	10.1
Arizona	282.7
Arkansas	85.3
California	5,229.3
Colorado	216.8
Connecticut	463.0
Delaware	122.3
Florida	2,599.8
Georgia	422.0
Hawaii	110.7
Idaho	38.9
Indiana	64.3
Iowa	119.8
Kentucky	181.9
Louisiana	81.0
Michigan	565.0
Mississippi	107.9
Missouri	565.6
Montana	21.8
Nevada	144.5
New Hampshire	102.4
New Mexico	85.8
North Dakota	19.3
Oklahoma	48.2
South Carolina	190.5
South Dakota	18.7
Tennessee	70.9
Texas	1,112.0
Utah	56.6
West Virginia	65.9
Wyoming	34.6

Source: Center on Budget and Policy Priorities

Endnotes

[1] Elizabeth McNichol, "Many States Are Decoupling from the Federal Estate Tax Cut," Center on Budget and Policy Priorities, August 7, 2003.

Estate Tax Decoupling

For more information...

Center for Policy Alternatives
1875 Connecticut Avenue NW, Suite 710
Washington, DC 20009
202-387-603
www.stateaction.org

Center on Budget and Policy Priorities
820 First Street NE, Suite 510
Washington, DC 20002
202-408-1080
www.cbpp.org

Estate Tax Decoupling

Decoupling from federal estate tax changes

Language based on law enacted in Rhode Island:

For decedents whose death occurred on or after January 1, 2002, a tax is imposed upon the transfer of the net estate of every resident or nonresident decedent as a tax upon the right to transfer. The tax is a sum equal to the maximum credit for state death taxes allowed by 26 U.S.C. Section 2011 *as it was in effect as of January 1, 2001*, provided, however, any scheduled increase in the unified credit provided in 26 U.S.C. Section 2010 in effect on January 1, 2001 or thereafter shall not apply.

Language based on law enacted in North Carolina:

The amount of the estate tax imposed by this section for estates of decedents dying on or after January 1, 2002, is the maximum credit for state death taxes allowed under section 2011 of the Code *without regard to the phase-out of that credit under subdivision (b) (2) of that section.*

Language based on law enacted in Maryland:

(a) Notwithstanding an Act of Congress that repeals or reduces the federal credit under § 2011 of the Internal Revenue Code, the provisions of this subtitle in effect before the passage of the Act of Congress shall apply with respect to a decedent who dies after the effective date of the Act of Congress so as to continue the state estate tax in force without reduction in the same manner as if the federal credit had not been repealed or reduced.

(b)(1) Except as provided in paragraph (2) of this subsection, after the effective date of an Act of Congress described in subsection (a) of this section, the state estate tax shall be determined using:
(i) the federal credit allowable by § 2011 of the Internal Revenue Code as in effect before the reduction or repeal of the federal credit pursuant to the Act of Congress; and
(ii) other provisions of federal estate tax law, including the applicable unified credit allowed against the federal estate tax, as in effect on the date of the decedent's death.

(2) If the federal estate tax is not in effect on the date of the decedent's death, the Maryland estate tax shall be determined using:
(i) the federal credit allowable by § 2011 of the Internal Revenue Code as in effect before the reduction or repeal of the federal credit pursuant to the Act of Congress; and
(ii) other provisions of federal estate tax law, including the applicable unified credit allowed against the federal estate tax, as in effect on the date immediately preceding the effective date of the repeal of the federal estate tax.

Family Leave Benefits

Millions of American workers who qualify for family or medical leave don't take it because they cannot go without pay. States are enacting innovative programs to provide family leave benefits.

Family Leave Benefits

Summary

- Millions of American workers who qualify for family or medical leave don't take it because they cannot go without pay.
- Nearly one in ten workers who take family leave are forced onto public assistance.
- Family leave benefits support the needs of working families in today's economy.
- Family leave benefits strengthen businesses.
- Some states currently provide limited forms of family leave benefits.
- States have recently enacted innovative programs to provide family leave benefits through flexible sick leave.
- Americans strongly support paid family leave.

Millions of American workers who qualify for family or medical leave don't take it because they cannot go without pay.

Although the federal Family and Medical Leave Act of 1993 (FMLA) guarantees *unpaid* leave for child-birth or family illness, many Americans simply can't afford it. Of American workers who qualify for leave under the FMLA, 78 percent say they do not take it because they cannot afford to go without pay. For those who take leave, the financial hardship can be great. Nearly one in ten workers who take unpaid family leave are actually forced onto public assistance to make ends meet.[1] The right to take leave is meaningless if a worker can't afford it.

Family leave benefits support the needs of working families in today's economy.

Family and work patterns have shifted dramatically in recent decades, yet workplace policies have not kept pace with these changes. The proportion of mothers with children ages 6-17 in the workforce between 1955 and 2001 increased from 38 to 78 percent, and for mothers with children under six, from 18 to 64 percent.[2] About 25 percent of Americans have elderly relatives to care for, and many of them reduce their work hours or take a brief leave from work to care for them. Americans shouldn't have to choose between paying the bills and caring for family.

WHY WORKERS HAVE TAKEN FAMILY AND MEDICAL LEAVE:[3]

- 52% to care for their own serious illness
- 26% to care for a new child or for a maternity-related disability
- 13% to care for a seriously ill parent
- 12% to care for a seriously ill child
- 6% to care for a seriously ill spouse

(Sum is greater than 100% because some take more than one leave.)

Family leave benefits strengthen businesses.

The vast majority of employers—84 percent—found that the benefits of providing leave under the FMLA offset or outweighed the costs, according to the bipartisan Commission on Family Leave. Nearly 42 percent reported a positive return on their leave programs, and another 42 percent said the costs had a neutral effect. Furthermore, 98 percent of employees who took family leave returned to work for the same employer, and 77 percent of employers reported cost savings because of decreased turnover.[4]

Some states currently provide limited forms of family leave benefits.

California, Hawaii, New Jersey, New York, Rhode Island, and Puerto Rico have Temporary Disability Insurance (TDI) systems that provide partial wage replacement for employees who are temporarily disabled for medical reasons, including pregnancy and childbirth. Minnesota pioneered a public program that provides low-income working parents with subsidies for caring for infants under age one. Montana adopted a similar program in 2003. And in 2002, Oklahoma became the 25th state to require state and/or local governments to allow employees to use paid sick leave to care for certain ill family members.

In 2002, California enacted the first comprehensive family leave benefits statute.

Building on its existing TDI program, California's law allows workers to collect partial wages for up to six weeks while they take time off to care for a new infant or a seriously ill family member. The law is entirely employee-funded and is estimated to cost employees an average of $27 a year. Workers will be eligible for benefits of up to 55 percent of their wages, receiving no more than $728 a week.

Three states enacted flexible sick leave programs in 2002-03.

Connecticut, Hawaii and Washington gave employees—public and private—the right to use their sick leave as necessary to care for a newborn or a family member in need of personal care. Although these new laws do not provide additional leave to workers, they make legal what many employees have had to do covertly in order to balance their work and family responsibilities.

Americans strongly support paid family leave.

Eighty-two percent of women and 75 percent of men surveyed in 1998 favored the idea of developing a new insurance program that would provide families with partial wage replacement when a worker takes family or medical leave.[5] In 2002, 79 percent of working women surveyed said that access to paid family and medical leave is more important to them than increased pay, promotions and job flexibility.[6]

This policy brief relies in large part on information from the National Partnership for Women and Families.

Endnotes

[1] Department of Labor, "Balancing the Needs of Families and Employers: Family and Medical Leave Surveys," 2000.

[2] U.S. Department of Labor, Bureau of Labor Statistics, 2001.

[3] "Balancing the Needs of Families and Employers."

[4] Ibid.

[5] Lake Snell Perry and Associates, "Family Matters: A National Survey of Women and Men," conducted for the National Partnership for Women and Families, February 1998.

[6] Lake Snell Perry and Associates, "Ask a Working Woman Survey," conducted for AFL-CIO, March 2002.

Family Leave Benefits

For more information...

Center for Policy Alternatives
1875 Connecticut Avenue NW, Suite 710
Washington, DC 20009
202-387-6030
www.stateaction.org

AFL-CIO
815 16th Street NW
Washington, DC 20006
202-637-5064
www.aflcio.org/women

Economic Opportunity Institute
1900 North Northlake Way, Suite 237
Seattle, WA 98103
206-633-6580
www.eoionline.org

National Employment Law Project
55 John Street, 7th Floor
New York, NY 10038
212-285-3025
www.nelp.org

National Parenting Association
1841 Broadway, Room 808
New York, NY 10023
212-315-2333
www.parentsunite.org

National Partnership for Women and Families
1875 Connecticut Avenue NW, Suite 650
Washington, DC 20009
202-986-2600
www.nationalpartnership.org

Family Leave Benefits

Flexible Sick Leave Act

Summary: The Flexible Sick Leave Act allows employees to use employer-granted leave to care for family members with serious medical conditions.

SECTION 1. SHORT TITLE

This Act shall be called the "Flexible Sick Leave Act."

SECTION 2. FLEXIBLE SICK LEAVE

After section XXX, the following new section XXX shall be inserted:

(A) DEFINITIONS—In this section:

1. "Child" means a biological, adopted, or foster child, a stepchild, a legal ward, or a child of a person standing in loco parentis who is:

   a. Under eighteen years of age; or
   b. Eighteen years of age or older and incapable of self-care because of a mental or physical disability.

2. "Grandparent" means a parent of a parent.

3. "Parent" means a biological parent or an individual who stood in loco parentis when a person was a child.

4. "Parent-in-law" means a parent of the spouse.

5. "Sick leave or other paid time off" means time allowed under the terms of a collective bargaining agreement or employer policy, as applicable, to an employee for illness, vacation, or personal holiday.

6. "Spouse" means a husband, wife or domestic partner.

(B) USE OF SICK LEAVE

1. If, under the terms of an employment contract, a collective bargaining agreement or employer policy, an employee is entitled to sick leave or other paid time off, then the employer shall allow the employee to use any or all of the employee's choice of sick leave or other paid time off to care for:

   a. A child of the employee with a health condition that requires treatment or supervision; or
   b. A spouse, parent, parent-in-law, or grandparent of the employee who has a serious health condition or an emergency condition.

2. An employee may not exercise a right under this section to take leave until it has been earned. The employee taking leave under the circumstances described in this section must comply with the terms of the collective bargaining agreement or employer policy applicable to the leave, except for any terms which contradict this section.

Family Leave Benefits

(C) ENFORCEMENT

1. This section shall be enforced by [appropriate state agency], which shall promulgate such regulations as are necessary to implement and administer compliance. Regulations shall include procedures to receive, investigate and attempt to resolve complaints; and bring actions in any court of competent jurisdiction to recover appropriate relief for aggrieved employees.

2. An employer shall not discharge, threaten to discharge, demote, suspend, discipline, or otherwise discriminate against an employee because the employee exercised, or attempted to exercise, any right under this section, or filed a complaint, testified, or assisted in any proceeding to enforce this section.

SECTION 3. EFFECTIVE DATE

This Act shall take effect on July 1, 2004.

Family Leave Benefits

Family Leave Benefits Insurance Act

Summary: The Family Leave Benefits Insurance Act establishes a fund to provide a safety net for men and women who are temporarily unable to work due to their own serious illness, or their need to provide care to a newborn, newly adopted or newly placed foster child, or to a seriously ill child, spouse or parent.

SECTION 1. SHORT TITLE

This Act shall be called the "Family Leave Benefits Insurance Act."

SECTION 2. FINDINGS AND PURPOSE

(A) FINDINGS—The legislature finds:

1. Although family leave laws have assisted employees to balance the demands of the workplace with their family responsibilities, more needs to be done to achieve the goals of workforce stability and economic security.
2. Many employees do not have access to family leave, and those who do may not be in a financial position to take leave that is unpaid.
3. Employer-paid benefits meet only a small part of this need.
4. The establishment of paid family leave benefits will reduce the impact on state income-support programs by increasing the ability of workers to recover from illness or provide caregiving services for family members while maintaining employment.

(B) PURPOSE—This law is enacted to establish a Family Leave Benefits Insurance Program to provide limited income support for a reasonable period while an employee is away from work on family leave, a policy which protects the health and safety of [STATE] residents and strengthens the [STATE] economy.

SECTION 3. FAMILY LEAVE BENEFITS INSURANCE

After section XXX, the following new section XXX shall be inserted:

(A) DEFINITIONS—In this section:

1. "Application year" means the 12-month period beginning on the first day of the calendar week in which an employee files an application for family leave benefits and, thereafter, the 12-month period beginning with the first day of the calendar week in which the employee files a subsequent application for family leave benefits after the expiration of the employee's last preceding application year.
2. "Child" means a person who is a biological, adopted, or foster child, a stepchild, a legal ward, or a child of a person standing in loco parentis, and who is:
    a. Under 18 years of age; or
    b. Eighteen years of age or older and incapable of self-care because of a mental or physical disability.
3. "Department" means the [Department of Labor].
4. "Employer" means the same as the definition in [cite workers compensation law] and the state and its political subdivisions.
5. "Employment" means the same as the definition in [cite workers compensation law].
6. "Family leave" means leave taken by an employee who is temporarily disabled and unavailable to work because she or he has to care for a newborn, newly-adopted or foster child (and leave is completed within 12 months after the birth or the placement of the child for foster care or adoption), to care for a family member who has a serious health condition, or because of the employee's own serious health condition, making them unable to perform the functions of the employee's position.

Family Leave Benefits

7. "Family member" means a child, spouse, domestic partner or the parent of the employee or employee's spouse or domestic partner.

8. "Healthcare provider" means a person licensed as a physician under [cite applicable code section].

9. "Parent" means a biological or adoptive parent, a stepparent, or a person who stood in loco parentis to an employee or an employee's spouse or domestic partner.

10. "Premium" means the money payments required by this chapter to be made to the Department for the Family Leave Benefits Insurance Account.

11. "Qualifying year" means the first four of the last five completed calendar quarters or the last four completed calendar quarters immediately preceding the first day of the employee's application year.

12. "Serious health condition" means an illness, injury, impairment, or physical or mental condition that involves inpatient care in a hospital, hospice, or residential medical care facility, or continuing treatment by a healthcare provider.

(B) APPLYING FOR FAMILY LEAVE BENEFITS

1. The Department shall establish and administer a Family Leave Benefits Insurance Account, and establish procedures and forms for filing benefit claims. The Department shall notify the employer within two business days of a claim being filed.

2. The Department may require that a claim for benefits under this chapter be supported by a certification issued by a healthcare provider who is providing care to the employee or the employee's family member, as applicable.

3. Information contained in the files and records pertaining to an employee under this chapter is confidential and not open to public inspection, other than to public employees in the performance of their official duties. However, the employee or an authorized representative of an employee may review the records or receive specific information from the records on the presentation of the signed authorization of the employee. An employer or the employer's duly authorized representative may review the records of an employee in connection with a pending claim. At the Department's discretion, other persons may review records when such persons are rendering assistance to the Department at any stage of the proceedings on any matter pertaining to the administration of this chapter.

(C) QUALIFYING FOR FAMILY LEAVE BENEFITS—Family leave benefits are payable to an employee during a period in which the employee is on unpaid family leave if the employee:

1. Files a claim for benefits as required by rules adopted by the Department.

2. Has been employed for at least 520 hours during the employee's qualifying year.

3. Establishes an application year. An application year may not be established if the qualifying year includes hours worked before establishment of a previous application year.

4. Documents that he or she has provided the employer from whom family leave is to be taken with written notice of his or her intention to take family leave as follows:

   a. If the necessity for family leave was foreseeable based on an expected birth, placement or treatment, notice was given at least 30 days before the family leave was to begin, stating the anticipated starting date and ending date of the family leave.

   b. If the date of birth, placement or treatment requiring family leave will begin in less than 30 days, as much notice as practicable was given.

   c. In the case of medical treatment, the employee made reasonable efforts to schedule the treatment so as not to unduly disrupt the operations of the employer, subject to the approval of the healthcare provider of the employee or his or her ill family member.

5. Discloses whether or not she or he owes child support obligations.

Family Leave Benefits

(D) DISQUALIFICATION FROM BENEFITS

1. An employee is disqualified from family leave insurance benefits beginning with the first day of the calendar week, and continuing for the next 52 consecutive weeks, if the employee:

   a. Willfully made a false statement or misrepresentation regarding a material fact, or willfully failed to report a material fact, to obtain benefits under this chapter; or

   b. Seeks benefits based on a willful and intentional self-inflicted serious health condition or a serious health condition resulting from the employee's perpetration of a felony.

2. Benefits are not payable for any weeks in which compensation is payable to the employee under Title XXX or another federal or state workers compensation program.

3. An employee is not disqualified for benefits for any week when there is a strike or lockout at the factory, establishment, or other premises at which the employee is or was last employed.

(E) DURATION AND AMOUNT OF BENEFITS

1. In an application year, family leave benefits are payable for a maximum of 12 weeks.

2. The first payment of benefits shall be made to an employee within two weeks after the claim is filed or the family leave began, whichever is later. Subsequent payments must be made twice a month thereafter.

3. Family leave benefits shall be paid as follows:

   a. For family leave beginning before July 1, 2004, benefits shall be $250 per week for an employee who at the time family leave began was regularly working 40 hours or more per week, or a prorated amount based on the weekly hours regularly worked for an employee regularly working less than 40 hours per week.

   b. By June 30, 2005, and by each subsequent June 30, the Department shall calculate to the nearest dollar an adjusted maximum benefit to account for inflation using the consumer price index for urban wage earners and clerical workers, CPI-W, or a successor index. The adjusted maximum benefit takes effect for family leave beginning after the relevant June 30.

   c. If an employee was regularly working 40 hours a week or more per week at the beginning of family leave, and during family leave is working less than 40 hours but at least eight hours a week, the employee's weekly payment shall be .025 times the maximum benefit times the number of hours of family leave taken in the week. Benefits are not payable for less than eight hours of family leave taken in a week.

   d. If an employee discloses that he or she owes child support obligations and the Department determines that the employee is eligible for benefits, the Department shall notify the applicable state or local child support enforcement agency and deduct and withhold an amount from benefits pursuant to [insert appropriate citation].

   e. If an employee elects to have federal income tax deducted and withheld from benefits, the Department shall deduct and withhold the amount specified in the federal Internal Revenue Code.

4. If family leave benefits are paid erroneously or as a result of fraud, or if a claim for benefits is rejected after benefits are paid, the Department shall seek repayment of benefits from the recipient.

5. If an employee dies before receiving payment of benefits, the payment shall be made by the Department to the surviving spouse or the child or children if there is no surviving spouse. If there is no surviving spouse and no child or children, the payment shall be made and distributed consistent with the terms of the decedent's will or, if the decedent dies intestate, consistent with the terms of [insert appropriate citation].

(F) EXISTING BENEFITS NOT DIMINISHED

1. Nothing in this chapter shall be construed to limit an employee's right to leave from employment under other laws or employer policy.

Family Leave Benefits

2. If an employer provides paid family leave or an employee is covered by disability insurance, the employee may elect whether first to use the paid family leave or to receive temporary disability benefits. An employee may not be required to use his or her paid family leave to which she or he is entitled before receiving benefits under this chapter.

3. An employer may require that family leave for which an employee is receiving or received benefits under this chapter be taken concurrently with leave under the federal Family and Medical Leave Act or other applicable federal, state or local law, except that:

    a. Family leave taken for sickness or temporary disability because of pregnancy or childbirth is in addition to leave under the federal Family and Medical Leave Act or other applicable federal, state or local law.

    b. Family leave during which the employee is receiving or received benefits under this chapter is in addition to leave from employment during which benefits are paid or are payable under XXX or a similar federal or state workers compensation law and that is designated as leave under the federal Family and Medical Leave Act.

    c. If an employer requires that family leave for which an employee is receiving or received benefits under this chapter be taken concurrently with leave under the federal Family and Medical Leave Act, or other applicable federal, state or local law, the employer must give all employees written notice of the requirement.

4. This entitlement is supplementary to a federal, state or local law establishing a similar entitlement, and if a federal, state or local law applying to the employee establishes a more favorable right to return to his or her position than is established under this section, the application of that federal, state or local law is not affected by this section.

5. An employee who has received benefits under this chapter shall not lose any employment benefit, including seniority or pension rights accrued before the date that family leave commenced. However, this chapter does not entitle an employee to accrue employment benefits during a period of family leave or to a right, benefit or position of employment other than a right, benefit or position to which the employee would have been entitled had the employee not taken family leave.

6. This chapter is not to be construed to diminish an employer's obligation to comply with a collective bargaining agreement or an employment benefit program or plan that provides greater benefits to employees than family leave insurance benefits provided under this chapter.

7. An agreement by an employee to waive his or her rights under this chapter is void as against public policy. The benefits provided to employees under this chapter may not be diminished by a collective bargaining agreement or an employment benefit program or plan entered into or renewed after the effective date of this section.

(G) ELECTION OF COVERAGE

1. An employer of employees not covered by this chapter or a self-employed person may elect coverage under the Family Leave Benefits Insurance Program for an initial period of not less than three years or a subsequent period of not less than one year immediately following another period of coverage. The employer or self-employed person must file a notice of election in writing with the Department. The election becomes effective on the date of filing the notice.

2. An employer or self-employed person who has elected coverage may withdraw from coverage within 30 days after the end of the three-year period of coverage, or at such other times as the Department may prescribe by rule, by filing written notice with the Department. Such withdrawal shall take effect not sooner than 30 days after the filing of the notice.

3. The Department may cancel elective coverage if the employer or self-employed person fails to provide required payments or reports. The Department may collect due and unpaid premiums and may levy an additional premium for the remainder of the period of coverage. The cancellation shall be effective no later than 30 days from the date of the notice in writing advising the employer or self-employed person of the cancellation.

Family Leave Benefits

(H) RECORDS AND REPORTS

1. The Department shall specify the forms and times for employers to provide reports, furnish information and remit premiums. If the employer is a temporary services agency that provides employees on a temporary basis to its customers, the temporary services agency is considered the employer for purposes of this section. However, if the temporary services agency fails to remit the required premiums, the customer to whom the employees were provided is liable for paying the premiums.

2. An employer must keep at its place of business a record of employment from which the information needed by the Department for purposes of this chapter may be obtained. This record shall at all times be open to the inspection of the Department pursuant to rules promulgated by the Department.

3. Information obtained from employer records under this chapter is confidential and not open to public inspection, other than to public employees in the performance of their official duties. However, an interested party shall be supplied with information from employer records to the extent necessary for the proper presentation of the case in question. An employer may authorize inspection of its records by written consent.

(I) DISPOSAL OF BUSINESS

1. When an employer quits business, or sells out, exchanges, or otherwise disposes of the business or stock of goods, any premium payable under this chapter is immediately due and payable, and the employer must, within 10 days thereafter, make a return and pay the premium due. Any person who becomes a successor to the business is liable for the full amount of the premium and must withhold from the purchase price a sum sufficient to pay any premium due from the employer until the employer produces a receipt from the Department showing payment in full of any premium due or a certificate that no premium is due and, if the premium is not paid by the employer within 10 days from the date of the sale, exchange, or disposal, the successor is liable for the payment of the full amount of premium. The successor's payment thereof is, to the extent thereof, a payment upon the purchase price, and if the payment is greater in amount than the purchase price, the amount of the difference is a debt due the successor from the employer.

2. A successor is not liable for any premium due from the person from whom the successor has acquired a business or stock of goods if the successor gives written notice to the Department of the acquisition and no assessment is issued by the Department within 180 days of receipt of the notice against the former operator of the business and a copy is mailed to the successor.

(J) FAMILY LEAVE BENEFITS INSURANCE ACCOUNT

1. The Family Leave Benefits Insurance Account is created in the custody of the [state treasurer]. All receipts from the premium or penalties imposed under this chapter must be deposited in the account. Expenditures from the account may be used only for the purposes of the Family Leave Benefits Insurance Program.

2. Each employer shall retain from the earnings of each employee a premium of one cent per hour worked, up to a maximum of 40 hours per week. The employer shall match the amount retained by an equal amount, and the money retained shall be paid to the Department in the manner and at such intervals as the Department directs for deposit in the Family Leave Benefits Insurance Account.

3. The Department shall adjust the amount of the premium from time to time to ensure that the amount is the lowest rate necessary to pay family leave benefits and administrative costs, and maintain actuarial solvency in accordance with recognized insurance principles.

4. The Department may adopt rules to permit an employee with multiple employers and his or her employers to petition for refunds or credits of amounts paid to the Department for hours in excess of 40 hours per week worked by the employee.

Family Leave Benefits

(K) TAXATION OF FAMILY LEAVE BENEFITS—The Department must advise an employee filing a new claim for family leave benefits, at the time of filing such claim, that:

1. Benefits are subject to federal income tax.

2. Requirements exist pertaining to estimated tax payments.

3. The employee may elect to have federal income tax deducted and withheld from the employee's payment of benefits at the amount specified in the Internal Revenue Code.

4. The employee is permitted to change a previously elected withholding status.

(L) NO DISCRIMINATION AGAINST CLAIMANTS—An employer, temporary services agency, employment agency, employee organization, or other person may not discharge, expel, or otherwise discriminate against a person because he or she has filed or communicated to the employer an intent to file a claim, a complaint, or an appeal, or has testified or is about to testify or has assisted in any proceeding under this chapter.

(M) NO ENTITLEMENT

1. Family leave benefits are payable under this chapter only to the extent that moneys are available in the Family Leave Benefits Insurance Account for this purpose. Neither the state nor the Department is liable for any amount in excess of these limits.

2. This chapter does not create a continuing entitlement or contractual right. There is no vested private right of any kind against amendment or repeal of this chapter.

(N) RULES AND REGULATIONS—The Department may adopt rules as necessary to implement this chapter. In adopting rules, the Department shall maintain consistency with the rules adopted to implement the federal Family and Medical Leave Act, to the extent such rules are not in conflict with this chapter.

SECTION 4. APPROPRIATION

The sum of $XXXXXX is appropriated for the purposes of administering the Family Leave Benefits Insurance Program. This sum shall be repaid from the Family Leave Benefits Insurance Account by June 30, 2005.

SECTION 5. SEVERABILITY

The provisions of this Act shall be severable, and if any phrase, clause, sentence, or provision is declared to be invalid or is preempted by federal law or regulation, the validity of the remainder of this Act shall not be affected.

SECTION 6. EFFECTIVE DATE

This Act shall take effect on July 1, 2004.

Gay and Transgender

Anti-Discrimination

Seventy-four percent of gay, lesbian and bisexual individuals have been discriminated against because of their sexual orientation. States can amend existing civil rights statutes to include sexual orientation and gender identity or expression.

Gay and Transgender Anti-Discrimination

Summary

- Seventy-four percent of gay, lesbian and bisexual individuals have been discriminated against because of their sexual orientation.
- In 36 states, individuals can legally be fired from their jobs, or denied access to housing, educational institutions, credit, and public accommodations simply because they are gay, lesbian, bisexual or transgender (GLBT).
- The American business community adopted anti-discrimination policies years ago.
- Americans strongly support laws prohibiting discrimination based on sexual orientation and gender identity or expression.
- An increasing number of jurisdictions are including "gender identity or expression" in their anti-discrimination laws.
- The GLBT Anti-Discrimination Act amends existing civil rights statutes to include sexual orientation and gender identity or expression.

Seventy-four percent of gay, lesbian and bisexual individuals have been discriminated against because of their sexual orientation.[1]

For example, thousands of individuals report employment discrimination based on sexual orientation in the states that forbid such discrimination.[2] Gays, lesbians and bisexuals also experience discrimination in such areas as applying to a college, university or other school; renting an apartment or buying a house; or getting health care or health insurance.[3] People of color in the GLBT community often face heightened discrimination. A survey of gay and transgender Asian American women found that 87 percent experienced verbal intimidation, while 15 percent reported physical injury because they were or were thought to be gay.[4]

In 36 states, individuals can legally be fired from their jobs, or denied access to housing, educational institutions, credit, and public accommodations simply because they are gay, lesbian, bisexual or transgender (GLBT).

Only 14 states (CA, CT, HI, MD, MA, MN, NV, NH, NJ, NM, NY, RI, VT and WI) and the District of Columbia prohibit discrimination based on sexual orientation. Without anti-discrimination laws, GLBT people have no legal recourse when landlords deny housing or employers fire or refuse to hire them.

The American business community adopted anti-discrimination policies years ago.

More than 300 of the Fortune 500 companies and more than 1,200 private companies, nonprofits and unions in the United States have adopted anti-discrimination policies covering sexual orientation. These policies do not require employers to hire gay, lesbian, bisexual or transgender individuals. Rather, they serve to prevent an employer from refusing to hire, or demoting or discharging an employee, simply because of the individual's sexual orientation or gender identity or expression.

Americans strongly support laws prohibiting discrimination based on sexual orientation, and gender identity or expression.

A 2001 survey for the Kaiser Family Foundation found that three-quarters of Americans believe there should be laws protecting gays and lesbians from prejudice and discrimination in job opportunities and housing.[5] Sixty-one percent of Americans also favor laws to prevent employment discrimination against transgender people.[6]

An increasing number of jurisdictions are including "gender identity or expression" in their anti-discrimination laws.

Transgender people—whether they are transsexual or simply identify with the gender opposite from their biological sex—are often targeted for discrimination. Four states (CA, MN, NM, RI), the District of Columbia, and more than 40 local jurisdictions have passed laws that explicitly prohibit discrimination based on an individual's gender identity or expression.

The GLBT Anti-Discrimination Act amends existing civil rights statutes to include sexual orientation and gender identity or expression.

This model, which is similar to laws in several states:

- Prohibits discrimination in employment, public accommodations, education, credit/lending, and housing based on sexual orientation and gender identity or expression.

- Creates a private right of action for aggrieved individuals.

- Provides for enforcement through a state agency.

This policy summary relies in large part on information from Human Rights Campaign and the National Gay and Lesbian Task Force.

GLBT ANTI-DISCRIMINATION LAWS AND POLICIES
■ 14 states and the District of Columbia
■ More than 270 cities or counties
■ 333 of the Fortune 500 companies
■ More than 1,200 private companies, nonprofit organizations, and labor unions
■ Almost 400 colleges and universities

Endnotes

[1] The Henry J. Kaiser Family Foundation, "Inside-OUT: A Report on the Experiences of Lesbians, Gays and Bisexuals in America and the Public's Views on Issues and Policies Related to Sexual Orientation," November 2001.

[2] General Accounting Office, "Sexual Orientation-Based Employment Discrimination," July 9, 2002. www.gao.gov/new.items/d02878r.pdf

[3] "Inside-OUT."

[4] Asian Pacific Islander Lesbian, Bisexual, Queer and Transgender Task Force (APLBQT) Survey, October 2000.

[5] "Inside-OUT."

[6] "Public Perceptions of Transgender People", Human Rights Campaign, 2002.

Gay and Transgender Anti-Discrimination

For more information...

Center for Policy Alternatives
1875 Connecticut Avenue NW, Suite 710
Washington, DC 20009
202-387-6030
www.stateaction.org

National Gay and Lesbian Task Force
1325 Massachusetts Avenue NW, Suite 600
Washington, DC 20005
202-393-5177
www.ngltf.org

The Federation of Lesbian, Gay, Bisexual and Transgender Advocacy Organizations
1222 South Dale Mabry, Suite 652
Tampa, FL 33629
813-870-3735
www.federationlgbt.org

Human Rights Campaign
1640 Rhode Island Avenue NW
Washington, DC 20036
202-628-4160
www.hrc.org

Lambda Legal Defense and Education Fund
120 Wall Street, Suite 1500
New York, NY 10005
212-809-8585
www.lambdalegal.org

National Center for Lesbian Rights
870 Market Street, Suite 570
San Francisco, CA 94102
415-392-6257
www.nclrights.org

Gay and Transgender Anti-Discrimination

GLBT Anti-Discrimination Act

SECTION 1. SHORT TITLE

This Act shall be called the "GLBT Anti-Discrimination Act."

SECTION 2. FINDINGS AND PURPOSE

(A) FINDINGS – The legislature finds that:

1. It is very common for gay, lesbian, bisexual and transgender (GLBT) individuals to be the victims of discrimination. They are fired from jobs, denied access to housing and educational institutions, refused credit, and excluded from public accommodations because of their sexual orientation or gender identity or expression.

2. It is essential that the state of [STATE] protect the civil rights of all its residents.

(B) PURPOSE – This law is enacted to protect civil rights by prohibiting discrimination against gay, lesbian, bisexual and transgender individuals.

SECTION 3. DEFINITIONS

In section XXX, the following new paragraphs shall be inserted:

"sexual orientation" means an individual's actual or perceived heterosexuality, bisexuality or homosexuality.

"gender identity or expression" means having, or being perceived as having, a gender-related identity, appearance, expression or behavior, whether or not that identity, appearance, expression or behavior is different from that stereotypically associated with the person's assigned sex at birth.

SECTION 4. GLBT ANTI-DISCRIMINATION

In section XXX, after each occurrence of the words, ["race, gender, national origin"—alter to fit state law], following new section XXX shall be inserted:

"sexual orientation, gender identity or expression,"

SECTION 5. EFFECTIVE DATE

This Act shall take effect on July 1, 2004.

Gun Violence Prevention

Americans strongly support gun restrictions as a means to reduce violence. States can and have enacted gun restrictions that are much stronger and more effective than federal law.

Gun Violence Prevention

Summary

- Gun violence claimed the lives of 29,573 people in the United States in 2001.
- The Brady law has proven to be one of the most efficient law enforcement tools available, preventing more than 975,000 illegal firearms transactions from occurring through licensed gun dealers.
- Forty percent of gun transactions nationwide occur through unlicensed sellers and private deals that require no background check, no questions asked.
- 88 percent of traced crime guns have changed hands at least once after they were purchased from a licensed dealer.
- There are over 65 million handguns in circulation in the United States today, and that number increases by 2 million each year.
- Many states already have strong laws regulating firearms transfers by unlicensed sellers.
- Americans, including gun owners, strongly support gun restrictions.

Gun violence claimed the lives of 29,573 people in the United States in 2001, according to the Centers for Disease Control and Prevention.

For every American who dies from a gunshot, at least two others are seriously wounded. All told, nearly 100,000 Americans pass through the doors of hospital emergency rooms every year with serious or fatal gun injuries. The medical and social costs of gun violence to our country are estimated at $100 billion per year.[1]

Since its enactment in 1993, the Brady law has proven to be one of the most efficient law enforcement tools available, preventing more than 975,000 illegal firearms transactions from occurring through licensed gun dealers.[2]

Federal law prohibits convicted felons, individuals convicted of violent misdemeanors, domestic abusers, juveniles, and people with serious mental illnesses from buying or owning guns. The Brady law calls for background checks on individuals who seek to purchase handguns, in order to screen out prohibited purchasers. But the Brady law's application, and therefore its effectiveness, is limited because the law only applies to licensed gun dealers.

Forty percent of gun transactions nationwide occur through unlicensed sellers and private deals that require no background check, no questions asked.[3]

In most states, private gun sales are totally unregulated. Guns can be sold anonymously from homes, in alleys, and on the street, without any legal oversight. The lack of an enforceable barrier between the legal and the illegal markets means that criminals and other prohibited gun buyers can still obtain guns, and they do so *easily*. This gaping loophole in federal law, and most state laws, may explain why 88 percent of traced crime guns have changed hands through at least one private transaction.

There are over 65 million handguns in circulation in the United States today, and that number increases by 2 million each year.

Handguns are extremely durable products that can be circulated from buyer to buyer, easily outliving their owners. These dangerous weapons remain functional and deadly for years. That is why it is essential to apply commonsense regulations, like the Brady law's background checks, to all gun transactions.

There are several policy options that would reduce the violence by regulating the distribution of firearms.

In the absence of federal standards, states can curtail the flow of guns into the illegal market by giving police the tools they need to keep guns out of the wrong hands. The harder it is for gun sellers to hide their activities, the easier it is to prevent criminal access to firearms. States can:

■ Require background checks for all transactions at gun shows.

■ Institute background checks on all gun sales.

■ Require handgun licensing and registration.

■ Prohibit the transfer of semiautomatic assault weapons. This is especially urgent because the federal assault weapon ban will likely expire in September 2004.

Many states already have strong laws regulating firearms transfers by unlicensed sellers.

IN, MD, MI, MO, NE, NC, and PA have laws that require criminal background checks on all handgun sales. CA, CT, HI, MA, NJ and NY have taken regulation a step further, requiring the licensing and registration of handguns.

Americans, including gun owners, strongly support gun restrictions.

A 2001 Lake Snell Perry and Associates poll found that: 92 percent of Americans and 86 percent of gun owners favor criminal background checks for all gun sales; 85 percent of Americans and 73 percent of gun owners favor handgun licensing; and 83 percent of Americans and 72 percent of gun owners favor the registration of all new handguns. A 2001 Zogby poll found that 86 percent of Americans and 78 percent of gun owners favor closing the gun show loophole.

This policy summary relies in large part on information from the Coalition to Stop Gun Violence.

Endnotes

[1] Cook and Ludwig, "Gun Violence: The Real Costs," 2000.

[2] Bureau of Justice Statistics, "Background Checks for Firearm Transfers," NCJ 195235, September 2001.

[3] Cook and Ludwig, "Guns in America: National Survey on Private Ownership and Use of Firearms, National Institute of Justice Research in Brief," May 1997.

Gun Violence Prevention

For more information...

Center for Policy Alternatives
1875 Connecticut Avenue NW, Suite 710
Washington, DC 20009
202-387-6030
www.stateaction.org

Coalition to Stop Gun Violence
1023 15th Street NW, Suite 600
Washington, DC 20005
202-408-0061
www.csgv.org

Brady Campaign to Prevent Gun Violence
1225 Eye Street NW, Suite 1100
Washington, DC 20005
202-898-0792
www.bradycampaign.org

Million Mom March
1225 Eye Street NW, Suite 1100
Washington, DC 20005
202-898-0792
www.millionmommarch.org

Americans for Gun Safety
2000 L Street NW, Suite 702
Washington, DC 20036
202-775-0300
www.americansforgunsafety.com

Johns Hopkins Center for Gun Policy and Research
624 N. Broadway
Baltimore, MD 21205
410-614-3243
www.jhsph.edu/gunpolicy/index.html

Violence Policy Center
1140 19th Street NW, Suite 600
Washington, DC 20036
202-822-8200
www.vpc.org

Join Together, Boston University School of Public Health
One Appleton Street, 4th floor
Boston, MA 02116
617-437-1500
www.jointogether.org/gv

Gun Violence Prevention

One Handgun A Month Act

Summary: The One Handgun A Month Act combats illegal gun trafficking by limiting individuals to the purchase of no more than one handgun in any 30 day period.

SECTION 1. SHORT TITLE

This Act shall be called the "One Handgun A Month Act."

SECTION 2. ONE HANDGUN A MONTH

After section XXX, the following new section XXX shall be inserted:

(A) DEFINITION—In this section:

"Handgun" means a firearm described in 18 USC 921(a)(29).

(B) LIMIT ON HANDGUN TRANSFERS

1. Except as provided in this section, no person shall receive transfer of more than one handgun in any 30 day period, and no person shall transfer to any individual more than one handgun in any 30 day period.

2. The [State Police] shall establish a centralized system for ensuring compliance with this section.

3. The limit on handgun transfers shall not apply to:

   a. Any law enforcement officer or agency; or
   b. Any person licensed under 18 U.S.C. 923 for the purposes of acquiring handguns as inventory.

(C) PENALTIES

Any person who violates any provision of this section shall, if convicted, be fined not more than $5,000 or be imprisoned for not more than one year, or both.

SECTION 3. EFFECTIVE DATE

This Act shall take effect on July 1, 2004.

Gun Violence Prevention

Universal Background Checks Act

Summary: The Universal Background Checks Act ensures that the transfer of a firearm is preceded by a thorough background check of the intended recipient of that firearm.

SECTION 1. SHORT TITLE

This Act shall be called the "Universal Background Checks Act."

SECTION 2. UNIVERSAL BACKGROUND CHECKS

After section XXX, the following new section XXX shall be inserted:

1. A person shall not transfer or receive transfer of any firearm unless the transferee has first passed a background check identical to the background check required under 18 U.S.C. 922(t) for transfers by federal firearms licensees. The background check required under this section may be conducted by a person licensed under 18 U.S.C. 923 or by a law enforcement agency.

2. Any person licensed under 18 U.S.C. 923 and whose licensed premises are within the state, shall, upon request by a transferor of a firearm who is not licensed under 18 U.S.C. 923 conduct a background check on the intended recipient of that firearm, following the same procedures as if the transfer involved a firearm in the inventory of the licensed dealer.

3. This section shall not apply to:

    a. The transfer of a firearm to a law enforcement officer or agency.
    b. The transfer of a curio or relic, as defined under 27 C.F.R. 178.11.
    c. The transfer of a firearm to a person licensed under 18 U.S.C. 923.

4. Any person who violates any provision of this section shall upon conviction be fined not more than $1,000 for the first offense, or $5,000 for each subsequent offense.

SECTION 3. EFFECTIVE DATE

This Act shall take effect on July 1, 2004.

Gun Violence Prevention

Gun Owner Accountability Act

Summary: The Gun Owner Accountability Act ensures that law enforcement officials have reliable information to trace the ownership of guns used in crime.

SECTION 1. SHORT TITLE

This Act shall be called the "Gun Owner Accountability Act."

SECTION 2. RECORDS OF TRANSFER

After section XXX, the following new section XXX shall be inserted:

1. For every firearm transferred in the state on or after January 1, 2005, the [State Police] shall maintain a record of transfer containing the name, current address, and driver license number or state identification card number of the recipient of the firearm; the date of the transfer; the make, model and serial number of the firearm; and the name, address and, if applicable, federal firearms license number of the transferor.

2. Once each year, the [State Police] shall inform each person for whom such a record exists that the person is the owner of record of that firearm, identified by make, model and serial number, unless and until the person provides to the [State Police] one of the following:

   a. Reliable evidence that the firearm has been lawfully transferred, including the name, current address, and driver license number or state identification card number of the legal recipient;
   b. A copy of a report of the theft of the firearm filed with a law enforcement agency; or
   c. Reliable evidence that the firearm has been destroyed.

3. The [State Police] may collect from each person for whom a record of transfer exists a fee, not to exceed $5.00 per firearm per year, to cover the costs of administering the program established by this section.

4. Any person who violates the provisions of this section, including a refusal to pay any fees authorized by this section, shall upon conviction be fined not more than $5,000 or be imprisoned for not more than one year, or both.

SECTION 3. EFFECTIVE DATE

This Act shall take effect on July 1, 2004.

Gun Violence Prevention

Handgun Buyer Licensing Act

Summary: The Handgun Buyer Licensing Act ensures that every person who wishes to acquire a handgun first demonstrates at least a minimum level of knowledge and skill in the safe and lawful handling, storage and use of handguns, and has demonstrated to a law enforcement agency that he or she is not prohibited by law from acquiring or possessing a handgun.

SECTION 1. SHORT TITLE

This Act shall be called the "Handgun Buyer Licensing Act."

SECTION 2. HANDGUN BUYER LICENSING

After section XXX, the following new section XXX shall be inserted:

(A) DEFINITIONS—In this section:

1. "Handgun" means a firearm described in 18 USC 921(a)(29).

2. "Law enforcement agency" means the office of Sheriff of any county or the office of the Chief of Police of any city or municipality.

(B) HANDGUN BUYER LICENSE

1. A person shall not transfer or receive transfer of any handgun unless the transferee displays a valid handgun buyer license and one other government-issued identification card bearing the transferee's name, date of birth, current address, signature, and photograph.

2. Upon receipt of a written application, a local law enforcement agency shall, within 14 days, provide a handgun buyer license, unless the local law enforcement agency finds that the applicant is not qualified to receive a handgun buyer license.

3. An applicant shall be qualified to receive a handgun buyer license if he or she:

    a. Has completed a safe handling course approved by the [Superintendent of State Police] and covering all of the following topics:
        (1) The basic operation of pistols and revolvers.
        (2) Safe procedures for loading and unloading pistols and revolvers.
        (3) The operation of safety devices found on pistols or revolvers.
        (4) Basic rules of safe handling of firearms.
        (5) Safe storage of firearms and ammunition.
        (6) Current laws governing the possession, transfer and use of firearms.
        (7) Current laws governing the lawful use of lethal force.
    b. Has passed a test of the knowledge and skills covered in the safe handling course.
    c. Has provided to the law enforcement agency a full set of fingerprints for the purpose of conducting a background check.
    d. Is not prohibited by the laws of [STATE] or of the United States from acquiring or possessing a firearm.

e. Is, at the time such determination is made, a current resident of [STATE], as demonstrated by a current mortgage stub, residential rental agreement, utility bill, or other comparable document in the name of the intended recipient and bearing a valid address in [STATE].

4. A handgun buyer license shall be valid for 4 years after it is issued. The local law enforcement agency may collect an application fee of up to $20 to defray costs.

5. The denial of, or failure to timely issue, a handgun buyer license may be appealed to the [Superintendent] of State Police. The Superintendent shall have the authority to promulgate rules in order to comply with this section.

6. A local law enforcement agency shall revoke a handgun buyer license if, after it is issued, the licensee becomes prohibited by the laws of [STATE] or of the United States from acquiring or possessing a firearm, or the licensee is no longer a current resident of [STATE].

7. This section shall not require the display of a handgun buyer license to:

   a. Any law enforcement officer or agency; or
   b. Any person licensed under 18 USC sec. 923 for the purposes of receiving a handgun as inventory.

8. No civil liability shall arise from any action or inaction on the part of a local law enforcement agency in connection with either the approval or denial of a handgun buyer license.

9. Any person who willfully violates the provisions of this section, or a person who attempts through misrepresentation to obtain a handgun in violation of this section, shall upon conviction be fined not more than $10,000 or imprisoned for not more than one year, or both.

SECTION 3. EFFECTIVE DATE

This Act shall take effect on July 1, 2004.

Gun Violence Prevention

Assault Weapons Protection Act

Summary: The Assault Weapons Protection Act bans the purchase, sale or transfer of semiautomatic assault weapons.

SECTION 1. SHORT TITLE

This Act shall be called the "Assault Weapons Protection Act."

SECTION 2. FINDINGS AND PURPOSE

(A) FINDINGS—The legislature finds:

1. Semiautomatic assault weapons are military-style guns designed to quickly kill large numbers of people. The shooter can simply point, rather than carefully aim, the weapon to quickly spray a wide area with a hail of bullets.

2. According to FBI data, between 1998 and 2001, one in five law enforcement officers slain in the line of duty was killed with an assault weapon.

3. Gun manufacturers have for many years made, marketed and sold to civilians semiautomatic versions of military assault weapons designed with features specifically intended to increase lethality for military applications.

4. Assault weapons have been used in some of America's most notorious murders, including the 1999 massacre at Columbine High School and the 2002 Washington, D.C.-area sniper shootings.

(B) PURPOSE—This law is enacted to protect the health and safety of state residents by prohibiting the purchase, sale and transfer of semiautomatic assault weapons.

SECTION 3. ASSAULT WEAPONS PROTECTION

After section XXX, the following new section XXX shall be inserted:

(A) DEFINITIONS—In this section:

1. "Assault weapon" means:

    a. Any semiautomatic or pump-action rifle or semiautomatic pistol that is capable of accepting a detachable magazine and that also possesses any of the following:
        1) If the firearm is a rifle, a pistol grip located behind the trigger.
        2) If the firearm is a rifle, a stock in any configuration, including but not limited to a thumbhole stock, a folding stock, or a telescoping stock, that allows the bearer of the firearm to grasp the firearm with the trigger hand such that the web of the trigger hand, between the thumb and forefinger, can be placed below the top of the external portion of the trigger during firing.
        3) If the firearm is a pistol, a shoulder stock of any type or configuration, including but not limited to a folding stock or a telescoping stock.
        4) A barrel shroud.
        5) A muzzle brake or muzzle compensator.

6) Any feature designed to be capable of functioning as a protruding grip that can be held by the hand that is not the trigger hand, except this does not include an extension of the stock along the bottom of the barrel that does not substantially or completely encircle the barrel.

b. Any pistol that is capable of accepting a detachable magazine at any location outside of the pistol grip.

c. Any semiautomatic pistol, or any semiautomatic center-fire rifle, with a fixed magazine that has the capacity to accept more than 10 rounds of ammunition.

d. Any shotgun capable of accepting a detachable magazine.

e. Any shotgun with a revolving cylinder magazine.

f. Any conversion kit or other combination of parts from which an assault weapon, as defined herein, can be assembled if the parts are in the possession or under the control of any person.

2. "Large-capacity detachable magazine" means a magazine, the function of which is to deliver one or more ammunition cartridges into the firing chamber, which can be removed from the firearm without the use of any tool, and which has the capacity to hold more than 10 rounds of ammunition.

3. "Barrel shroud" means a covering, other than a slide, that is attached to, or that substantially or completely encircles the barrel of a firearm and that allows the bearer of the firearm to hold the barrel with the non-shooting hand while firing the firearm, without burning that hand, except that the term shall not include an extension of the stock along the bottom of the barrel that does not substantially or completely encircle the barrel.

4. "Muzzle brake" means a device attached to the muzzle of a weapon that utilizes escaping gas to reduce recoil.

5. "Muzzle compensator" means a device attached to the muzzle of a weapon that utilizes escaping gas to control muzzle movement.

6. "Conversion kit" means any part or combination of parts designed and intended for use in converting a firearm into an assault weapon.

(B) PROHIBITION ON ASSAULT WEAPONS

1. No person shall manufacture, possess, purchase, sell or otherwise transfer any assault weapon, or assault weapon conversion kit.

2. No person shall possess or have under his or her control at one time both:

a. A semiautomatic or pump-action rifle or semiautomatic pistol capable of accepting a detachable magazine, and

b. A large-capacity detachable magazine capable of use with that firearm.

3. This section shall not apply to:

a. Any law enforcement agency or officer acting within the scope of his or her profession.

b. Any person licensed under 18 U.S.C. 923 for the purpose of selling an assault weapon or large-capacity detachable magazine to a law enforcement agency.

c. The possession of an unloaded assault weapon or large-capacity detachable magazine for the purpose of permanently relinquishing it to a law enforcement agency, pursuant to regulations adopted for such purpose by [the state police]. Any assault weapon relinquished pursuant to this paragraph shall be destroyed.

Gun Violence Prevention

d. An assault weapon that has been permanently disabled so that it is incapable of discharging a projectile.

e. The possession of an assault weapon while lawfully engaged in shooting at a duly licensed, lawfully operated shooting range.

f. The possession of an assault weapon while lawfully participating in a sporting event officially sanctioned by a club or organization established in whole or in part for the purpose of sponsoring sport shooting events.

g. The possession of an assault weapon or large-capacity detachable magazine by a person who received the weapon by inheritance, bequest or succession, as long as the person complies with this section within 30 days of receipt.

h. The possession of an assault weapon that was legally possessed on the effective date of this Act, only if the person legally possessing the assault weapon has complied with all of the requirements of paragraph 4 of this section.

4. In order to continue to possess an assault weapon that was legally possessed on the effective date of this Act, the person possessing the assault weapon must:

a. Within 90 days following the effective date of this Act, submit to a background check identical to the background check conducted in connection with the purchase of a firearm from a licensed gun dealer.

b. Unless the person is prohibited by law from possessing a firearm, immediately register the assault weapon with the [state police] pursuant to regulations adopted for such purpose.

c. Safely and securely store the assault weapon pursuant to regulations adopted for such purpose by the [state police]. The [state police] may, no more than once per year, conduct an inspection to ensure compliance with this subsection.

d. Annually renew both the registration and the background check.

e. Possess the assault weapon only on property owned or immediately controlled by the person, or while engaged in the legal use of the assault weapon at a duly licensed firing range, or while traveling to or from either of these locations for the purpose of engaging in the legal use of the assault weapon, provided that the assault weapon is stored unloaded and in a separate locked container during transport.

f. Pay a fee to the [state police] for each registration and registration renewal, provided that such fee may not exceed the costs incurred by the [state police] in administering the registration program.

(C) PENALTIES

Any person who willfully violates the provisions of this section shall upon conviction be fined not more than $10,000 or imprisoned for not more than two years, or both.

SECTION 4. EFFECTIVE DATE

This Act shall take effect on July 1, 2004.

Hate Crime
Prevention

Nearly every state has a law on the books regarding hate crimes, yet the laws vary in who they protect and what types of protection are provided. States need to strengthen hate crime statutes to offer better protections to their residents.

Hate Crime Prevention

Summary

- Thousands of hate crimes are reported each year.
- Hate crimes are not ordinary crimes—they are intended to send a threatening message to a particular group within a community.
- Hate crimes directed at Muslims, Sikhs and people of Middle Eastern or South Asian descent have increased.
- Hate crimes against transgender people are a serious problem.
- Hate crime laws send a clear message that hate will not be tolerated.
- Nearly every state has a hate crime statute—but they vary in who they protect and what protection they provide.
- States need to enact hate crime statutes if they do not already have them, or amend existing statutes to offer better protection to their residents.

Thousands of hate crimes are reported each year.

The FBI reported 7,462 hate crime incidents in 2002. Forty-nine percent of hate crimes were based on racial prejudice. Another 19 percent were attributed to religious bias, 17 percent were based on sexual orientation, and 15 percent were motivated by prejudice against the victim's ethnicity or national origin. Since it began collecting data in 1991, the FBI has reported almost 80,000 hate crimes.[1]

Hate crimes are not ordinary crimes—they are intended to send a threatening message to a particular group within a community.

Perpetrators are motivated by intolerance and bigotry, harassing or attacking victims because of their race, ethnicity, national origin, religion, sexual orientation, gender identity or expression, or disability. A hate crime is more serious than a conventional crime because it is directed at more than just the immediate victim. Hate crimes are intended to intimidate members of the victim's community.

Hate crimes directed at Muslims, Sikhs and people of Middle Eastern or South Asian descent have increased.

Since September 11, 2001, thousands of crimes directed at Muslims, Sikhs and people of Middle Eastern or South Asian descent have been documented. Anti-Islamic hate crimes reported to the FBI in 2001 increased by more than 1,600 percent over the 2000 volume.[2] Human Rights Watch reports that at least three and as many as seven individuals were murdered in the backlash of September 11.[3] In June 2003, an Indian-American man was robbed, beaten and stabbed in Boston. His assailants mistook the Hindu man for a Muslim.

Hate crimes against transgender people are a serious problem.

Violent crimes against transgender people happen with alarming frequency. The summer of 2003 alone saw murders of transgender people in Council Bluffs, Iowa and in Houston, Indianapolis and New Haven. In Washington, DC, three transgender people were murdered during a two-week span in August. It is imperative that legislators recognize these victims and include gender identity and expression in state hate crime laws.

Hate crime laws send a clear message that hate will not be tolerated.

While hate crimes cannot be legislated out of existence, separate charges or enhanced sentences make the state's position against bias-motivated crimes clear.

Nearly every state has a hate crime statute—but they vary in who they protect and what protection they provide.

Currently, a majority of states protect against hate crimes based on race, ethnicity and religion (44), while over half protect against hate crimes based on gender (26), sexual orientation (29), and disability (39). The District of Columbia protects against all these categories of hate crimes.[4]

Many states now include transgender people in their hate crime protections.

Seven states (CA, HI, MN, MO, NM, PA and VT) and the District of Columbia now include gender identity in their hate crime laws. Both Hawaii and New Mexico strengthened their hate crime laws in 2003 by including gender identity.

States need to enact hate crime statutes if they do not already have them, or amend existing statutes to offer better protection to their residents.

Model hate crime legislation includes three provisions:

■ Increasing penalties for crimes against people or property when the victim's race, ethnicity, national origin, religion, sexual orientation, gender identity or expression, or disability motivates the underlying offense.

■ Allowing hate crime victims to sue for civil damages.

■ Collecting data on hate crime incidents and training police how to recognize, respond to, and report such crimes.

Endnotes

[1] Federal Bureau of Investigations, "Uniform Crime Reports," November 2003.

[2] Federal Bureau of Investigations, "Hate Crimes Statistics, 2001," November 2002.

[3] Human Rights Watch, "'We Are Not The Enemy': Hate Crimes Against Arabs, Muslims, and Those Perceived to be Arab or Muslim after September 11," November 2002.

[4] Anti-Defamation League, "Hate Crimes Laws," 2003.

Hate Crime Prevention

For more information...

Center for Policy Alternatives
1875 Connecticut Avenue NW, Suite 710
Washington, DC 20009
202-387-6030
www.stateaction.org

Anti-Defamation League
1100 Connecticut Avenue NW, Suite 1020
Washington, DC 20036
202-452-8320
www.adl.org

Arab American Institute
1600 K Street NW, Suite 601
Washington, DC 20006
202-429-9210
www.aaiusa.org

Human Rights Campaign
1640 Rhode Island Avenue NW
Washington, DC 20036
202-628-4160
www.hrc.org

Leadership Conference on Civil Rights
1629 K Street NW, Suite 1000
Washington, DC 20006
202-466-3311
www.civilrights.org

National Gay and Lesbian Task Force
1700 Kalorama Road NW
Washington, DC 20009
202-332-6483
www.ngltf.org

Hate Crime Prevention

Hate Crime Prevention Act

Summary: The Hate Crime Prevention Act establishes enhanced sentences for crimes motivated by bias, provides civil remedies, and directs the state police to maintain records and provide training.

SECTION 1. SHORT TITLE

This Act shall be called the "[STATE] Hate Crime Prevention Act."

SECTION 2. HATE CRIME PREVENTION

After section XXX, the following new section XXX shall be inserted:

(A) HATE CRIMES—ENHANCED PENALTIES

If a person charged with any felony, misdemeanor, or petty misdemeanor offense is found to have intentionally selected the victim or the victim's property because of the victim's actual or perceived race, color, creed, religion, ancestry, gender, sexual orientation, gender identity or expression, physical or mental disability, national origin, or age, that person may be found guilty of a hate crime with the penalty imposed as follows:

1. Where the underlying offense is a petty misdemeanor, it shall be punishable as a misdemeanor.

2. Where the underlying offense is a misdemeanor, it shall be punishable as a class C felony.

3. Where the underlying offense is a class C felony, it shall be punishable as a class B felony.

4. Where the underlying offense is a class B felony, it shall be punishable as a class A felony.

5. Where the underlying offense is a class A felony, the maximum fine authorized shall be doubled and a 20-year term of imprisonment shall be imposed.

(B) CIVIL ACTION FOR HATE CRIMES

1. If a person commits an intentional tort and has selected the victim or the victim's property because of the victim's actual or perceived race, color, creed, religion, ancestry, gender, sexual orientation, gender identity or expression, physical or mental disability, national origin, or age, any victim of that tort may file a civil action to secure an injunction, damages or other appropriate relief at law or equity. In this subsection, a victim can be a person, corporation, association or other organization.

2. In any such action, whether a tort has occurred shall be determined according to the burden of proof used in other civil actions for similar relief.

3. Upon prevailing in such civil action, the plaintiff may recover:

   a. Both special and general damages, including damages for emotional distress;
   b Punitive damages; and/or
   c. Reasonable attorney fees and costs.

Hate Crime Prevention

4. Notwithstanding any other provision of law to the contrary, the parent(s) or legal guardian(s) of any unemancipated minor shall be liable for any judgment rendered against such minor under this section.

(C) HATE CRIME REPORTING AND TRAINING

1. The state police shall establish and maintain a central repository for the collection and analysis of information regarding hate crimes. Upon establishing such a repository, the state police shall develop a procedure to monitor, record, classify and analyze information relating to crimes apparently directed against individuals or groups, or their property, by reason of their actual or perceived race, color, creed, religion, ancestry, gender, sexual orientation, gender identity or expression, physical or mental disability, national origin, or age.

2. All local law enforcement agencies shall report monthly to the [state superintendent of police] concerning such offenses in such form and manner as prescribed by rules and regulations adopted by the [state superintendent of police]. The [state superintendent of police] must summarize and analyze the information received and file an annual report with the governor and the state legislature.

3. All information, records and statistics collected in accordance with this subsection shall be available for use by any local law enforcement agency, unit of local government, or state agency, to the extent that such information is reasonably necessary or useful to such agency in carrying out the duties imposed upon it by law. Dissemination of such information shall be subject to all confidentiality requirements otherwise imposed by law.

4. The [state superintendent of police] shall provide training for law enforcement officers in identifying, responding to, and reporting all hate crimes.

SECTION 3. EFFECTIVE DATE—This Act shall take effect on July 1, 2004.

Health and Sexuality
Education

Despite the rise in federal funding for abstinence-only education, there is no strong evidence that it works. However, teenagers who receive comprehensive sexuality education are more likely to delay sexual activity, practice safe sex, and have fewer partners.

Health and Sexuality Education

Summary:

- Millions of teenagers are sexually active, yet many of them do not receive adequate sexuality education.
- Young Americans, particularly minority youth, are at high risk of contracting sexually transmitted diseases, including HIV/AIDS.
- Comprehensive sexuality education is critical to the health and well-being of America's teenagers.
- Comprehensive sexuality education works.
- Since 1996, Congress has committed more than a half-billion dollars to fund abstinence-only education.
- There is no credible evidence that abstinence-only education works.
- American parents overwhelmingly favor sexuality education programs that cover all aspects of sexuality, including contraception and safe sex.
- Only 22 states require schools to provide sexuality education.

Millions of teenagers are sexually active, yet many of them do not receive adequate sexuality education.

Nearly 46 percent of all high school students have engaged in sexual intercourse, and 42 percent of sexually active students had not used a condom when they last had sexual intercourse.[1] About four out of ten young women become pregnant at least once before age 20.[2] Despite the clear need for information to help teens abstain from sex and protect themselves if they become sexually active, many local school boards and curriculum committees across the country are moving in the opposite direction—toward abstinence-only education.

Young Americans, particularly minority youth, are at high risk of contracting sexually transmitted diseases (STDs) including HIV/AIDS.

Teenagers continue to be at high risk for acquiring and transmitting STDs. In fact two-thirds of all STDs occur in people 25 years of age or younger, and one in four new STD cases occur in adolescents.[3] Young women of color are particularly at risk; Latinas, African-American, Asian-American, and Native-American women all have substantially higher rates of chlamydia than white women. And, although African-American women and Latinas together represent about 25 percent of the female population, they account for over three-fourths of all reported female cases of AIDS.[4]

Comprehensive sexuality education is critical to the health and well-being of America's teenagers.

Comprehensive sexuality education addresses the full range of issues that arise during adolescence, including sexual development, reproductive health, interpersonal relationships, body image, decision-making, and gender roles. In a society where teens are continually exposed to sexual overtones and innuendoes—in the media, in popular culture, and in everyday life—providing comprehensive and medically-accurate sexuality education can help children and teenagers process what they see and hear regarding sex, deal effectively with societal and peer pressure, and make responsible decisions regarding their own sexuality. In fact, former Surgeon General David Satcher recently declared that teaching comprehensive sex education in schools is "vital," noting that "the gap between what we know and what we do is lethal."[5]

Comprehensive sexuality education works.

For example, a comprehensive sexuality education program taught by a Maine community group around the state contributed to a 35 percent decline in the teen pregnancy rate over the 20 years the program has been in existence. Because of its success, the Maine legislature expanded the program in 2002 to cover every school in the state. Further, a 2001 report noted that many comprehensive sexuality education programs successfully delayed the initiation and decreased the frequency of sexual activity among students.[6]

Since 1996, Congress has committed more than a half-billion dollars to fund abstinence-only education programs.

These programs teach abstinence from sexual activity as the only acceptable form of behavior outside of marriage (for people of any age). Programs receiving these federal funds are prohibited from discussing contraceptives, unless they portray them as ineffective.

There is no credible evidence that abstinence-only education works.

Despite years of evaluation of abstinence-only education, no reliable evidence exists to prove that it actually delays the initiation of teen sex or reduces its frequency. In fact, recent research shows that abstinence-only strategies may deter contraceptive use among sexually active teenagers, increasing their risk of unintended pregnancy and STDs.[7] A 2002 Human Rights Watch report found that some abstinence-only education programs falsely claimed that condoms are inefficient in preventing HIV transmission, and that "condoms don't work."[8]

American parents overwhelmingly favor sexuality education programs that cover all aspects of sexuality, including contraception and safe sex.

Nearly 9 in 10 American parents believe that sexuality education programs should cover all aspects of sexuality, including contraception and safe sex.[9] Major medical, public health, and research institutions support comprehensive sexuality education, including the American Medical Association, the American Academy of Pediatrics, the American Nurses Association, the American College of Obstetricians and Gynecologists, and the American Public Health Association.

Only 22 states require schools to provide sexuality education.

Education on HIV/AIDS and other STDs is mandated in 38 states and the District of Columbia, but only 22 states and D.C. require a broader sexuality education curriculum (AK, DE, FL, GA, HI, IL, IA, KS, KY, ME, MD, MN, NV, NJ, NC, RI, SC, TN, UT, VT, WV, WY).

This policy summary relies in large part on information from Planned Parenthood Federation of America and NARAL Pro-Choice America.

Endnotes

[1] Centers for Disease Control, "Youth Risk Behavior Surveillance—United States, 2001," 2002.

[2] National Campaign to Prevent Teen Pregnancy, "Whatever Happened to Childhood? The Problem of Teen Pregnancy in the United States," 1997.

[3] American Social Health Association, "STD Statistics," 2001.

[4] AIDS Action, "What Works in HIV Prevention for Women of Color," 2001.

[5] Jim Kirksey, "Official: Sex Ed Gap Hurts All of Us: Ex-Surgeon General Calls it a Health Risk," *The Denver Post*, September 12, 2002.

[6] Douglas Kirby, "Emerging Answers: Research Findings on Programs to Reduce Teen Pregnancy," National Campaign to Prevent Teen Pregnancy, 2001.

[7] Martha Kempner, "Toward a Sexually Healthy America: Abstinence-Only-Until-Marriage Programs that Try to Keep Our Youth 'Scared Chaste,'" Sexuality Information and Education Council of the United States, 2001.

[8] Human Rights Watch, "Ignorance Only: HIV/AIDS, Human Rights and Federally Funded Abstinence-Only Programs in the United States," 2002.

[9] Kaiser Family Foundation, "Sex Education in America: A View from Inside the Nation's Classrooms," 2000.

Health and Sexuality Education

For more information...

Center for Policy Alternatives
1875 Connecticut Avenue NW, Suite 710
Washington, DC 20009
202-387-6030
www.stateaction.org

Advocates for Youth
2000 M Street NW, Suite 750
Washington, DC 20036
202-419-3420
www.advocatesforyouth.org

Alan Guttmacher Institute
1120 Connecticut Avenue NW, Suite 460
Washington, DC 20036
202-296-4012
www.agi-usa.org

NARAL Pro-Choice America
1156 15th Street NW, Suite 700
Washington, DC 20005
202-973-3000
www.prochoiceamerica.org

National Campaign to Prevent Teen Pregnancy
1776 Massachusetts Avenue NW, Suite 200
Washington, DC 20036
202-478-8500
www.teenpregnancy.org

Planned Parenthood Federation of America
444 West 33rd Street
New York, NY 10001
212-541-7800
www.plannedparenthood.org

Sexuality Information and Education Council of the United States
130 W 42nd Street, Suite 350
New York, NY 10036
212-819-9770
www.siecus.org

Health and Sexuality Education

Responsible Sexuality Education in Schools Act

SECTION 1. SHORT TITLE

This Act shall be called "The Responsible Sexuality Education in Schools Act."

SECTION 2. FINDINGS AND PURPOSE

(A) FINDINGS—The legislature finds that:

1. Effective sexuality education programs discussing condoms and contraception help delay the onset of sexual activity, reduce the frequency of underage sex, and reduce the number of sex partners.

2. Abstinence-only programs in schools do not delay the initiation of teen sex or reduce its frequency.

3. It is essential for the health and safety of young people that they receive medically and factually accurate and objective information about sexuality, pregnancy and sexually transmitted diseases.

(B) PURPOSE—This law is enacted to protect the health and safety of young people and reduce the incidence of sexually transmitted disease in the state.

SECTION 3. RESPONSIBLE SEXUALITY EDUCATION IN SCHOOLS

(A) DEFINITION—In this section, "medically accurate" means information:

1. Supported by the weight of research conducted in compliance with accepted scientific methods.

2. Recognized as accurate and objective by leading professional organizations and agencies with relevant expertise in the field, such as the American College of Obstetricians and Gynecologists or the Centers for Disease Control.

(B) RESPONSIBLE SEXUALITY EDUCATION REQUIRED

1. The [Board of Education] shall adopt rules requiring all [high schools and middle schools] to teach age-appropriate, comprehensive and religiously neutral sexuality education, including education on both abstinence and contraception for the prevention of pregnancy and sexually transmitted diseases, including HIV.

2. All sexuality education courses taught in schools must provide medically accurate information.

SECTION 4. EFFECTIVE DATE

This Act shall take effect on July 1, 2004.

Health Clinic
Protection

An ongoing campaign of violence, vandalism and harassment endangers reproductive healthcare providers and patients. States can act to protect clinic staff and patients.

Health Clinic Protection

Summary:

- An ongoing campaign of violence, vandalism and harassment endangers reproductive healthcare providers and patients.
- Anti-abortion activists routinely try to intimidate doctors and their families, clinic staff, and patients in an attempt to block abortion services.
- Anti-choice violence and terror exacerbate the shortage of abortion providers, further limiting vital reproductive healthcare options.
- Clinic protection laws have proven effective, reducing incidents of violence and intimidation to clinic employees and patients.
- One approach to reduce violence and intimidation is mandating a buffer zone around clinics to protect workers and patients.

An ongoing campaign of violence, vandalism and harassment endangers reproductive healthcare providers and patients.

Since 1993, three reproductive health clinic doctors, two employees, an escort, and a security guard have been murdered by anti-choice forces in the United States. In fact, since 1977, there have been over 4,000 reported acts of violence against abortion providers, including bombings, arsons, death threats, kidnappings, and assaults, and almost 80,000 reported acts of disruption, including bomb threats and harassing calls.[1]

Anti-abortion activists routinely try to intimidate doctors and their families, clinic staff, and patients in an attempt to block abortion services.

This conduct is part of a deliberate campaign to curtail women's access to abortion by closing clinics and terrorizing healthcare providers. As a result of clinic violence, physicians and other clinic workers must take extraordinary measures for protection. Clinics spend thousands of dollars on bulletproof glass, armed guards, security cameras, metal detectors, and other security measures. Clinic workers have been instructed by federal marshals to vary their routes to work and to call police if they receive a suspicious package. These measures instill fear in and impose undue burdens on those seeking and providing reproductive health care. Preventing acts of domestic terrorism against reproductive health clinics and providers must be part of our country's effort to eliminate all forms of terrorism.

Anti-choice violence and terror exacerbate the shortage of abortion providers, further limiting access to vital reproductive health services.

A severe and escalating shortage of physicians who are trained, qualified and willing to provide abortion services is drastically diminishing access in some areas. In 38 states and the District of Columbia, the number of physicians who perform abortions declined between 1996 and 2000.[2] In addition, clinic directors can have a difficult time hiring and retaining office staff because of daily threats and harassment from anti-choice activists.

Both Congress and state legislatures have recognized the importance of laws protecting clinic access.

In 1994, Congress enacted the Freedom of Access to Clinic Entrances Act (FACE), which provides both civil and criminal penalties for violent or threatening tactics used by abortion opponents. Fifteen states (CA, CO, CT, KS, ME, MD, MA, MI, MN, NV, NY, NC, OR, WA, and WI) and the District of Columbia have also enacted some form of clinic protection law.

Clinic protection laws have proven effective, reducing the violence and intimidation clinic employees and patients experience.

The percentage of clinics experiencing severe violence has declined overall since FACE became law, and the percentage of clinics experiencing no anti-abortion violence, harassment or intimidation rose from 33 to 56 percent between 1994 and 2002.[3]

Laws protecting access to reproductive health facilities are constitutional.

Both federal and state clinic protection laws have been repeatedly upheld by the courts, including the U.S. Supreme Court, which in 2000 upheld Colorado's clinic protection statute, ruling that it does not violate the First Amendment right to free speech.[4]

One effective approach to reduce violence and intimidation is mandating a buffer zone around clinics to protect workers and patients.

Massachusetts and Colorado have enacted laws to provide a zone of privacy between patients and protesters, allowing patients to safely seek the services they need without facing intimidating, unwanted and close physical encounters with aggressive protestors. Maintaining a zone of personal space provides an essential buffer against physical or psychological threat, and ensures patients' privacy and access to reproductive health services.

In addition to laws creating buffer zones, states can enact other measures to protect clinic staff and patients.

States can also establish task forces on violence against reproductive healthcare providers; authorize funds for reproductive health facilities to upgrade security; require Attorneys General to collect and analyze information relating to anti-reproductive rights crimes; and develop plans to prevent such crimes, report them when they occur, and apprehend and prosecute perpetrators.

This policy summary relies in large part on information from NARAL Pro-Choice America.

Endnotes

[1] National Abortion Federation (NAF), "NAF Violence and Disruption Statistics: Incidents of Violence & Disruption Against Abortion Providers in the U.S. & Canada," June 30, 2003.

[2] Lawrence Finer & Stanley Henshaw, "Abortion Incidence and Services in the United States in 2000," *Perspectives on Sexual and Reproductive Health*, Vol. 35, No. 1, 2003.

[3] Feminist Majority Foundation, "2002 National Clinic Violence Survey Report," March 2003.

[4] *Hill v. Colorado*, 530 U.S. 703 (2000).

Health Clinic Protection

For more information...

Center for Policy Alternatives
1875 Connecticut Avenue NW, Suite 710
Washington, DC 20009
202-387-6030
www.stateaction.org

ACLU Reproductive Freedom Project
125 Broad Street
New York, NY 10004
212-344-3005
www.aclu.org

Feminist Majority Foundation
1600 Wilson Boulevard, Suite 801
Arlington, VA 22209
703-522-2214
www.feminist.org

NARAL Pro-Choice America
1156 15th Street NW, Suite 700
Washington, DC 20005
202-973-3000
www.prochoiceamerica.org

National Abortion Federation
1755 Massachusetts Avenue NW, Suite 600
Washington, DC 20036
202-667-5881
www.prochoice.org

Planned Parenthood Federation of America
434 West 33rd Street
New York, NY 10001
212-541-7800
www.plannedparenthood.org

Health Clinic Protection

Reproductive Health Clinic Protection Act

SECTION 1. SHORT TITLE

This Act shall be called the "[STATE] Reproductive Health Clinic Protection Act."

SECTION 2. FINDINGS AND PURPOSE

(A) FINDINGS—The legislature finds that:

1. Citizens of [STATE] have a right to access reproductive health facilities for the purpose of obtaining or providing reproductive health care, counseling and treatment.

2. A campaign of violence and intimidation is curtailing the availability of abortion services and endangering providers and patients. Since 1977, there have been over 4,000 reported acts of violence against abortion providers, including bombings, arsons, death threats, and assaults, as well as almost 80,000 reported acts of disruption, including bomb threats and harassing calls.

NOTE: National Abortion Federation (NAF), "NAF Violence and Disruption Statistics: Incidents of Violence & Disruption Against Abortion Providers in the U.S. and Canada," June 30, 2003. (NAF's statistics include incidents from both the United States and Canada. NAF derives most of its statistics from its members, most of which are in the United States.)

3. [Insert facts regarding clinic violence and obstruction of clinic access in the state.]

4. Intimidating, unwanted, and close physical encounters with aggressive anti-abortion activists can exacerbate a patient's stress and create increased health risks. Maintaining a zone of personal space is essential to sustain privacy, and to provide a buffer against physical or psychological threat.

5. The U.S. Supreme Court has recognized the importance of protecting access to reproductive health facilities and maintaining a zone of separation between protestors and patients. In *Hill v. Colorado* (2000), the U.S. Supreme Court upheld a Colorado law establishing a zone of separation between protestors and patients, ruling that the state has "a substantial and legitimate interest" in protecting persons attempting to enter health facilities from "unwanted encounters, confrontations, and even assaults." *Hill v. Colorado*, 530 U.S. 703 (2000).

(B) PURPOSE—This law is enacted to protect the health, safety and welfare of the citizens of [STATE].

SECTION 3. PROTECTING ACCESS TO REPRODUCTIVE HEALTH FACILITIES

After section XXX, the following new section XXX shall be inserted:

(A) DEFINITIONS—In this section:

1. "Reproductive health facility" means a hospital, clinic, physician's office, or other facility that provides reproductive health services, and includes the building or structure in which the facility is located.

2. "Reproductive health services" means medical, surgical, counseling or referral services relating to the human reproductive system, including services relating to pregnancy or the termination of pregnancy.

Health Clinic Protection

(B) PROTECTION AROUND REPRODUCTIVE HEALTH FACILITIES

1. No person shall knowingly obstruct, detain, hinder, impede or block another person's entry to or exit from a reproductive health services facility.

2. No person shall knowingly approach within eight feet of another person in the public way or sidewalk area within a radius of 100 feet from any entrance door to a reproductive health facility for the purpose of passing a leaflet or handbill to, displaying a sign to, or engaging in oral protest, education or counseling with such other person, unless the other person consents.

(C) REMEDIES

1. Any person who violates this section shall be guilty of a [CLASS A] misdemeanor.

2. In addition to, and not in lieu of, criminal penalties set forth in this section, a person who violates the provisions of this section shall be subject to civil liability. Any person aggrieved by reason of conduct prohibited by this section may commence a civil action for relief. The court may award appropriate relief, including temporary, preliminary or permanent injunctive relief and compensatory and punitive damages, as well as the costs of the suit and reasonable fees for attorneys and expert witnesses.

SECTION 4. EFFECTIVE DATE

This Act shall take effect July 1, 2004.

*This model is based on legislation developed by **NARAL Pro-Choice America.***

High Road -

Apprenticeship Training

High Road policies promote high-wage, low-waste, worker-friendly, publicly-accountable economic development.

High Road - Apprenticeship Training

Summary

- High Road policies promote high-wage, low-waste, worker-friendly, publicly-accountable economic development.
- Education and training are essential elements of a sustainable economic development strategy.
- Apprenticeship moves workers from low-skill to high-skill employment.
- States can expand access to apprenticeship programs by requiring that apprentices perform at least a certain percentage of hours worked on public construction projects.
- Local governments have successfully implemented laws mandating minimum apprenticeship requirements in public works contracts.
- Washington operates a statewide program requiring apprenticeship training.

High Road policies promote high-wage, low-waste, worker-friendly, publicly-accountable economic development.

Current government subsidy programs tend to support "low road" economic development: the creation of low-wage, dead-end jobs by businesses that are fundamentally unfriendly to the surrounding community, the environment, and their own employees. But there is another way. A "high road" strategy uses the levers of government, especially economic incentives and disincentives, to compel businesses to act in a socially responsible manner. High Road policies result in better and more secure jobs, a stronger tax base, and more efficient, environmentally friendly community development.[1]

Education and training are essential elements of a sustainable economic development strategy.

To attract businesses over the long-term, a region must develop the skills of its workforce. One straightforward way to make job training more accessible is to require it in projects that are paid for or heavily subsidized by the government.

Apprenticeship moves workers from low-skill to high-skill employment.

In the building trades, individuals become skilled craftsmen through a probationary training program called apprenticeship. The idea behind apprenticeship is centuries old. An apprentice learns a skilled trade by working alongside a journeyman who provides on-the-job training. The apprentice is paid at a lower rate until he or she attains the degree of proficiency needed to advance to the level of journeyman. Most apprenticeship programs are operated by labor unions.

States can expand access to apprenticeship programs by requiring that apprentices perform at least a certain percentage of hours worked on public construction projects.

Project Labor Agreements are comprehensive contracts among building contractors, their clients, and trade unions that govern working conditions and hiring practices on specific projects. Such agreements commonly make some provision for apprentices. The state can ensure that Project Labor Agreements for public works projects require that a substantial percentage of construction workers receive training through state-certified programs, a policy called Apprenticeship Utilization Requirements. The state can also require that a minimum percentage of apprenticeships go to low-income workers, minorities and women.

Local governments have successfully implemented laws mandating minimum apprenticeship requirements in public works contracts.

Local governments in Washington's Puget Sound area have such laws for public works projects costing over one million dollars. As a result, since 1994, 782 residents have been placed into building trades apprenticeships or jobs in other industries with comparable wages and career prospects.

Ninety-six percent of them came from low-income backgrounds, 21 percent had no income before enrolling in training, 44 percent reported incomes below poverty, and 35 percent had been receiving some form of public assistance. In recent years, similar apprenticeship requirements have been used with success in Boston, Philadelphia, Milwaukee and Washington D.C.

Washington operates a statewide program requiring apprenticeship training.

Through an Executive Order in 2000, Governor Gary Locke directed state agencies to require that apprentices enrolled in state-approved training programs work a certain percentage of the total labor hours in public works projects. State legislation enacted in 2003 expands on the Governor's order. It mandates that from July 1, 2003 through December 31, 2003, all public works projects estimated to cost $2 million or more shall require that at least ten percent of the labor hours within each trade be performed by apprentices of that trade. The requirement increases to 12 percent in 2004 and 15 percent in 2005.

This policy summary relies in large part on information from the AFL-CIO Working for America Institute.

Endnotes

[1] For a comprehensive discusson of High Road economic development, see www.highroadnow.org.

High Road - Apprenticeship Training

For more information...

Center for Policy Alternatives
1875 Connecticut Avenue NW, Suite 710
Washington, DC 20009
202-387-6030
www.stateaction.org

Center on Wisconsin Strategy
University of Wisconsin-Madison
1180 Observatory Drive, Room 7122
Madison, WI 53706
608-263-3889
www.cows.org

AFL-CIO Working for America Institute
815 16th Street NW
Washington, DC 20006
202-974-8100
www.workingforamerica.org

Policy Matters Ohio
2912 Euclid Avenue
Cleveland, OH 44115
216-931-9922
www.policymattersohio.org

Worker Center
King County Labor Council, AFL-CIO
2800 1st Avenue, Room 252
Seattle, WA 98121
206-461-8408
www.wc-kclc.org

High Road - Apprenticeship Training

High Road Apprenticeship Utilization Act

SECTION 1. SHORT TITLE

This Act shall be called the "High Road Apprenticeship Utilization Act."

SECTION 2. FINDINGS AND PURPOSE

(A) FINDINGS—The legislature finds that:

1. A well-trained construction trades workforce is critical to the economic future of the state and its political subdivisions.

2. The efficient and economical construction of public works projects will be hindered if there is not an ample supply of trained construction workers.

3. Apprenticeship training programs are particularly effective in providing training and experience to individuals seeking to enter or advance in the workforce.

4. By providing for apprenticeship utilization on public works projects, state and local governments can provide training and experience that will help assure that a skilled workforce will be available in sufficient numbers for the construction of public works in the future.

(B) PURPOSE—This law is enacted to promote job training, improve the skills of the workforce, and enhance the economic vitality of the state.

SECTION 3. APPRENTICESHIP UTILIZATION

After section XXX, the following new section XXX shall be inserted:

(A) DEFINITIONS—In this section:

1. "Apprentice" means an apprentice enrolled in a state-approved apprenticeship training program.

2. "Apprentice utilization requirement" means the requirement that the appropriate percentage of labor hours within each separate craft or trade be performed by apprentices of that craft or trade.

3. "Labor hours" means the total hours of workers receiving an hourly wage who are directly employed on the site of the public works project. "Labor hours" includes hours performed by workers employed by the contractor and all subcontractors working on the project. "Labor hours" does not include hours worked by foremen, superintendents, owners and workers who are not subject to prevailing wage requirements.

4. "Public works" means construction projects financed by state or local government funds, and includes those projects encompassed by [appropriate statute].

5. "Secretary" means the Secretary of the Department of [Labor], or the Secretary's designee(s).

6. "State-approved apprenticeship training program" means an apprenticeship training program approved by the [State Apprenticeship Council].

High Road - Apprenticeship Training

(B) MINIMUM STANDARDS FOR APPRENTICESHIP UTILIZATION

1. From July 1, 2004, through December 31, 2004, for all public works projects estimated to cost two million dollars or more, all specifications shall require that no less than 10 percent of the labor hours within each trade be performed by apprentices of that trade.

2. From January 1, 2005, through December 31, 2005, for all public works projects estimated to cost two million dollars or more, all specifications shall require that no less than 12 percent of the labor hours within each trade be performed by apprentices of that trade.

3. From January 1, 2006, and thereafter, for all public works projects estimated to cost one million dollars or more, all specifications shall require that no less than 15 percent of the labor hours within each trade be performed by apprentices of that trade.

4. Work shall not be divided among contractors or subcontractors in order to evade the requirements of this section. Where two or more contractors or subcontractors perform work within a trade, all such contractors or subcontractors shall comply with the requirements of this section.

5. All contractors and subcontractors subject to this section shall provide payroll reports on at least a monthly basis to the awarding agency or political subdivision awarding the work, certifying the names of all workers performing labor hours, their trade, hours worked, and designation as journey level worker or apprentice.

6. The awarding agency or political subdivision may adjust the requirements of this section for a specific project for the following reasons:

    a. The demonstrated lack of availability of apprentices in specific geographic areas;
    b. A disproportionately high ratio of material costs to labor hours, which does not make feasible the required minimum levels of apprentice participation; or
    c. Other criteria the awarding agency director deems appropriate, which are subject to prior review and approval by the Secretary.

7. The failure by a contractor to comply with the apprentice utilization requirement shall be deemed a breach of contract for which the state or municipality is entitled to all remedies allowed by law and under the contract. Failure to comply with the apprentice utilization requirement shall be considered evidence bearing on a contractor's qualification for award of future contracts.

8. This section does not apply to agencies and political subdivisions that adopt requirements for apprenticeship utilization on public works projects that equal or exceed those set forth in this section.

(C) ENFORCEMENT

1. The Secretary shall promulgate such regulations as are necessary to implement and administer compliance.

2. No person, association, corporation or other entity shall discharge, demote, harass or otherwise take adverse actions against any individual because such individual seeks the enforcement of this section, or testifies, assists or participates in any manner in an investigation, hearing or other proceeding to enforce this section.

SECTION 4. EFFECTIVE DATE

This Act shall take effect on July 1, 2004.

High Road - Apprenticeship Training

Minimum Standards for Subsidized Jobs Act

SECTION 1. SHORT TITLE

This Act shall be called the "Minimum Standards for Subsidized Jobs Act."

SECTION 2. FINDINGS AND PURPOSE

(A) FINDINGS—The legislature finds that:

1. Every year, [STATE] awards more than [INSERT AMOUNT] dollars in economic development subsidies to for-profit businesses.

2. When government invests in economic development, it makes no economic sense to support the creation or promotion of jobs that do not give workers the chance to earn a decent living.

3. When state-subsidized jobs provide low wages and poor benefits, they increase the need for government services, including public assistance for food, housing, health care, and childcare.

(B) PURPOSE—This law is enacted to improve the effectiveness of economic development expenditures, take pressure off state social service programs, and improve the public health and welfare by ensuring that major state subsidies are used to support at least minimum living standards for working families.

SECTION 3. MINIMUM STANDARDS FOR SUBSIDIZED JOBS

After section XXX, the following new section XXX shall be inserted:

(A) DEFINITIONS—In this section:

1. "Economic development subsidy" means any expenditure of public funds with a value of at least [$100,000], for the purpose of stimulating economic development within the state, including but not limited to bonds, grants, loans, loan guarantees, enterprise zones, empowerment zones, tax increment financing, grants, fee waivers, land price subsidies, matching funds, tax abatements, tax exemptions, and tax credits.

2. "Secretary" means the Secretary of the Department of [LABOR], or the Secretary's designee(s).

(B) MINIMUM STANDARDS FOR WAGES AND BENEFITS

1. No person, association, corporation or other entity shall be eligible to receive any economic development subsidy unless that entity:

    a. Pays all its employees in the state a minimum wage that is at least $1 per hour higher than the [federal/state as appropriate] minimum wage provided in [section number].
    b. Offers to all its employees in the state who work at least 35 hours per week a health insurance benefits plan for which the employer pays at least 80 percent of the monthly premium, and the coverage pays at least 80 percent of the costs of physician office visits, emergency care, surgery, and prescriptions with an annual deductible of no more than $1,000.

High Road - Apprenticeship Training

c. Offers to at least 20 percent of its workers in the state a worker training program that meets minimum standards issued by the Secretary.

2. This section does not apply to:

a. A not-for-profit entity that is exempt from taxation under [cite section].
b. An intern or trainee who is under 21 years of age and who is employed for a period not longer than three months.

3. If the Secretary determines that application of this section would conflict with a federal program requirement, the Secretary, after notice and public hearing, may grant a waiver from the requirements of this section.

(C) ENFORCEMENT

1. The Secretary shall promulgate such regulations as are necessary to implement and administer compliance.

2. No person, association, corporation or other entity shall discharge, demote, harass or otherwise take adverse actions against any individual because such individual seeks the enforcement of this section, or testifies, assists or participates in any manner in an investigation, hearing or other proceeding to enforce this section.

3. No entity shall pay an employee through a third party, or treat an employee as a subcontractor or independent contractor, to avoid the requirements of this section.

SECTION 4. EFFECTIVE DATE

This Act shall take effect on July 1, 2004 and shall apply to any economic development subsidy awarded or renewed on or after October 1, 2004.

Housing -
Expanding
Low-Income Access

States can expand the supply of low-income housing by allowing families with Section 8 vouchers to use them at any available rental unit.

Housing - Expanding Low-Income Access

Summary

- The flagging economy is creating an affordable housing crisis for low-income Americans.
- Over 14 million households—one in seven—spend more than half their incomes on housing.
- The number of available public housing units is rapidly declining, as long-term contracts expire and profit-hungry owners scramble to rent or sell properties at current market value.
- In communities where rental vacancy rates are low, public housing agencies struggle to place families in rental units.
- States can expand the supply of low-income housing by allowing families with Section 8 vouchers to use them at any available rental unit.
- Permitting families to use vouchers at any available rental unit is an inexpensive way to create mixed-income neighborhoods.
- Currently, nine states prohibit discrimination against prospective renters based upon their source of income.

The flagging economy is creating an affordable housing crisis for low-income Americans.

A single worker earning the minimum wage cannot afford adequate family housing anywhere in the country. In 37 states, two workers earning the federal minimum wage do not make enough to afford adequate family housing, while up to three times the federal minimum wage is still insufficient in the 10 least affordable states.[1]

Over 14 million households—one in seven—spend more than half their incomes on housing.[2]

While some family incomes have risen in tandem with rising rent costs, lower-income workers are being priced out of the housing market. As a result, many affected Americans are forced to live in housing beyond their means, squeeze their families into overcrowded dwellings, or live in housing that is out of compliance with health and safety codes.

The number of available public housing units is rapidly declining, as long-term contracts expire and profit-hungry owners scramble to rent or sell properties at current market value.

While public housing availability shrinks, the federal government has expanded its supply of Section 8 vouchers. As a result, families who are lucky enough to receive a voucher—some waiting lists have thousands of names—are unable to find Section 8 approved housing in increasingly tight rental markets.

In communities where rental vacancy rates are low, public housing agencies struggle to place families in rental units.

Local housing agencies are required to meet a 97 percent placement rate of eligible applicants in order to qualify for additional funding. Meeting that threshold is increasingly difficult for precisely those areas with the strongest need. The lack of available housing jeopardizes current and future Section 8 voucher recipients, because if counties fail to meet this strict federal guideline, they cannot apply for additional funding.

States can expand the supply of low-income housing by allowing families with Section 8 vouchers to use them at any available rental unit.

When "source of income" is included in a state's non-discrimination code for housing, families in need can have access to a wider range of rental options. Prohibiting source of income discrimination permits Section 8 voucher holders to look beyond the current federal housing stock, and helps poor families move away from areas of high-poverty concentration.

Permitting families to use vouchers at any available rental unit is an inexpensive way to create mixed-income neighborhoods.

Research consistently shows that communities with a range of family incomes have the resources to provide better schools, social services, and job opportunities, and are better able to help low-income families break the cycle of poverty. Families who spend less on housing are able to spend more of their money in the community, boosting local economies, building individual assets, and reducing personal debt.

Nine states prohibit discrimination against prospective renters based upon their source of income.

Since the mid 1990s, nine states with diverse housing needs—California, Connecticut, Maine, Massachusetts, New Jersey, North Dakota, Oklahoma, Utah, and Vermont—have amended their housing anti-discrimination laws to include source of income as a protected category.

Endnotes

[1] Noam Neusner and Matthew Benjamin, "Shelter from the Storm," US News & World Report, July 29, 2002.

[2] Joint Center for Housing Studies and Harvard University, "The State of the Nation's Housing," 2003.

Housing - Expanding Low-Income Access

For more information...

Center for Policy Alternatives
1875 Connecticut Avenue NW, Suite 710
Washington, DC 20009
202-387-6030
www.stateaction.org

National Low Income Housing Coalition
1012 14th Street NW, Suite 610
Washington, DC 20005
202-662-1530
www.nlihc.org

National Rural Housing Coalition
1250 Eye Street NW, Suite 902
Washington, DC 20005
202-393-5229
www.nrhcweb.org

Housing - Expanding Low-Income Access

Source of Income Anti-Discrimination Act

SECTION 1. SHORT TITLE

This Act shall be called the "Source of Income Anti-Discrimination Act."

SECTION 2. DEFINITION

After section XXX, paragraph XXX, the following new paragraph XXX shall be inserted:

"Source of income" means any lawful source of money paid directly or indirectly to a renter or buyer of housing, including:
1. Any lawful profession or occupation.
2. Any government or private assistance, grant or loan program.
3. Any gift, inheritance, pension, annuity, alimony, child support, or other consideration or benefit.
4. Any sale or pledge of property or interest in property.

SECTION 3. NO DISCRIMINATION IN HOUSING BASED ON SOURCE OF INCOME

In section XXX, after the word [religion], the following shall be inserted:
"source of income,".

[This is to be placed within the current statute against housing discrimination, e.g., "It is unlawful to discriminate in the sale or rental, or otherwise make unavailable or deny, a dwelling to any buyer or renter because of race, color, religion, source of income, sex…]

SECTION 4. EXCEPTIONS CONCERNING SOURCE OF INCOME

After section, paragraph XXX, the following new paragraph XXX shall be inserted:

The prohibitions in this subtitle against discrimination based on source of income do not prohibit a person from:
1. Refusing to consider income derived from any criminal activity; or
2. Determining the ability of a potential buyer or renter to pay a purchase price or pay rent by:
   a. Verifying, in a commercially reasonable manner, the source and amount of income of the potential buyer or renter; or
   b. Evaluating, in a commercially reasonable manner, the stability, security and credit worthiness of the potential buyer or renter or any source of income of the potential buyer or renter.

SECTION 5. EFFECTIVE DATE

This Act shall take effect on July 1, 2004.

Housing -
Predatory Lending

A dramatic increase in the incidence of predatory lending has created a crisis for communities of color, elderly homeowners, and low-income Americans. States have been moving to curtail predatory lending practices in the home mortgage industry.

Housing - Predatory Lending

Summary

- A dramatic increase in the incidence of predatory lending practices has created a crisis for communities of color, elderly homeowners, and low-income Americans.
- Predatory lending occurs predominantly in the subprime mortgage industry, and nationally the practice of subprime lending has skyrocketed, growing by 900 percent in only six years.
- The increase in predatory lending has been most damaging to the elderly and in minority communities.
- About half of subprime borrowers could qualify for a traditional mortgage.
- The victims of predatory lending practices are compelled to accept unreasonable loan terms and abusively high fees.
- There is a long history of states limiting abusive lending practices through usury laws, but financial industry deregulation and statutory loopholes have made those laws ineffective.
- Since 1999, many states have implemented laws to curtail predatory lending practices in the home mortgage industry.

A dramatic increase in the incidence of predatory lending practices has created a crisis for communities of color, elderly homeowners, and low-income Americans.

The overwhelming majority of abusive loan practices occur in the subprime mortgage industry. Subprime loans are intended for people unable to obtain a conventional prime loan at standard mortgage rates. For legitimate reasons, these loans have higher interest rates to compensate for the potentially greater risk that the borrowers represent. Lending practices are predatory when loan terms or conditions become abusive, or when borrowers who would qualify for credit on better terms are targeted instead for higher cost loans.

Nationally, the practice of subprime lending has skyrocketed, growing by 900 percent in only six years.

In 1993, only 100,000 home purchase or refinance loans were brokered in the subprime market; that number jumped to nearly 1 million loans in 1999. During this same period, all other home purchase and refinance loans declined by 10 percent.[1]

The increase in subprime and predatory lending has been most damaging to the elderly and in minority communities.

Subprime lenders now account for 51 percent of all refinance loans made in predominantly African-American neighborhoods, compared to just nine percent of the refinance loans made in predomi-

nantly white neighborhoods.[2] Similarly, almost one in three refinance loans made to low-income Latino families were subprime. One study found that borrowers 65 years of age or older were three times more likely to hold a subprime mortgage than borrowers under 35 years of age.[3]

About half of subprime borrowers could qualify for a traditional mortgage.

The Chairman of Fannie Mae Corporation estimates that as many as half of the borrowers who receive high-cost subprime loans could have instead qualified for traditional mortgages at lower interest rates.[4]

The victims of predatory lending practices are compelled to accept unreasonable terms and abusively high fees.

Borrowers who are not in a position to qualify for an "A" loan are too often required to pay unreasonable rates and fees in the subprime market. Contributing to the problem are incentive systems that reward brokers and loan officers for charging more. Other abusive loan practices found in the subprime industry include: requiring borrowers to purchase single-premium credit insurance, saddling credit-challenged borrowers with unwanted balloon payments and prepayment penalties, and using high-pressure tactics to encourage repeated refinancing by existing customers, tacking on extra fees each time, in a practice known as "flipping."

Predatory lending practices are even more insidious because they specifically target the members of our society who can least afford to be stripped of their equity or life savings.

These same citizens have the fewest resources to fight back when they are cheated—they lack the money to seek legal counsel and the knowledge to contact an appropriate enforcement agency.

There is a long history of states limiting abusive lending practices through usury laws, but financial industry deregulation and statutory loopholes have made those laws ineffective.

Usury laws have been so weakened over the past 20 years that predatory lending practices—modern day loan-sharking—are legal. Although federal law prohibits specific predatory practices, those provisions cover only certain types of loans, and the threshold for what is considered a high-cost loan is set so high that many homeowners are left unprotected.

Since 1999, many states have implemented laws to curtail predatory lending practices in the home mortgage industry.

North Carolina became the first state to prohibit predatory lending in 1999. Since then, legislatures in California, Georgia, New Jersey, New Mexico, New York, and South Carolina have enacted strong predatory lending restrictions, and predatory lending regulations have been adopted in Illinois and Massachusetts as well. A number of other states, including AR, FL, KY, OH, OK and PA have enacted bills that purport to address the problem, but actually provide no additional substantive consumer protections.

State legislation against predatory lending has proven to work.

An economic study of the North Carolina law found that predatory lending practices were reduced while full access to credit for subprime borrowers was maintained.[5]

Effective legislation to prohibit predatory lending practices includes the following elements:

■ Limits balloon payments, call provisions, and negative amortization in high-cost home loans.

■ Limits prepayment penalties for the first three years of the loan, increased interest rates after a default, and improper payments to home improvement contractors.

■ Limits fees to modify, renew, extend or amend high-cost home loans.

■ Prohibits "flipping" of home loans—in which refinancing worsens the borrower's financial position.

■ Prohibits mandatory arbitration or required broker licensing.

■ Requires homeownership counseling for borrowers who seek high-cost loans.

Endnotes

[1] "Unequal Burden: Income and Racial Disparities in Subprime Lending in America," U.S. Department of Housing and Urban Development, April 2000.

[2] "Curbing Predatory Home Mortgage Lending: A Joint Report," U.S. Department of the Treasury and U.S. Department of Housing and Urban Development, June 2000.

[3] AARP, "Subprime Mortgage Lending and Older Borrowers," citing "Subprime Lending: An Investigation of Economic Efficiency," February 2000.

[4] Business Wire, "Fannie Mae Has Played Critical Role in Expansion of Minority Homeownership," March 2, 2000.

[5] Roberto Quercia, Michael Stegman, and Walter Davis, "The Impact of North Carolina's Anti-Predatory Lending Law: A Descriptive Assessment," Center for Community Capitalism, University of North Carolina, 2003.

Housing - Predatory Lending

For more information...

Center for Policy Alternatives
1875 Connecticut Avenue NW, Suite 710
Washington, DC 20009
202-387-6030
www.stateaction.org

AARP
601 E Street NW
Washington, DC 20049
202-434-2277
www.aarp.org

Association of Community Organizations for Reform Now
88 3rd Avenue, 3rd Floor
Brooklyn, NY 11217
718-246-7900
www.acorn.org

Center for Responsible Lending
P.O. Box 77513
Washington, DC 20013
202-207-0153
www.responsiblelending.org

Community Reinvestment Association of North Carolina
114 W. Parrish Street, Second Floor
P.O. Box 1929
Durham, NC 27702-1929
919-667-1557
www.cra-nc.org

Fannie Mae Corporation
3900 Wisconsin Avenue NW
Washington, DC 20016
202-752-7000
www.fanniemae.com

North Carolina Fair Housing Center
114 W. Parrish Street
Durham, NC 27701
919-667-0888
www.fairhousing.com

U.S. Department of Housing and Urban Development
451 7th Street SW
Washington, DC 20410
202-708-1112
www.hud.gov/offices/fheo/lending/predatory.cfm

Housing - Predatory Lending

Predatory Lending Prevention Act

Summary: The Predatory Lending Prevention Act prohibits specific unfair practices in the sale of residential home loans, and provides civil and administrative enforcement procedures.

SECTION 1. SHORT TITLE

This Act shall be called the "[STATE] Predatory Lending Prevention Act."

SECTION 2. FINDINGS AND PURPOSE

(A) FINDINGS—The legislature finds that:

1. A dramatic increase in the practice of subprime lending has occured in the state. Nationally, subprime lending grew 900 percent from 1993 to 1999 and a similar trend occurred in [STATE].

2. Subprime loans are intended for people who, because of blemished credit, are unable to obtain conventional prime loans at standard mortgage rates.

3. While subprime lending is a legitimate practice, expanding access to credit for home ownership, most predatory practices occur in the subprime lending market.

4. Predatory lenders tend to target groups that can least afford to be stripped of their assets—lower income families, minorities, and elderly citizens.

5. The state of [STATE] must act to protect its residents from the most abusive loan practices.

(B) PURPOSE—This law is enacted to protect the equity and property of homeowners, provide needed consumer protections, and safeguard the economic vitality of our state.

SECTION 3. PREDATORY LENDING PREVENTION

After section XXX, the following new section XXX shall be inserted:

(A) DEFINITIONS—In this section:

1. "Annual percentage rate" means the annual percentage rate for a loan, calculated according to the provisions of the federal Truth In Lending Act (15 U.S.C. 1601, et seq.), and the regulations promulgated thereunder by the Board of Governors of the Federal Reserve System (as said Act and regulations are amended from time to time).

2. "Borrower" means any individual obligated to repay the loan, including a co-borrower, cosigner or guarantor.

3. "Flipping" means knowingly refinancing an existing home loan when any of the following occurs:
    a. More than 50 percent of the prior debt refinanced bears a lower interest rate than the new loan.
    b. It will take more than five years of reduced interest rate payments for the borrower to recoup the

Housing - Predatory Lending

transaction's prepaid finance charges and closing costs.

c. Refinancing a special mortgage originated, subsidized or guaranteed by or through a state, tribal or local government, or nonprofit organization, which either bears a below-market interest rate, or has nonstandard payment terms beneficial to the borrower, such as payments that vary with income or are limited to a percentage of income, or where no payments are required under specified conditions, and where, as a result of the refinancing, the borrower will lose one or more of the benefits of the special mortgage.

4. "High-cost home loan" means a home loan where—

a. The total points and fees on the loan exceed five percent of the total loan amount, or

b. The annual percentage rate of interest of the home loan equals or exceeds eight percentage points over the yield on U.S. Treasury securities that have comparable periods of maturity to the loan maturity, as of the 15th day of the month immediately preceding the month in which the application for credit is received by the lender.

5. "Home loan" means a loan, other than a reverse mortgage transaction, where the principal amount of the loan does not exceed the conforming loan size limit for a single-family dwelling as established from time to time by the Federal National Mortgage Association and Federal Home Loan Mortgage Corporation, and the loan is secured by a mortgage or deed of trust on real estate upon which there is located or is to be located a structure or structures, designed principally for occupancy of from one to four families, which is or will be occupied by a borrower as the borrower's principal dwelling. Home loan does not include an open-end line of credit as defined in Part 226 of Title 12 of the Code of Federal Regulations.

6. "Lender" means any entity that originated, or acted as a mortgage broker for, more than five home loans within the previous 12 months.

7. "Points and fees" means—

a. All items required to be disclosed as finance charges under Sections 226.4(a) and 226.4(b) of Title 12 of the Code of Federal Regulations, including the Official Staff Commentary, as amended from time to time, except interest.

b. All compensation and fees paid to mortgage brokers in connection with the loan transaction.

c. All items listed in Section 226.4(c)(7) of Title 12 of the Code of Federal Regulations, only if the person originating the covered loan receives direct compensation in connection with the charge.

8. "Total loan amount" means the same as in section 226.32 of Title 12 of the Code of Federal Regulations.

(B) PROHIBITED PRACTICES FOR ALL HOME LOANS

1. **Deceptive and unfair business practices**—No lender shall:

a. Recommend or encourage non-payment of an existing loan or other debt prior to, and in connection with, the closing or planned closing of a home loan that refinances all or any portion of such existing loan or debt.

b. Coerce, intimidate or directly or indirectly compensate an appraiser for the purpose of influencing his or her independent judgment concerning the value of real estate that is to be covered by a home loan or is being offered as security according to an application for a home loan.

c. Leave blanks in any loan documents to be filled in after they are signed by the borrower.

2. **Financing credit insurance**—No lender shall require or allow the advance collection of a premium, on a single premium basis, for any credit life, credit disability, credit unemployment, or credit property insurance, or the advance collection of a fee for any debt cancellation or suspension agreement or contract, in

connection with any home loan, whether such premium or fee is paid directly by the consumer or is financed by the consumer through such loan. For purposes of this section, credit insurance does not include a contract issued by a government agency or private mortgage insurance company to insure the lender against loss caused by a mortgagor's default.

(C) PROHIBITED PRACTICES FOR HIGH-COST HOME LOANS

1. **Balloon payments**—No high-cost home loan may contain a scheduled payment that is more than twice as large as the average of earlier scheduled payments during the first seven years of the loan. This provision does not apply to a payment schedule that is adjusted to the seasonal or irregular income of the borrower, or a bridge loan with a maturity of less than 12 months that requires only payments of interest until the entire unpaid balance is due.

2. **Prepayment penalties**—No high-cost home loan shall contain a prepayment penalty of more than 3% of the original principal amount of the note in the first year, 2% in the second year, 1% in the third year, or any prepayment penalty beyond the third year.

3. **Negative amortization**—No high-cost home loan may include payment terms under which the outstanding principal balance will increase at any time over the course of the loan because the regular periodic payments do not cover the full amount of interest due. This provision does not apply to a payment schedule that is adjusted to the seasonal or irregular income of the borrower.

4. **Increased interest rate**—No high-cost home loan may contain a provision that increases the interest rate after default. This provision does not apply to interest rate changes in a variable rate loan otherwise consistent with the provisions of the loan documents, provided the change in the interest rate is not triggered by a default or the acceleration of indebtedness.

5. **Advance payments**—No high-cost home loan may include terms under which more than two periodic payments required under the loan are consolidated and paid in advance from the loan proceeds provided to the borrower.

6. **Call provisions**—No high-cost home loan may contain a provision that permits the lender, in its sole discretion, to accelerate indebtedness. This provision does not prohibit acceleration of the loan in good faith due to the borrower's failure to abide by the material terms of the loan.

7. **Home improvement contracts**—A lender may not pay a contractor under a home improvement contract from the proceeds of a high-cost home loan unless the instrument is payable to the borrower or jointly to the borrower and the contractor, or, at the election of the borrower, through a third-party escrow agent in accordance with terms established in a written agreement signed by the borrower, the lender, and the contractor prior to disbursement.

8. **Flipping**—A lender may not offer a high-cost home loan while engaged in the practice of flipping.

9. **Modification or deferral fees**—A lender may not charge a borrower any fees or other charges to modify, renew, extend or amend a high-cost home loan, or to defer any payment due under the terms of a high-cost home loan, except when the borrower is in default of the loan.

10. **Homeownership counseling**—A lender may not originate a high-cost home loan without first receiving certification from a counselor approved by the U.S. Department of Housing and Urban Development, a state housing financing agency, or the regulatory agency which has jurisdiction over the lender, that the borrower has received counseling on the advisability of the loan transaction.

Housing - Predatory Lending

(D) ENFORCEMENT

1. **Civil remedies**—This Act may be enforced by a private cause of action under [appropriate section of state statutes].

2. **Administrative remedies**—This Act shall be enforced by [appropriate state oversight agency], which shall promulgate such rules and regulations as are necessary to implement and administer compliance with the Act.

SECTION 4. SEVERABILITY

The provisions of this Act shall be severable, and if any phrase, clause, sentence or provision is declared to be invalid or is preempted by federal law or regulation, the validity of the remainder of this Act shall not be affected thereby.

SECTION 5. EFFECTIVE DATE

This Act shall take effect on July 1, 2004.

Immigrants -
Driver's Licenses

There is no question that states should use rigorous procedures to ensure the identity of a driver's license recipient. But those procedures should not exclude persons who *can* prove their identity.

Immigrants - Driver's Licenses

Summary

- Immigrants are too often unable to obtain state driver's licenses.
- Granting immigrants the right to obtain licenses saves lives.
- Denying driver's licenses increases the likelihood of identity fraud.
- Denying driver's licenses is an ineffective means of enforcing immigration law.
- Denying driver's licenses is an ineffective tool for preventing terrorism or improving security.
- Law enforcement officials support providing driver's licenses to immigrants.
- States should adopt policies that allow all residents to obtain driver's licenses, regardless of their immigration status.

Immigrants are too often unable to obtain state driver's licenses.

Federal law does not require states to deny driver's licenses to undocumented immigrants. However, states often require applicants to provide specific types of identification, such as Social Security numbers, and refuse to accept foreign-issued identity documents. As a result, many immigrants, including legal permanent residents, are unable to obtain driver's licenses.

Granting immigrants the right to obtain licenses saves lives.

Traffic accidents are the leading cause of death for persons aged six to 33, with over 40 thousand traffic fatalities each year. According to a study conducted by the AAA Foundation for Traffic Safety, unlicensed drivers are five times more likely to be in fatal crashes than drivers with valid licenses. Providing access to licenses ensures that drivers are trained, tested and can secure insurance. In addition, registering and photographing all drivers helps the state monitor driving records and better protect the safety of communities.

Denying driver's licenses increases the likelihood of identity fraud.

There is no question that states should use rigorous procedures to ensure the identity of a driver's license recipient. But those procedures should not exclude persons who *can* prove their identity, whether by consular identification, foreign passport, birth certificate, or other verifiable documents. Excluding verifiable documents creates conditions for false documents and false identities to flourish. New Jersey, New York, and Virginia, among other states, have been rocked by scandals involving corrupt issuance of hundreds of fraudulent documents to persons who were precluded from obtaining licenses legally.

Denying driver's licenses is an ineffective means of enforcing immigration law.

Driver's license restrictions have neither deterred immigration nor encouraged existing immigrants to return to their countries of origin. It is a policy without a purpose. In the meantime, states have a responsibility to protect the health and safety of all their residents.

Denying driver's licenses is an ineffective tool for preventing terrorism or improving security.

Proponents of restrictions on immigrants have linked driver's licenses to security concerns, by pointing out that many of the September 11 hijackers were able to obtain licenses. However, proposals that restrict immigrants' ability to obtain driver's licenses as a means to fight terrorism or to enhance security are red herrings. First, immigrant driver's license restrictions would not have prevented September 11. Most of the hijackers were in the United States lawfully and would have been able to secure licenses even with such a restriction. Second, to improve security, driver's license regulations should focus on ensuring the identity of the applicant. Providing access to a legitimate and secure means of identification for all drivers will help states prevent identification fraud.

Law enforcement officials support providing driver's licenses to immigrants.

In most states, law enforcement officials are part of coalitions supporting the elimination of restrictions on driver's licenses. They cite public safety, fraud prevention, and the desire to reduce courtroom congestion as reasons for their support. They also note that police officers are better able to protect communities with the cooperation of all residents, regardless of immigration status. For example, when some Tennessee policymakers suggested repealing the state law permitting driver's licenses for immigrants in the name of national security, the state Safety Department opposed the suggestion, pointing out that issuing licenses allows the state to clearly document its residents.

States should adopt policies that allow all residents to obtain driver's licenses, regardless of their immigration status.

The Immigrant Drivers Inclusion Act eliminates the state's "lawful presence" requirement and allows driver's license applicants who do not have a Social Security number (SSN) to submit alternative proof of identity, including a birth certificate or record of birth issued by a foreign country, a military identification, a passport, a license issued by another state or country, a consular identification document issued by the government of Mexico (matricula consular), or another document, specified by the Department of Motor Vehicles, that confirms the identity of the applicant.

Currently, 40 states allow some alternatives to the SSN. Motor vehicle administrations in 18 states (HI, IL, MI, MT, NE, NV, NH, NM, NY, NC, ND, OR, RI, TN, UT, VT, WA and WI) do not require driver's license applicants to be legal residents.

This policy summary relies in large part on information from the National Council of La Raza.

Immigrants - Driver's Licenses

For more information...

Center for Policy Alternatives
1875 Connecticut Avenue NW, Suite 710
Washington, DC 20009
202-387-6030
www.stateaction.org

California Immigrant Welfare Collaborative
926 J Street, Suite 701
Sacramento, CA 95814
916-448-6762
www.nilc.org/ciwc/ciwcindex.htm

National Council of La Raza
1111 19th Street NW, Suite 1000
Washington, DC 20036
202-785-1670
www.nclr.org

National Immigration Law Center
1101 14th Street NW, Suite 410
Washington, DC 20005
202-216-0261
www.nilc.org

Immigrant Drivers Inclusion Act

Summary: This Act allows immigrants to obtain driver's licenses by listing forms of identification that can be accepted in lieu of a Social Security number.

SECTION 1. SHORT TITLE

This Act shall be called the "Immigrant Drivers Inclusion Act."

SECTION 2. IMMIGRANT DRIVERS INCLUSION

After section XXX, the following new section XXX shall be inserted:

If the applicant for a driver's license does not have a Social Security number, the [Department of Motor Vehicles] is authorized to accept any of the following documents for identification purposes:

1. An Individual Tax Identification Number (ITIN) issued by the Internal Revenue Service.

2. A U.S. Social Security Administration letter (L-676) stating that the applicant is ineligible to obtain a Social Security number.

3. An alien registration receipt card, resident alien card, employment authorization card, temporary resident card or other authorized document from the Immigration and Naturalization Service (INS).

4. A passport, a federal identification card, or other verifiable certificate or document issued by a federal governmental agency other than the INS.

5. Military papers issued by the defense department of a foreign country.

6. Any type of generally recognized governmental registration document issued by a governmental agency of a foreign country, including a Mexican Matricula Consular.

7. An original birth certificate, or certified copy of a birth certificate issued by this or another state, or by another country, if accompanied by supportive documentation required by [Department of Motor Vehicles] rule.

8. Any other certificate or document issued by the government of a foreign country, if such certificate or document includes a photo of the person to whom the certificate or document has been issued.

9. Any other proof of identity satisfactory to the [Department of Motor Vehicles].

SECTION 3. REPEAL OF AUTHORIZED PRESENCE REQUIREMENT

Section XXX is repealed. [This section would repeal any provision requiring applicants to prove that their presence in the United States is authorized under federal law.]

SECTION 4. EFFECTIVE DATE

This Act shall take effect on July 1, 2004.

Immigrants -
In-State Tuition

Many immigrant children are ineligible for in-state college tuition rates, effectively denying them access to higher education. Placing college education out of reach for students is an enormous loss for the economy and for society. States should enact laws to make higher education more accessible to long-term residents.

Immigrants - In-State Tuition

Summary

- Many immigrant children are ineligible for in-state college tuition rates, effectively denying them access to higher education.
- Placing college education out of reach for immigrant students is an enormous loss for the economy and for society.
- To excel in school and attend college, many children of low-income immigrant families overcome tremendous obstacles.
- The denial of in-state tuition rates disproportionately affects Latino students.
- States should enact laws to make higher education more accessible to long-term resident immigrant students.

Many immigrant children are ineligible for in-state college tuition rates, effectively denying them access to a college education.

Despite the fact that numerous foreign-born children have lived in the United States for most of their lives, many are denied in-state college tuition rates if they are undocumented or in the process of obtaining legal status. These children are subject to international student tuition rates, which tend to be three to ten times higher than in-state tuition. For example, the annual in-state tuition rate to attend the University of California-Berkeley is $5,842, compared to $20,068 for international students. The in-state rate at California community colleges is $18 per semester unit, compared to $141 per unit for international students. At these rates, college is not a viable option for most immigrant students in lower-income families.

Placing college education out of reach for immigrant students is an enormous loss for the economy and for society.

At a time when state economies need a more highly educated workforce, it makes no sense to deny higher education to immigrant students. College graduates have higher earnings than high school graduates; they pay more state taxes and provide a better trained workforce for high-paying employers. States that block students who are capable of excelling in college are shooting themselves in the foot.

To excel in school and attend college, many children of low-income immigrant families overcome tremendous obstacles.

Often they must overcome language and cultural barriers, in addition to the economic hardships faced by other minority groups. These students have attended and graduated from local high schools in communities where their parents work and pay taxes. Given the opportunity, immigrant students stand to make great contributions to our society.

The denial of in-state tuition rates disproportionately affects Latino students.

Recent Census data show that Latino children are among the fastest-growing populations in the United States. In fact, more than one-third of all Latinos in the United States are under the age of 18. These young people will make up a large proportion of our nation's future workforce. It is especially important to encourage young Latinos and other immigrant students to continue in school and pursue their dreams through higher education.

States should enact laws to make higher education more accessible to long-term resident immigrant students.

Illinois, Oklahoma and Washington adopted legislation in 2003 to allow resident immigrant students who meet certain criteria to attend state colleges and universities at in-state tuition rates. California, New York, Texas and Utah adopted similar legislation in 2001-02. To be eligible, students are required to be state residents, have attended a high school within the state for two or three years, have graduated from a state high school (or attained an equivalent certification), and be currently attending, or have been accepted at, a state college or university. Students are also required to file an affadavit stating that the student has filed an application to legalize his or her immigration status, or will file such an application as soon as he or she is eligible to do so.

In recent years, in-state tuition laws have enjoyed strong bi-partisan support in many states.

In 2003, Illinois legislation allowing immigrant students access to in-state tuition rates passed the House by a vote of 112 to 4, and the Senate by a vote of 55 to 1. Similar legislation in New York and Utah was broadly supported by both parties, and by businesses, unions, educators and the civil rights community.

This policy summary relies in large part on information from the National Council of La Raza and the National Immigration Law Center.

Immigrants - In-State Tuition

Center for Policy Alternatives
1875 Connecticut Avenue NW, Suite 710
Washington, DC 20009
202-387-6030
www.stateaction.org

California Immigrant Welfare Collaborative
926 J Street, Suite 701
Sacramento, CA 95814
916-448-6762
www.nilc.org/ciwc

National Council of La Raza
1111 19th Street NW, Suite 1000
Washington, DC 20036
202-785-1670
www.nclr.org

National Immigration Law Center
1101 14th Street NW, Suite 410
Washington, DC 20005
202-216-0261
www.nilc.org

Access to Postsecondary Education Act

Summary: The Access to Postsecondary Education Act provides in-state university and college tuition rates to qualified immigrant students who have attended state high schools for at least two years.

SECTION 1. SHORT TITLE

This Act shall be called the "Access to Postsecondary Education Act."

SECTION 2. FINDINGS AND PURPOSE

(A) FINDINGS—The legislature finds:

1. Many [STATE] immigrant high school students have lived in the state most of their lives, and are likely to remain residents. These students are nevertheless precluded from obtaining an affordable college education because they do not qualify for in-state tuition rates. Without in-state tuition, many of these students are not able to attend college.

2. These students have already proven their academic eligibility and merit by being accepted into the state college and university system.

3. Making it possible for these students to attend college will increase the state's college-educated workforce and stimulate economic growth.

4. This Act does not confer postsecondary education benefits on the basis of residence within the meaning of Section 1623 of Title 8 of the United States Code.

(B) PURPOSE—This law is enacted to provide educational opportunity to children who are long-time residents of [STATE], improving the overall economic condition of the state.

SECTION 3. ACCESS TO POSTSECONDARY EDUCATION

After section XXX, the following new section XXX shall be inserted:

(A) QUALIFICATIONS FOR IN-STATE TUITION RATES

A student, other than a nonimmigrant alien within the meaning of paragraph 15 of subsection (a) of Section 1101 of Title 8 of the United States Code, shall qualify for in-state tuition rates at [STATE] state universities and colleges if the student meets all of the following requirements:

1. High school attendance in [STATE] for two or more years.

2. Graduation from a [STATE] high school or attainment of the equivalent thereof.

3. Registration as an entering student at, or current enrollment in, a public institution of higher education in [STATE].

Immigrants - In-State Tuition

4. In the case of a person without legal immigration status, the filing of an affidavit with the institution of higher education stating that the student has filed an application to legalize his or her immigration status, or will file an application as soon as he or she is eligible to do so.

(B) ADMINISTRATION

1. The [Trustees of the University System] and the [Board of Governors of the Community College System] shall prescribe rules and regulations for the implementation of this section.

2. Student information obtained in the implementation of this section shall be confidential.

(C) ENFORCEMENT

A state court may award only prospective injunctive and declaratory relief to a party in any lawsuit based upon this section or based upon rules and regulations prescribed to implement this section.

SECTION 4. EFFECTIVE DATE

This Act shall take effect on July 1, 2004.

Initiative
Campaign
Funding Disclosure

States need to improve initiative donor disclosure laws before soft money dollars overwhelm the process of direct democracy with millions in undisclosed or poorly disclosed spending.

Initiative Campaign Funding Disclosure

Summary

- In the 24 states that permit ballot initiatives, wealthy individuals and organizations routinely spend millions of dollars on initiative campaigns to change public policy.
- Soft money, now banned from federal campaigns, may be diverted to fund state initiative campaigns.
- Accurate and timely disclosure of ballot initiative funding helps voters make informed decisions.
- Ballot initiative campaigns are usually subject to insufficient or infrequent filing deadlines.
- Organizations working for or against ballot initiatives too often obscure their involvement.
- Ballot committees often disclose little information about their donors.
- Most states do not require electronic filing, making information virtually inaccessible to voters.
- The Initiative Campaign Funding Disclosure Act would provide voters with essential information about donors to ballot initiative campaigns.

In the 24 states that permit ballot initiatives, wealthy individuals and organizations routinely spend millions of dollars on initiative campaigns to change public policy.

In 1998 alone, $400 million was spent on ballot measures. A 2002 study of seven states found that over 57 percent of the contributions to ballot committees were raised in amounts of $50,000 or more. That same year, special interests, corporations, advocacy organizations, and individuals spent over $173 million on 117 measures on the 2002 ballot.[1]

Soft money, now banned from federal campaigns, may be diverted to fund state initiative campaigns.

Because there are no limits on contributions to ballot measures, former soft money donors may turn to funding ballot measures. Initiative campaigns not only influence public policy directly, but they can also influence candidate elections by increasing voter turnout and framing the overarching policy debate. Now more than ever, states need to improve initiative donor disclosure laws, before soft money dollars overwhelm the process of direct democracy with millions in undisclosed or poorly disclosed spending.

Accurate and timely disclosure of ballot initiative funding helps voters make informed decisions.

The initiative process lacks the deliberative qualities of legislative lawmaking. Initiative voters don't have the information that legislators receive from official reports, formal hearings, and two-sided debates. Further, titles and descriptions of initiatives on the ballot are often misleading. Therefore, voters look at which groups are supporting or opposing a measure when considering their vote. But in most states, donor disclosure requirements are woefully inadequate, and fail to provide citizens with the identities of key initiative supporters and opponents.

Ballot initiative campaigns are usually subject to insufficient or infrequent filing deadlines.

Most state filing schedules fail to provide enough time for voters and opinion leaders to evaluate the money behind ballot measures prior to Election Day. The best states require regular committee reporting (CO, FL, OR, WA), while the worst states leave voters in the dark about initiative campaign funders until late October (MI, NV, ND, OH, SD). Gaps in the filing schedule, particularly close to the election, substantially hinder full and accurate disclosure. Oregon is the only state that specifically requires finance reports during the critical signature-gathering period of an initiative campaign.

Organizations working for or against ballot initiatives too often obscure their involvement.

Ballot committees are often deceptively named, and many state disclosure forms fail to link committee names to the ballot initiatives they support or oppose. In many circumstances, organizations are not required to register as ballot committees at all, even when they are the chief political force opposing a measure.

Ballot committees often disclose little information about their donors.

Many states fail to require two essential pieces of information about campaign contributors: occupation and employer. Without this information, voters cannot assess the economic interests of contributors. Furthermore, ballot measure donors are increasingly funneling their contributions through 501(c)(3) organizations and out-of-state entities in order to conceal their involvement.

Most states do not require electronic filing, making information virtually inaccessible to voters.

Only six states (AZ, CA, IL, MA, OH, WA) require ballot campaigns to file donor disclosure information electronically. Four states (AR, MT, OK, WY) fail to provide any disclosure information online. The rest offer at least partial online access. But, because disclosure agencies consider ballot measure reports a lower priority than candidate reports, the information posted is usually incomplete and late. Mandatory electronic filing would ensure timelier reporting and require less work for understaffed disclosure agencies. Several studies also show that electronic filing generates long-term savings.

The Ballot Measure Campaign Disclosure Act would provide voters with essential information.

The Act requires:

■ Every entity spending $100 or more to support or oppose a ballot measure must register as a ballot measure committee, ensuring a full reporting of campaign spending by all parties.

■ Ballot measure committees to clearly identify their cause to the state enforcement agency before a ballot number or letter is assigned. After a number or letter assignment, ballot measure committees must clearly disclose that designation and whether the organization is in favor or opposed.

■ Ballot measure committees to meet donor disclosure deadlines during the signature-gathering period, regularly during the campaign season, and, for large contributions, within 48 hours during the final weeks prior to the election.

■ Ballot measure committees to list occupations and employers for all donations of $100 or more.

■ Electronic filing of campaign funding disclosure information for ballot measure committees.

■ The state disclosure agency to make all electronic data easy to access, search and sort online.

This policy summary relies in large part on information from the Ballot Initiative Strategy Center Foundation.

Endnotes

[1] Ballot Initiative Strategy Center Foundation, "The Campaign Finance Reform Blind Spot," 2002.

Initiative Campaign Funding Disclosure

For more information...

Center for Policy Alternatives
1875 Connecticut Avenue NW, Suite 710
Washington, DC 20009
202-387-6030
www.stateaction.org

Ballot Initiative Strategy Center Foundation
1025 Connecticut Avenue NW, Suite 205
Washington, DC 20009
202-223-2373
www.ballotfunding.org

Brennan Center For Justice
New York University School of Law
161 Avenue of the Americas, 12th Floor
New York, NY 10013
212-998-6730
www.brennancenter.org

Initiative Campaign Funding Disclosure

Ballot Measure Campaign Disclosure Act

SECTION 1. SHORT TITLE

This Act shall be called the "Ballot Measure Campaign Disclosure Act."

SECTION 2. FINDINGS AND PURPOSE

(A) FINDINGS – The legislature finds that:

1. In various ways, current campaign disclosure laws are less sufficient for ballot measure campaigns than they are for political candidate campaigns.

2. Because of the absence of contribution limits, and the potential damage to state policy, it is especially important for ballot measure campaigns to provide accurate and timely disclosure of their fundraising and spending.

3. Strengthening disclosure requirements is particularly important because soft money contributions, recently banned from federal campaigns, may soon be diverted to fund ballot measure campaigns.

(B) PURPOSE – This law is enacted to improve the democratic process for the adoption or defeat of ballot measures by providing crucial information to the public in a timely, accessible manner.

SECTION 3. DEFINITIONS

After subsection XXX, the following new subsection XXX shall be inserted:

"Ballot measure" means an initiative, referendum, ballot question, or any other matter on the ballot other than the election of a candidate to public office.

SECTION 4. BALLOT MEASURE CAMPAIGN REGISTRATION REQUIREMENTS

After subsection XXX, the following new subsection XXX shall be inserted:

In addition to all other registration requirements, the following requirements shall apply to ballot measure campaigns:

1. Within 10 days after first collecting or spending $100 or more in an attempt to place a ballot measure on the ballot, or to support or oppose a ballot measure, a person, group or entity shall register with the [Board of Elections] as a ballot measure committee. However, if it is within 30 days of Election Day when the measure appears on the ballot, the person, group or entity shall register as a ballot measure committee within 24 hours after first collecting or spending $100 or more.

Initiative Campaign Funding Disclosure

2. If a ballot measure committee registers before a ballot measure number/letter is assigned by the [Board of Elections], the registration shall clearly describe the nature of the ballot measure, and whether the committee supports or opposes such measure. If a ballot measure committee registers after a ballot measure number/letter is assigned by the [Board of Elections], the registration shall list that number/letter and whether the committee supports or opposes such measure.

SECTION 5. BALLOT MEASURE CAMPAIGN REPORTING REQUIREMENTS

After subsection XXX, the following new subsection XXX shall be inserted:

In addition to all other reporting requirements, the following requirements shall apply to any ballot measure committee:

1. After registering with the [Board of Elections], a ballot measure committee shall file a campaign disclosure report, as described in [citation], within 10 days after the end of each calendar quarter.

2. If a ballot measure committee receives a contribution of $1,000 or more between the closing date of the last pre-election disclosure report and Election Day, the committee shall disclose that contribution within 48 hours of receipt in a manner designated by the [Board of Elections].

3. In each campaign disclosure report, a ballot measure committee shall list, for any donation of $100 or more, the occupation and employer of an individual, or the nature of business of a contributor that is not an individual.

4. If a ballot measure committee files a campaign disclosure report before a ballot measure number/letter is assigned by the [Board of Elections], the report shall clearly describe the nature of the ballot measure, and whether the committee supports or opposes such measure. If a ballot measure committee files a campaign disclosure report after a ballot measure number/letter is assigned by the [Board of Elections], the report shall list that number/letter and whether the committee supports or opposes such measure.

5. If a ballot measure committee collects or spends, or expects to collect or spend, over $10,000 throughout the ballot measure campaign, the committee shall file all financial disclosure reports by electronic means, in such form as the [Board of Elections] directs.

SECTION 6. BALLOT MEASURE CAMPAIGN REPORTING REQUIREMENTS

After subsection XXX, the following new subsection XXX shall be inserted:

The [Board of Elections] shall make all registration forms and campaign finance reports for ballot measure committees easily accessible, searchable and sortable through the Internet.

SECTION 7. EFFECTIVE DATE

This Act shall take effect on July 1, 2004.

Living
Wage

States are not innocent bystanders in the payment of sub-poverty level wages. Workers who directly or indirectly serve the state should be paid at least a living wage.

Living Wage

Summary

- Millions of hardworking Americans live in poverty.
- States are not innocent bystanders in the payment of sub-poverty level wages.
- State support of sub-poverty wages strains government public assistance programs.
- When the state helps create jobs that pay sub-poverty level wages, it is pursuing a shortsighted economic policy.
- The Living Wage Act can lift thousands of families above the poverty line while improving the quality of services received under state contracts.
- The living wage is a far more appropriate base earnings rate than the minimum wage.
- Since 1994, more than 80 cities and counties have adopted a living wage.
- The public strongly supports the living wage.

Millions of hardworking Americans live in poverty.

In every state there are hundreds of thousands, or even millions, of men and women who work full-time, but don't earn enough to climb out of poverty. Unfortunately, the federal minimum wage of $5.15 per hour is simply insufficient. A wage earner working full-time at the minimum wage earns approximately $10,700 a year—$4,500 below the 2003 poverty line for a family of three, and $7,700 below the poverty line for a family of four. All too often in America, hard work goes unrewarded.

States are not innocent bystanders in the payment of sub-poverty level wages.

Most states award billions of dollars in service contracts each year, resulting in the employment of thousands of individuals. Many of these individuals employed indirectly by the state—such as janitorial, healthcare and clerical workers—are paid wages that keep them in poverty. Workers who directly or indirectly serve the state should be paid at least enough to feed their families.

State support of sub-poverty wages strains the state's public assistance programs.

When they are paid wages at or near the minimum wage, workers and their families must rely on public assistance to survive. They need Medicaid, subsidized housing, childcare programs, and free school lunches. It simply makes no sense for the state to use taxpayer funds to promote sub-poverty wage jobs.

When the state helps create jobs that pay sub-poverty level wages, it is pursuing a shortsighted economic policy.

A rational economic development policy promotes the creation of good jobs, not bad ones. The creation of sub-poverty level jobs does not lead to a self-sufficient workforce. Such jobs cannot provide the basis for sustainable economic growth. Public dollars should be leveraged for the public good—supporting "high road" private sector employers that demonstrate a commitment to providing decent, family-supporting jobs throughout the state.

The Living Wage Act can lift thousands of families above the poverty line while improving the quality of services received under state contracts.

The Act requires employers who receive major service contracts from the state to pay a living wage to employees working on those contracts. The living wage will not only make sure that companies accepting public money are creating good jobs for state residents, it will mean that work for the state will be performed by workers who are more productive, with lower turnover and training costs, and less absenteeism.[1]

The living wage is a far more appropriate base earnings rate than the minimum wage.

In the 1960s and 70s, the federal minimum wage gave Americans an income slightly above the poverty line. If the minimum wage of 1968 were adjusted for inflation, it would equal about $8.50 today.[2] The Living Wage Act's proposed rate of $8.50 per hour provides an income that is just slightly below the 2003 federal poverty level for a family of four, plus health insurance. The living wage proposed in cases where the employer does not provide health insurance is $10 per hour, just above the 2003 federal poverty level for a family of four.

Since 1994, more than 110 cities and counties have adopted a living wage.

Living Wage laws have been enacted in more than 110 cities and counties, including Baltimore, Boston, Chicago, Cleveland, Des Moines, Detroit, Los Angeles, Milwaukee, Minneapolis, New York City, San Antonio, San Francisco, and St. Louis.[3] Many studies demonstrate that the living wage is a success, lifting families out of poverty without adversely affecting local economies.[4]

The public strongly supports the living wage.

Americans overwhelmingly support the living wage in public opinion polls. Seventy percent of Los Angeles voters surveyed, for example, said they favored that city's Living Wage law. Moreover, according to a Lake Snell Perry & Associates poll, 84 percent of Americans support the idea that anyone who works full-time should not have to live in poverty.[5]

Endnotes

[1] Michael Reich, Peter Hall and Ken Jacobs, "Living Wages, Airport Security and Worker Performance: The San Francisco Model," Institute of Industrial Relations, University of California at Berkeley, 2002.

[2] Based on the Consumer Price Index for Urban Wage Earners and Clerical Workers (CPI-W) calculated by the U.S. Bureau of Labor Statistics.

[3] Living Wage Resource Center, "Living Wage Successes: A Compilation of Living Wage Policies on the Books," 2003.

[4] Public Policy Institute of California, "How Living Wage Laws Affect Low-Wage Earners and Low-Income Families," 2002.

[5] Lake Snell Perry & Associates, "A National Survey of American Attitudes Towards Low-Wage Workers and Welfare Reform," April 2000.

Living Wage

Center for Policy Alternatives

1875 Connecticut Avenue NW, Suite 710
Washington, DC 20009
202-387-6030
www.stateaction.org

Association of Community Organizations for Reform Now

1486 Dorchester Avenue
Boston, MA 02122
617-740-9500
www.livingwagecampaign.org

AFL-CIO

815 16th Street NW
Washington, DC 20006
202-637-5000
www.aflcio.org

The Brennan Center for Justice

161 Avenue of the Americas, 12th Floor
New York, NY 10013
212-998-6730
www.brennancenter.org

Service Employees International Union

1313 L Street NW
Washington, DC 20005
202-898-3200
www.seiu.org

Living Wage

Living Wage Act

SECTION 1. SHORT TITLE

This Act shall be called the "[STATE] Living Wage Act."

SECTION 2. FINDINGS AND PURPOSE

(A) FINDINGS – The legislature finds that:

1. The state of [STATE] awards contracts that result in the employment of thousands of individuals. Many of these individuals, employed indirectly by the state, receive sub-poverty level wages.

2. The creation or promotion of jobs that pay sub-poverty level wages is shortsighted economic and social policy. Such jobs do not lead to a self-sufficient workforce or support sustainable community development. Instead, they increase the need for government services, such as public assistance for food, housing, health care, and child care.

3. The state is not an innocent bystander in the payment of sub-poverty level wages. It is necessary and appropriate for the state to require that contractors working on state business pay at least a living wage.

(B) PURPOSE – Recognizing that the state is a major contractor for services, this law is enacted to increase the wages of service employees who indirectly work for the state in order to improve public health and welfare, promote the economic strength of our society, and take pressure off state social service programs.

SECTION 3. LIVING WAGE

After section XXX, the following new section XXX shall be inserted:

(A) DEFINITIONS – In this section:

1. "Secretary" means the Secretary of the Department of [LABOR], or the Secretary's designee(s).

2. "State" means the state or a principal unit of state government.

3. "State contractor" means a for-profit or not-for-profit entity that has a state contract.

4. "State contract" means:

    a. A contract for services with the state valued at $100,000 or more; or

    b. A subcontract valued at $25,000 or more for providing part or all of the services covered by another entity's contract for services with the state valued at $100,000 or more.

5. "Basic health insurance benefits" means an insurance plan where an employer pays 100 percent of the premium for individual coverage or 80 percent of the premium for family coverage if the health insurance:

Living Wage

a. Covers at least 80 percent of the costs of office visits, emergency care, surgery, and prescriptions; and

b. Has an annual deductible of no more than $1,000.

(B) PAYMENT OF LIVING WAGE

1. Any state contract for services must require state contractors to pay an hourly wage rate that is at least the living wage.

2. During the duration of a state contract, a state contractor shall pay to each employee who is working on the state contract an hourly wage rate that is at least the living wage.

3. If a state contract is subject to prevailing wage requirements under [appropriate citation], the state contractor shall pay the living wage or the prevailing wage, whichever is higher.

(C) CALCULATION OF LIVING WAGE

1. The initial living wage shall be $10 per hour without basic health insurance benefits or $8.50 per hour with basic health insurance benefits.

2. On July 1 of each year, the Secretary shall adjust the living wage in direct proportion to any increase or decrease in the Consumer Price Index for [insert region], as reported by the U.S. Department of Labor, except that the hourly wage rate shall not be set at less than $10 per hour without basic health insurance benefits or $8.50 per hour with basic health insurance benefits.

(D) WAIVERS AND EXEMPTIONS

1. A not-for-profit entity that is subject to this section may apply to the state agency that is responsible for the state contract for a waiver of the living wage requirement, based on economic hardship. The state agency may only grant such a waiver after:

a. A review of the not-for-profit entity's financial situation, including salary levels of the entity's management personnel; and

b. A determination that the application of this section would cause an undue hardship to the entity's operation.

2. Any granted waiver of the living wage requirement must be renewed annually.

3. The living wage does not apply to a trainee who is enrolled for less than six months in a job readiness or job training program run by a non-profit entity.

4. The living wage does not apply to an intern who is under 21 years of age, employed by a non-profit entity before or after school, or during the summer for a period not longer than three months.

5. If a state agency responsible for a state contract determines that application of this section would conflict with a federal program requirement, this section does not apply to that contract.

(E) ENFORCEMENT

1. No state contractor shall discharge, demote, harass or otherwise take adverse actions against any individual because such individual seeks to enforce this section, or testifies, assists, or participates in any manner in an investigation, hearing, or other proceeding to enforce this section.

2. No state contractor shall split or subdivide a contract, pay an employee through a third party, or treat an employee as a subcontractor or independent contractor to avoid payment of a living wage.

3. This section shall be enforced by [appropriate state agency], which shall promulgate such regulations as are necessary to implement and administer compliance. Regulations shall include procedures to receive, investigate, and attempt to resolve complaints; and bring actions in any court of competent jurisdiction to recover appropriate relief for aggrieved employees.

4. In any action under this section in which an employee prevails:

   a. The employee shall be awarded monetary relief, including back pay in an amount equal to the difference between the employee's actual earnings and what the employee would have earned but for the employer's unlawful practices.

   b. The employer shall be enjoined from continuing to underpay employees, and the employer may be ordered to take such additional affirmative steps as are necessary, to ensure compliance with this section.

   c. The employer shall pay a reasonable attorney's fee, reasonable expert witness fees, and other costs of the action.

SECTION 4. EFFECTIVE DATE

This Act shall take effect on July 1, 2004. The living wage shall apply to state contracts executed or renewed on or after October 1, 2004.

Mandatory
Arbitration Clauses

Mandatory arbitration clauses are used to deny millions of Americans their right to sue in court. State legislatures have three options to attack unfair arbitration clauses.

Mandatory Arbitration Clauses

Summary

- Mandatory arbitration clauses are used to deny millions of Americans their right to sue in court.
- Mandatory arbitration clauses undermine consumer protections that were designed to level the playing field between big businesses and individuals.
- Private arbitration is much more expensive than going to court.
- A pro-business bias is built into the arbitration system.
- Arbitration clauses affect the most important aspects of people's lives, including their jobs, homes and health.
- The courts continue to enforce the most egregious arbitration clauses, even when judicial discretion allows them to be struck down.
- State legislatures have three options to attack unfair arbitration clauses.

Mandatory arbitration clauses are used to deny millions of Americans their right to sue in court.

Buried in the fine print of many form contracts—for employment, rental, credit, phone service, and insurance—are mandatory arbitration clauses that waive the right to access the courts. They force individuals to argue their cases through private arbitration, a costly private legal system that favors defendants.

Mandatory arbitration clauses undermine consumer protections that were designed to level the playing field between big businesses and individuals.

Since 1970, a wide range of laws have been enacted to protect Americans from defective products, negligent business practices, and discrimination in the workplace. Mandatory arbitration clauses circumvent many of these laws and deny Americans their day in court. In addition, the long-standing tendency among arbitrators to "split the difference" between the two sides results in awards to plaintiffs that are substantially lower than court-ordered awards.

Private arbitration is much more expensive than going to court.

Claimants must pay steep filing fees just to initiate a case—seldom less than $750—not including the arbitrator's hourly charges, which range from $200-$300 per hour, split between the parties. Further, these fees must be paid in advance, and almost always amount to thousands of dollars.[1]   For example, an $80,000 consumer claim that would cost $221 to bring in the Circuit Court for Cook County, IL, would cost $11,625 at the National Arbitration Forum, a major arbitration firm.[2] In addition, individuals filing claims have usually already sustained a serious economic loss in their dispute with the business—foreclosure on a home, firing from a job, termination of a franchise or dealership. As a result, many people cannot afford the costs of arbitration and are forced to drop their cases.

Mandatory arbitration clauses are used to defeat class action lawsuits.

Nearly every arbitration clause prohibits participation in class action lawsuits. Class actions are the only effective remedy for wide-scale scams. Individuals seldom have the time or resources to recognize, investigate or prove the existence of such fraudulent practices in order to recover their losses.

A pro-business bias is built into the arbitration system.

Arbitration providers are organized to serve businesses, not consumers. Their marketing is targeted entirely at businesses, and their panels of arbitrators consist primarily of corporate executives and their lawyers. Since only businesses are repeat users of an arbitrator, there is a disincentive for an arbitrator to rule in favor of a consumer or employee. In arbitration, discovery is a privilege, not a right, and many businesses draft arbitration clauses to severely restrict a claimant's ability to obtain necessary evidence.

Arbitration clauses affect the most important aspects of people's lives, including their jobs, homes and health.

■ **At work:** Arbitration firms have convinced employers that the solution to discrimination lawsuits is not to monitor offices and shop floors for harassment, but to impose so-called "early dispute resolution" requirements, including mandatory arbitration. This process reduces an employer's incentive to keep workplaces free from harassment and discrimination.

■ **Small business:** Operating a franchise or dealership is difficult enough without worrying about termination or unfair treatment by a powerful corporate partner. Mandatory arbitration clauses make it harder to redress bad faith practices and easier to mistreat franchisees, dealers and contract farmers.

■ **Homeownership:** In an era of increased complaints about defective construction, homebuilders use mandatory arbitration clauses to deflect lawsuits. Mandatory arbitration clauses are also an important tool in the predatory mortgage lender's bag of tricks, preventing a victim of predatory practices from suing lenders.

■ **Health care:** Insurance companies frequently use mandatory arbitration clauses to fend off appeals of denied medical coverage, and HMOs have also used them to avoid medical malpractice suits. More recently, nursing homes and even physicians are using them.

The courts continue to enforce the most egregious arbitration clauses, even when judicial discretion allows them to be struck down.

Judges have the power to invalidate mandatory arbitration clauses that are unconscionable, but few have done so. Many judges see arbitration as a way of clearing their dockets quickly. Unfortunately, judges' desire to reduce their workloads eliminates the deterrent—the possibility of court action—that motivates businesses to voluntarily comply with the law.

State legislatures have three options to attack unfair arbitration clauses.

Preemption by the 1925 Federal Arbitration Act forbids states from banning mandatory arbitration outright. But states can:

■ Use existing powers through the federal McCarran-Ferguson Act to prohibit arbitration clauses in insurance policies.

■ Ban contract provisions that forbid a party from bringing or benefitting from a class action lawsuit.

■ Adopt the California approach of disclosure, access and impartiality. It requires full disclosure of consumer arbitration outcomes, so that any patterns of bias can be detected. Texas enacted a similar provision for residential construction arbitrations in 2003. It increases access to justice by requiring that fees be waived for indigent claimants and banning any shift of arbitration fees to a claimant who does not prevail. It also improves impartiality of arbitrators by prohibiting conflicts of interest.

This policy summary is based in large part on information from Public Citizen.

Endnotes

[1] Public Citizen, "Mandatory Arbitration Clauses: Undermining the Rights of Consumers, Employees, and Small Businesses," 2002.

[2] Public Citizen, "The Costs of Arbitration," 2002.

Mandatory Arbitration Clauses

For more information...

Center for Policy Alternatives
1875 Connecticut Avenue NW, Suite 710
Washington, DC 20009
202-387-6030
www.stateaction.org

Public Citizen
1600 20th Street NW
Washington, DC 20009
202-588-1000
www.citizen.org

Mandatory Arbitration Clauses

Voluntary Arbitration for Insurance Consumers Act

SECTION 1. SHORT TITLE

This Act shall be called the "Voluntary Arbitration for Insurance Consumers Act."

SECTION 2. MANDATORY ARBITRATION CLAUSES UNENFORCEABLE

After section, paragraph XXX, the following new paragraph XXX shall be inserted:

Any contract or agreement between an insurance carrier and the beneficiary of such contract or agreement, or a third party acting on the beneficiary's behalf, that contains any clause or provision providing for an adjustment by arbitration shall not preclude any party or beneficiary under the contract or agreement from instituting a suit or legal action on the contract at any time, and the compliance with the clause or provision shall not be a condition precedent to the right to bring or recover in the action. A party is bound by an arbitration provision only when the agreement to arbitrate is entered into knowingly and voluntarily by the parties involved after the dispute has arisen, or exists pursuant to the terms of a collective bargaining agreement.

SECTION 3. EFFECTIVE DATE

This Act shall take effect on July 1, 2004.

Preservation of Class Action Remedies Act

SECTION 1. SHORT TITLE

This Act shall be called the "Preservation of Class Action Remedies Act."

SECTION 2. RESTRICTIONS ON CLASS ACTION REMEDIES UNENFORCEABLE

After section, paragraph XXX, the following new paragraph XXX shall be inserted:

Every contract, or restriction contained in any contract, that waives or has the practical effect of waiving a party's right to resolve a dispute by obtaining class-wide relief is void and unenforceable, unless the parties agree to such a waiver after the dispute has arisen.

SECTION 3. EFFECTIVE DATE

This Act shall take effect on July 1, 2004.

Mandatory Arbitration Clauses

Arbitration Reform Act

SECTION 1. SHORT TITLE

This Act shall be called the "Arbitration Reform Act."

SECTION 2. FAIR ARBITRATION OF CONSUMER CONTRACTS

After section XXX, the following new section XXX shall be inserted:

(A) DEFINITIONS—In this section:

1. "Consumer arbitration" means an arbitration conducted under a predispute arbitration provision where: the contract is with a consumer party; the contract was drafted by or on behalf of the nonconsumer party; and the consumer party was required to accept the arbitration provisions in the contract. "Consumer arbitration" excludes arbitration proceedings conducted under or arising out of public or private sector labor relations laws, regulations, or agreements.

2. "Consumer party" means a party to an arbitration agreement who, in the context of that arbitration agreement, is any of the following:

   a. An individual who seeks or acquires, including by lease, any goods or services, including but not limited to financial services and insurance, primarily for personal, family, or household purposes.
   b. An individual who is an enrollee, subscriber or insured under a health care plan or health care insurance, or an individual with a medical malpractice claim; or
   c. An employee or applicant for employment, in a dispute arising out of or relating to the employee's employment or the applicant's prospective employment that is subject to the arbitration agreement.

3. "Financial interest" means holding a position in a business as officer, director, trustee or partner or holding any position in management; or ownership of more than five percent interest in a business.

(B) FAIR DISCLOSURE BY ARBITRATION COMPANIES

1. Any private arbitration company that administers or is otherwise involved in 50 or more consumer arbitrations a year shall collect, publish at least quarterly, and make available to the public in a computer-searchable format, which shall be accessible at the Internet Web site of the private arbitration company, if any, and on paper upon request, all of the following information regarding each consumer arbitration within the preceding five years:

   a. The nonconsumer party, if the nonconsumer party is a corporation or other business entity that is a party to the arbitration, specifying the posture of the nonconsumer party as claimant or respondent;
   b. The type of dispute involved, including goods, banking, insurance, health care, employment, and, if it involves employment, the amount of the employee's annual wage divided into the following ranges: less than $100,000, $100,000 to $250,000, and over $250,000.
   c. Whether the consumer or nonconsumer was the prevailing party.
   d. On how many occasions, if any, the nonconsumer has previously been a party in an arbitration or mediation administered by the private arbitration company.

Mandatory Arbitration Clauses

e. Whether the consumer party was represented by an attorney.

f. The date the private arbitration company received the demand for arbitration, the date the arbitrator was appointed, and the date of disposition by the arbitrator or private arbitration company.

g. The type of disposition of the dispute, if known, including withdrawal, abandonment, settlement, award after hearing, award without hearing, default, or dismissal without hearing.

h. The amount of the claim, the amount of the award, and any other relief granted, if any.

i. The name of the arbitrator, his or her total fee for the case, fees assessed by the private arbitration company, and the percentage of the arbitrator's fee allocated to each party.

2. If the required information is provided by the private arbitration company in a computer-searchable format at the company's Internet Web site and may be downloaded without any fee, the company may charge the actual cost of copying to any person who requests the information on paper. If the information required is not accessible by the Internet, the company shall provide that information without charge to any person who requests the information on paper.

3. A private arbitration company that administers or conducts fewer than 50 consumer arbitrations per year may collect and publish the information required by subdivision (a) semiannually, provide the information only on paper, and charge the actual cost of copying.

4. No private arbitration company shall have any liability for collecting, publishing, or distributing the information in accord with this section.

(C) LIMITS ON COST SHIFTING

1. All fees and costs charged to or assessed upon a consumer by a private arbitration company in a consumer arbitration, [exclusive of arbitrator fees] shall be waived for any person having a gross monthly income that is less than 300 percent of the federal poverty guidelines.

2. Nothing in this section shall affect the ability of a private arbitration company to shift fees that would otherwise be charged or assessed upon a consumer party to another party.

3. Prior to requesting or obtaining any fee, a private arbitration company shall provide written notice of the right to obtain a waiver of fees in a manner calculated to bring the matter to the attention of a reasonable consumer, including, but not limited to, prominently placing a notice in its first written communication to a consumer and in any invoice, bill, submission form, fee schedule, rules, or code of procedure.

4. Any consumer requesting a waiver of fees or costs may establish eligibility by making a declaration under oath on a form provided by the private arbitration company for signature stating his or her monthly income and the number of persons living in the household. No private arbitration company may require a consumer to provide any further statement or evidence of indigence.

5. Any information obtained by a private arbitration company about a consumer's identity, financial condition, income, wealth, or fee waiver request shall be kept confidential and may not be disclosed to any adverse party or any nonparty to the arbitration, except a private arbitration company may not keep confidential the number of waiver requests received or granted, or the total amount of fees waived.

Mandatory Arbitration Clauses

(D) NEUTRALITY OF ARBITRATOR

1. No arbitrator or private arbitration company shall administer a consumer arbitration under any agreement or rule requiring that a consumer who is a party to the arbitration pay the fees and costs incurred by an opposing party if the consumer does not prevail in the arbitration, including, but not limited to, the fees and costs of the arbitrator, provider organization, attorney, or witnesses.

2. No private arbitration company may administer a consumer arbitration or provide any other services related to such a consumer arbitration, if:

> a. the private arbitration company has, or within the preceding year has had, a financial interest in any party or attorney for a party; or
> b. any party or attorney for a party has, or within the preceding year has had, any type of financial interest in the private arbitration company.

SECTION 3. SEVERABILITY

The provisions of this Act shall be severable, and if any phrase, clause, sentence or provision is declared to be invalid or is preempted by federal law or regulation, the validity of the remainder of this Act shall not be affected.

SECTION 4. EFFECTIVE DATE

This Act shall take effect on July 1, 2004.

Medical
Marijuana

Tens of thousands of seriously ill Americans endure severe pain and suffering that could be eased by the medicinal use of marijuana.

Medical Marijuana

Summary

- Tens of thousands of seriously ill Americans endure severe pain and suffering that could be eased by the medicinal use of marijuana.
- Marijuana is widely recognized as a medicine that is as effective and safe as other prescription medications.
- Medical associations support patients' legal access to medical marijuana.
- States can help the users of medical marijuana despite federal law.
- Ten states have enacted effective medical marijuana laws.
- The public overwhelmingly supports the legalization of medical marijuana.
- Medical marijuana laws do not increase use of the drug among youth.

Tens of thousands of seriously ill Americans endure severe pain and suffering that could be eased by the medicinal use of marijuana.

For cancer and HIV/AIDS patients, marijuana can very effectively treat nausea, vomiting and lost appetite caused by chemotherapy and HIV/AIDS medications. For glaucoma patients, it reduces buildup of pressure in the eye, alleviating pain and slowing vision loss. For multiple sclerosis patients, it lessens muscle pain and spasticity and relieves tremors and unsteadiness. For some epileptics, it prevents seizures. And for many other medical conditions, marijuana alleviates chronic, debilitating pain. It is simply inhumane to stand between suffering people and a medication that can help them.

Marijuana is widely recognized as a medicine that is as effective and safe as other prescription medications.

After a nearly two-year review of the medical literature, commissioned by the White House Office of National Drug Control Policy, investigators at the National Academy of Sciences, Institute of Medicine concluded that marijuana clearly has therapeutic uses for relief from pain, control of nausea and vomiting, and appetite stimulation.[1] In fact, government-sponsored reports have found marijuana to be an effective and acceptably safe medicine for many years. Those reports include the conclusions of the 1997 National Institutes of Health Workshop on the Medical Utility of Marijuana, and the 1988 findings of Administrative Law Judge Francis Young for the U.S. Department of Justice's Drug Enforcement Administration.[2] It is irrational to forbid doctors to prescribe marijuana while permitting them to prescribe morphine.

Medical professionals support patients' legal access to medical marijuana.

Medical professionals and public health officials support the legalization of medical marijuana for patients suffering from particular illnesses. Organizations favoring medical marijuana include: the American Academy of Family Physicians, American Nurses Association, American Public Health Association, Federation of American Scientists, Lymphoma Foundation of America, and the New England Journal of Medicine. Individual doctors have recommended marijuana therapy to their patients for years. A 1991 Harvard study found that 44 percent of oncologists had previously advised marijuana therapy to their patients.[3]

States can help the users of medical marijuana despite federal law.

Federal law continues to prohibit the possession of marijuana, even for medical use. But 99 percent of marijuana arrests are made by state authorities enforcing state law.[4] Furthermore, the U.S. Supreme Court in October 2003 blocked federal authorities from punishing doctors for recommending marijuana to their sick patients. This order let stand a

Court of Appeals ruling that doctors have a First Amendment right to discuss the possible benefits of marijuana for relief of pain, nausea and other symptoms.[5] So a well-crafted state medical marijuana law can protect both doctors and patients.

Ten states have enacted effective medical marijuana laws.

Ten very diverse states have now adopted medical marijuana statutes. Eight states adopted the policy by referendum: AK, AZ, CA, CO, ME, NV, OR and WA. The Hawaii legislature enacted a law in 2000 that dropped all criminal penalties for medical marijuana. And the Maryland legislature acted in 2003 to provide a "medical necessity" defense to patients who are arrested for marijuana possession, with a $100 fine as the maximum penalty.

The public overwhelmingly supports the legalization of medical marijuana.

A November 2002 CNN/Time poll found that 80 percent of Americans "think adults should be allowed to legally use marijuana for medical purposes if their doctor prescribes it." Only 17 percent "think marijuana should remain illegal even for medical purposes."

Medical marijuana laws do not increase use of the drug among youth.

Contrary to critics' fears, the availability of medical marijuana has not increased use of the drug among young people. In fact, after the passage of California's medical marijuana law in 1996, marijuana use among both junior high and high school students declined significantly.[6]

Endnotes

[1] National Academy of Sciences, Institute of Medicine, "Marijuana and Medicine: Assessing the Science Base," 1999.

[2] Conclusions of the National Institutes of Health, "Workshop on the Medical Utility of Marijuana: Report to the Director," 1997; Administrative Law Judge Francis L. Young, final ruling *In the Matter of Marijuana Rescheduling Petition*, Drug Enforcement Administration, U.S. Department of Justice, Docket No. 86-22, September 6, 1988.

[3] Richard Doblin and Mark Kleiman, "Marijuana as Anti-emetic Medicine: A Survey of Oncologists' Experiences and Attitudes," *Journal of Clinical Oncology*, Vol. 9, No. 7, 1991.

[4] Marijuana Policy Project, *Marijuana Policy Report*, Vol. 7 Num. 3, Fall 2001, based on a comparison of Federal Bureau of Investigation, "Crime in the United States: 2000 Uniform Crime Reports," 2001, and U.S. Department of Justice, "Compendium of Federal Justice Statistics, 1999," April 2001.

[5] *Walters v. Conant*, Case #03-40, October 14, 2003.

[6] Rodney Skager and Gregory Austin, "Report to Attorney General Bill Lockyer: Eighth Biennial California Student Survey 1999-2000," sponsored by the California Department of Justice, Office of the Attorney General, and California Department of Education, August 2002.

This policy summary relies in large part on information from the Marijuana Policy Project.

Medical Marijuana

For more information...

Center for Policy Alternatives
1875 Connecticut Avenue NW, Suite 710
Washington, DC 20009
202-387-6030
www.stateaction.org

Drug Policy Alliance
70 West 36th Street, 16th Floor
New York, NY 10018
212-613-8020
www.drugpolicy.org

Marijuana Policy Project
P.O Box 77492
Washington, DC 20013
www.mpp.org

National Organization for the Reform of Marijuana Laws
1600 K Street NW, Suite 501
Washington, DC 20006
202-483-5500
www.norml.org

Medical Marijuana

Medical Marijuana Decriminalization Act

SECTION 1. SHORT TITLE

This Act shall be called the "Medical Marijuana Decriminalization Act."

SECTION 2. FINDINGS AND PURPOSE

(A) FINDINGS – The legislature finds that:

1. Modern medical research has established beneficial uses for marijuana in treating or alleviating pain or other symptoms associated with certain debilitating illnesses. There is sufficient medical and anecdotal evidence to support the proposition that these diseases and conditions may respond favorably to a medically controlled use of marijuana.

2. Although federal law expressly prohibits the use of marijuana, at least ten states have legalized or decriminalized its use for medical purposes.

3. While the intent of this legislation is to make medical marijuana available for the health and welfare of residents with serious illnesses, it does not, and is not intended to, legalize marijuana for other purposes. This legislation does not in any way diminish the state's strong public policy and laws against illegal drug use.

(B) PURPOSE—This law is enacted to improve the health and welfare of seriously ill residents by ensuring that they are not penalized by the state for the use of marijuana for strictly medical purposes when the patient's treating physician provides a professional opinion that the benefits of medical use of marijuana would likely outweigh the health risks for the qualifying patient.

SECTION 3. MEDICAL MARIJUANA DECRIMINALIZATION

After section XXX, the following new section XXX shall be inserted:

(A) DEFINITIONS – In this section:

1. "Adequate supply" means an amount of marijuana collectively possessed between the qualifying patient and the qualifying patient's primary caregivers that is not more than is reasonably necessary to ensure the uninterrupted availability of marijuana for the purpose of alleviating the symptoms or effects of a qualifying patient's debilitating medical condition [provided that an "adequate supply" shall not exceed three mature marijuana plants, four immature marijuana plants, and one ounce of usable marijuana per each mature plant].

2. "Debilitating medical condition" means:

   a. cancer, glaucoma, positive status for human immunodeficiency virus, acquired immune deficiency syndrome, or the treatment of these conditions;
   b. a chronic or debilitating disease or medical condition or its treatment that produces one or more of the following: cachexia or wasting syndrome, severe pain, severe nausea, seizures including those characteristic of epilepsy, or severe and persistent muscle spasms including those characteristic of multiple sclerosis or Crohn's disease; or
   c. any other medical condition or its treatment approved by the Secretary.

Medical Marijuana

3. "Marijuana" shall have the same meaning as provided in section [cite current criminal code].

4. "Medical use" means the acquisition, possession, cultivation, use, transfer or transportation of marijuana or paraphernalia relating to the administration of marijuana to alleviate the symptoms or effects of a qualifying patient's debilitating medical condition. For the purposes of "medical use," the term "transfer" is limited to the transfer of marijuana and paraphernalia between primary caregivers and qualifying patients.

5. "Physician" means a person who is licensed under section [insert citation] and is authorized to prescribe drugs under section [insert citation].

6. "Primary caregiver" means a person who is at least 18 years old and who has agreed to undertake responsibility for managing the well-being of a person with respect to the medical use of marijuana.

7. "Qualifying patient" means a person who has been diagnosed by a physician as having a debilitating medical condition.

8. "Secretary" means the Secretary of the Department of [Health], or the Secretary's designee(s).

9. "Usable marijuana" means the dried leaves and flowers of marijuana, and any mixture or preparation thereof, that are appropriate for the medical use of marijuana, and does not include the seeds, stalks and roots of the plant.

10. "Written certification" means the qualifying patient's medical records or a written document signed by a physician, stating that in the physician's professional opinion, after having completed a full assessment of the qualifying patient's medical history and current medical condition made in the course of a bona fide physician-patient relationship, the qualifying patient has a debilitating medical condition, and the potential benefits of the medical use of marijuana would likely outweigh the health risks for the qualifying patient.

(B) DECRIMINALIZATION OF MEDICAL MARIJUANA

1. A qualifying patient who has in his or her possession written certification shall not be subject to arrest, prosecution or penalty in any manner for the medical use of marijuana, provided the quantity of marijuana does not exceed an adequate supply.

2. Paragraph 1 shall not apply to a qualifying patient under the age of 18 years, unless:

a. The qualifying patient's physician has explained the potential risks and benefits of the medical use of marijuana to the qualifying patient and to a parent, guardian or person having legal custody of the qualifying patient; and
b. A parent, guardian or person having legal custody consents in writing to allow the qualifying patient's medical use of marijuana, serves as the qualifying patient's primary caregiver, and controls the acquisition of the marijuana, the dosage, and the frequency of the medical use of marijuana by the qualifying patient.

3. When the acquisition, possession, cultivation, transportation or administration of marijuana by a qualifying patient is not practicable, the legal protections established by this section for a qualifying patient shall extend to the qualifying patient's primary caregivers, provided that the primary caregivers' actions are necessary for the qualifying patient's medical use of marijuana.

Medical Marijuana

4. A physician shall not be subject to arrest or prosecution, penalized in any manner, or denied any right or privilege for providing written certification for the medical use of marijuana to qualifying patients.

5. Any property interest that is possessed, owned or used in connection with the medical use of marijuana, or acts incidental to such use, shall not be harmed, neglected, injured or destroyed while in the possession of state or local law enforcement officials, provided that law enforcement agencies seizing live plants as evidence shall not be responsible for the care and maintenance of marijuana plants. Any such property interest shall not be forfeited under any provision of state or local law providing for the forfeiture of property other than as a sentence imposed after conviction of a criminal offense or entry of a plea of guilty to a criminal offense. Marijuana, paraphernalia or other property seized from a qualifying patient or primary caregivers in connection with the claimed medical use of marijuana shall be returned immediately upon the determination by a court or prosecutor that the qualifying patient or primary caregivers are entitled to the protections of this section, as may be evidenced by a decision not to prosecute, the dismissal of charges, or an acquittal.

6. No person shall be subject to arrest or prosecution for "constructive possession," "conspiracy," or any other offense for simply being in the presence or vicinity of the medical use of marijuana as permitted under this section.

(C) PROHIBITIONS AND RESTRICTIONS ON MEDICAL MARIJUANA

1. The authorization for the medical use of marijuana in this section shall not apply to:

   a. The medical use of marijuana that endangers the health or well-being of another person, such as driving or operating heavy machinery while under the influence of marijuana;
   b. The smoking of marijuana in a school bus, public bus, or other public vehicle; on any school grounds; in any correctional facility; or at any public park, public beach, public recreation center, or youth center; and
   c. The use of marijuana by a qualifying patient, primary caregiver, or any other person for purposes other than medical use permitted by this section.

2. Insurance companies shall not be required to cover the medical use of marijuana.

3. Fraudulent representation to a law enforcement official of any fact or circumstance relating to the medical use of marijuana to avoid arrest or prosecution shall be a petty misdemeanor and subject to a fine of $500. This penalty shall be in addition to any other penalties that may apply for the non-medical use of marijuana.

(D) ESTABLISHING A DEFENSE IN COURT--A person and a person's primary caregivers may assert the medical use of marijuana as a defense to any prosecution involving marijuana, and such defense shall be presumed valid where the evidence shows that:

1. The person's medical records indicate, or a physician has stated that, in the physician's professional opinion, after having completed a full assessment of the person's medical history and current medical condition made in the course of a bona fide physician-patient relationship, the potential benefits of the medical use of marijuana would likely outweigh the health risks for the person; and

2. The person and the person's primary caregivers were collectively in possession of a quantity of marijuana that was not more than was reasonably necessary to ensure the uninterrupted availability of marijuana for the purpose of alleviating the symptoms or effects of the person's medical condition.

Medical Marijuana

(E) ADMINISTRATION

1. The Secretary shall promulgate regulations to administer this section.

2. Not later than 90 days after the effective date of this act, the Secretary shall promulgate regulations governing the manner in which the Secretary will consider petitions from the public to add debilitating medical conditions to those included in this section. In considering such petitions, the Secretary shall include public notice of, and an opportunity to comment in a public hearing upon, such petitions. The Secretary shall, after public hearing, approve or deny such petitions within 180 days of submission. The approval or denial of such a petition shall be considered a final action, subject to judicial review.

(F) REGISTRY IDENTIFICATION CARDS
[This section is optional. It can be removed without affecting any other section of the bill.]

1. The Secretary shall create and administer a system of registry identification cards that identify qualifying patients and primary caregivers.

2. A qualifying patient or primary caregiver shall receive the legal protections of this section only if the qualifying patient or primary caregiver is in possession of a registry identification card.

3. Not later than 90 days after the effective date of this act, the Secretary shall promulgate regulations governing the manner in which it will consider applications for registry identification cards, and for renewing registry identification cards, for qualifying patients and primary caregivers.

4. The Secretary shall issue registry identification cards to qualifying patients, and to qualifying patients' primary caregivers, if any, who submit the following:

   a. Written certification that the person is a qualifying patient;
   b. Registration fee, not to exceed $25 per qualifying patient;
   c. Name, address and date of birth of the qualifying patient;
   d. Name, address and telephone number of the qualifying patient's physician; and
   e. Name, address and date of birth of the qualifying patient's primary caregivers, if the qualifying patient has designated any primary caregivers at the time of application.

5. The Secretary shall verify the information contained in an application submitted pursuant to this section, and shall approve or deny an application within 30 days of receipt of the application. The Secretary may deny an application only if the applicant did not provide the information required pursuant to this section, or if the Secretary determines that the information provided was falsified. Any person whose application has been denied may not reapply for six months from the date of the denial, unless so authorized by the Secretary or a court of competent jurisdiction.

6. The Secretary shall issue registry identification cards within five days of approving an application, which shall expire one year after the date of issuance. Registry identification cards shall contain:

   a. The name, address and date of birth of the qualifying patient and primary caregivers, if any;
   b. The date of issuance and expiration date of the registry identification card; and
   c. Other information that the Secretary may specify by regulation.

7. A person who possesses a registry identification card shall notify the Secretary of any change in the person's name, address, qualifying patient's physician, or qualifying patient's primary caregiver within 30 days of such change or the registry identification card shall be deemed null and void.

8. Possession of, or application for, a registry identification card shall not alone constitute probable cause to search the person or property of the person possessing or applying for the card, or otherwise subject the person or property of the person possessing the card to inspection by any governmental agency.

9. The Secretary shall maintain a confidential list of the persons to whom the Secretary has issued registry identification cards. Individual names on the list shall be confidential and not subject to disclosure, except to:

    a. Authorized employees of the department as necessary to perform official duties of the Secretary; or
    b. Authorized employees of state or local law enforcement agencies, only for the purpose of verifying that a person who is engaged in the suspected or alleged use of marijuana is lawfully in possession of a registry identification card.

SECTION 4. SEVERABILITY

The provisions of this Act shall be severable, and if any phrase, sentence or provision is declared to be invalid or is preempted by federal law or regulation, the validity of the remainder of this Act shall not be affected.

SECTION 5. EFFECTIVE DATE

This Act shall take effect on July 1, 2004.

Microenterprise
Development

Microenterprise development programs are cost effective investments that help create jobs and reduce reliance on public assistance.

Microenterprise Development

Summary

- For low-income families, self-employment is a significant source of jobs and income.
- Most low-income workers who want to start microenterprises cannot do so without help.
- Policies encouraging the creation of microenterprises help low-income families become economically self-sufficient.
- Microenterprise development programs are cost-effective investments that help create jobs and reduce reliance on public assistance.
- Training and technical assistance are the most urgent needs for microentrepreneurs.
- States are beginning to recognize the need to fund microenterprise development.

For low-income families, self-employment is a significant source of jobs and income.

Of the 10.5 million self-employed individuals in the United States, 2 million are low-income. Often, a small business is started in order to supplement income from a low-wage job, or to create a job when a worker becomes unemployed. For many low-income Americans, starting a microenterprise is the most effective way to support their families.

Most low-income workers who want to start microenterprises cannot do so without help.

There is a large unmet demand for microenterprise technical assistance, training and financing services in low-income communities. Community-based organizations exist in every state, offering some type of microenterprise development program targeted at non-traditional entrepreneurs, such as women of color, welfare recipients, immigrants, the disabled, and/or inner-city residents. But 90 percent of the existing low-income microentrepreneurs in the United States do not have access to these programs.[1]

Policies encouraging the creation of microenterprises can help low-income families become economically self-sufficient.

A large-scale study of low-income micro-entrepreneurs found that 72 percent experienced a substantial rise in pay—raising average annual household incomes from $13,889 to $22,374 over five years. More than 53 percent of low-income entrepreneurs gained enough income to move their families out of poverty.[2]

Microenterprise development programs are cost-effective investments that create jobs and reduce reliance on public assistance.

Low-income workers who start a microenterprise reduce their families' dependence on public assistance by up to 61 percent. According to the U.S. Small Business Administration, businesses created by low-income entrepreneurs have high survival rates—ranging from 57 to 90 percent over a five-year span—higher than the 47 percent survival rate for all small businesses.[3] A study of ten microenterprise programs supported by the Charles Stewart Mott Foundation found that participants' reliance on public assistance declined from 94 percent to 35 percent in just one year.[4]

Training and technical assistance are the most urgent needs for microentrepreneurs.

In microenterprise development programs, training and technical assistance are greatly in demand. On average, 89 percent of microenterprise program clients seek training and technical assistance in areas such as business management and economic literacy.[5] Currently, there is only one small source of federal funding for training and technical assistance services to low-income entrepreneurs. The Small Business Administration's Program for Investment in Microentrepreneurs was allocated just $5 million by Congress for fiscal year 2004.

States are beginning to recognize the need to fund microenterprise development.

Twenty states currently allocate funding for microenterprise program operations, training and technical assistance. Other programs offer direct loans to microenterprises. Vermont's Job Start Program, the oldest state microenterprise effort in the nation, administers a centralized loan pool through the state Economic Development Authority and uses state funds to support five local community action agencies which provide assistance and training to local entrepreneurs. Nebraska's longstanding microenterprise program created over 500 jobs in 2001 at a cost of only $729 per job. Oregon enacted legislation in 2001 that provides grants, technical assistance, and training to microentrepreneurs.

The Microenterprise Development Act helps support nonprofit organizations that provide training and technical assistance to low-income microentrepreneurs.

The Act directs the state economic development agency to create a grant program for nonprofit microenterprise development assistance programs. These programs will give low-income microentrepreneurs the support they need to succeed, including business planning, marketing, and financial management skills. All state funds must be matched at least dollar-for-dollar by other funding sources.

This policy summary relies in large part on information from the Corporation for Enterprise Development.

Endnotes

[1] Aspen Institute, "Microenterprise and the Poor: Findings from the Self-Employment Learning Project Five-Year Study of Microentrepreneurs," 1999.

[2] Ibid.

[3] Aspen Institute, "Microenterprise Development Works: Outcomes for Clients," 2002.

[4] Aspen Institute, "Welfare to Work: Microenterprise as Welfare to Work Strategy, One Year Findings," 2002.

[5] Aspen Institute, "Assessing the Effectiveness of Training and Technical Assistance," 1999.

Microenterprise Development

For more information...

Center for Policy Alternatives
1875 Connecticut Avenue NW, Suite 710
Washington, DC 20009
202-387-6030
www.stateaction.org

Corporation for Enterprise Development
777 North Capitol Street NE, Suite 800
Washington, DC 20002
202-408-9788
www.cfed.org

Microenterprise Fund for Innovation, Effectiveness, Learning and Dissemination
The Aspen Institute
One Dupont Circle NW, Suite 700
Washington, DC 20036
202-736-5800
www.fieldus.org

Small Business Administration
409 3rd Street SW
Washington, DC 20416
202-401-9600
www.sba.gov

Microenterprise Development

Microenterprise Development Act

SECTION 1. SHORT TITLE

This Act shall be called the "Microenterprise Development Act."

SECTION 2. FINDINGS AND PURPOSE

(A) FINDINGS – The legislature finds that:

1. There is a need to develop and expand businesses in economically distressed communities in both rural and urban areas, and there is a need to assist residents who are unemployed, underemployed or in low-income jobs.

2. Microenterprises can provide a means for unemployed, underemployed or low-income individuals to find and sustain productive work, and they can provide opportunities for economically distressed communities to thrive, one microentrepreneur at a time.

3. There is a lack of access to capital, training and technical assistance for low-income microentrepreneurs. Many low-income microentrepreneurs need technical assistance to start, operate or expand their businesses.

4. Local microenterprise support organizations have demonstrated cost-effective delivery methods to provide technical assistance.

5. Charitable foundation support, federal program funding, and private sector support can be leveraged by a statewide program for development of microenterprises.

(B) PURPOSE – This law is enacted to strengthen the [STATE] economy and enable low-income residents to become self-sufficient by encouraging microenterprise development.

SECTION 3. MICROENTERPRISE DEVELOPMENT

After section XXX, the following new section XXX shall be inserted:

(A) DEFINITIONS—In this section:

1. "Secretary" means the Secretary of the Department of [Economic Development].

2. "Microenterprise" means a sole proprietorship, partnership, or corporation that has fewer than five employees and generally lacks access to conventional loans, or other banking services.

3. "Microenterprise development organization or program" means a nonprofit entity, or a program administered by such an entity, including community development corporations or other nonprofit development organizations and social service organizations, that provides services to low-income microenterprises.

Microenterprise Development

4. "Training and technical assistance" means services and support provided to low-income owners and operators of microenterprises, such as assistance for the purpose of enhancing business planning, marketing, management, financial management skills, and assistance for the purpose of accessing financial services.

5. "Low income person" means a person with income adjusted for family size that does not exceed:
   a. For metropolitan areas, 80 percent of median income; or
   b. For nonmetropolitan areas, the greater of 80 percent of the area median income or 80 percent of the statewide nonmetropolitan area median income.

(B) ESTABLISHMENT OF MICROENTERPRISE DEVELOPMENT PROGRAM

1. The Secretary shall establish a microenterprise technical assistance and capacity building grant program to provide assistance in the form of grants to qualified organizations.

2. A qualified organization shall use grants made under this program to provide training and technical assistance to low-income entrepreneurs.

3. To be eligible for a grant, a qualified organization shall be a nonprofit microenterprise development organization that has a demonstrated record of delivering services to low-income individuals.

4. The Secretary shall ensure that not less than 50 percent of the funds made available are used to benefit persons whose income, adjusted for family size, is not more than 150 percent of the poverty line as defined in 42 U.S.C. 9902(2).

5. A qualified organization must provide at least one dollar in matching funds for every dollar of state financial assistance. Grants and gifts from public or private sources may be used to comply with the matching funds requirement.

6. The Secretary shall establish by regulation such requirements as may be necessary to carry out this section.

SECTION 4. AUTHORIZATION

During fiscal year 2005, $XXXXX is authorized to be appropriated to the Secretary to carry out this Act.

SECTION 5. EFFECTIVE DATE

This Act shall take effect on July 1, 2004.

Minimum Wage

A full-time job should be a bridge out of poverty, an opportunity to make a living from work. But for minimum wage earners, especially those with families, it is not.

Minimum Wage

Summary

- The current minimum wage of $5.15 per hour leaves millions of Americans in poverty.
- Because of inflation coupled with inaction by the federal government, the value of the minimum wage has plummeted.
- Only twelve states have a minimum wage greater than $5.15 per hour.
- Increasing the minimum wage would help millions of working families escape poverty.
- The current minimum wage strains state public assistance programs.
- Raising the minimum wage does not cost jobs.
- Three out of four Americans say the minimum wage should be increased by a dollar or more.

The current minimum wage of $5.15 per hour leaves millions of Americans in poverty.

A full-time job should be a bridge out of poverty, an opportunity to make a living from work. But for minimum wage earners, especially those with families, it is not. A wage earner working full-time at the minimum wage of $5.15 per hour earns about $10,700 a year—$4,500 below the 2003 poverty line for a family of three, and $7,700 below the poverty line for a family of four.

Because of inflation coupled with inaction by the federal government, the value of the minimum wage has plummeted.

The federal minimum wage is not adjusted for inflation, and it has not been increased since 1997. Each year the President and Congress neglect the minimum wage, low-wage workers fall further and further behind. If the minimum wage had just kept pace with inflation since 1979, when it was $2.90 per hour, it would now be over $7.65.[1] Without an increase, the real, inflation-adjusted value of the minimum wage in 2004 will be lower than in all but one year (1989) since 1955.[2]

Only twelve states have a minimum wage greater than $5.15 per hour.

Twelve states (AK, CA, CT, DE, HI, IL, ME, MA, OR, RI, VT, WA) and the District of Columbia have a minimum wage greater than the federal, the highest being $7.15 in Alaska and $7.16 in Washington. Twenty-nine states (AR, CO, GA, ID, IN, IA, KY, MD, MI, MN, MO, MT, NE, NV, NH, NJ, NM, NY, NC, ND, OK, PA, SD, TX, UT, VA, WV, WI, WY) match the federal minimum of $5.15. Two states (KS, OH) have a minimum wage that is lower than the federal, and seven (AL, AZ, FL, LA, MS, SC, TN) have no state minimum wage at all.

Increasing the minimum wage would help millions of working families escape poverty.

If the minimum wage were increased by $1.50, from $5.15 to $6.65, it would directly affect the wages of 5-10 percent of the workforce, depending on the state.[3] An additional 5-10 percent of workers, those who currently earn between $6.65 and $7.65 per hour, would see their wages increase because of the "spillover" effect of a rise in the minimum wage.

Increasing the minimum wage would especially help women and people of color.

Working women are the largest group that would benefit from a minimum wage increase. About 12.6 percent of working women—11 million Americans and their families—would be directly affected by a $1 increase in the minimum wage. Similarly, 18.1 percent of African American workers and 14.4 percent of Hispanic workers would directly benefit from such an increase.[4]

The current minimum wage strains state public assistance programs.

When they are paid at or near the current minimum wage, workers and their families must rely on public assistance to survive. They need Medicaid, subsidized housing, childcare programs, and free school lunches. Raising the minimum wage requires employers to shoulder more of the responsibility for the basic needs of their employees. This lowers costs for the state.

Raising the minimum wage does not cost jobs.

A comprehensive study by the Economic Policy Institute found that the 1996 and 1997 federal minimum wage increases did not cause job losses. Even teen employment, which some argue is the most vulnerable to minimum wage increases, suffered no job losses.[5] Increases in the minimum wage do not harm businesses because costs are offset by the benefits of higher employee productivity, lower recruiting and training costs, decreased absenteeism, and increased worker morale.

Three out of four Americans say the minimum wage should be increased by a dollar or more.

A 2001 poll for the *Christian Science Monitor* found that 75 percent of Americans support an increase in the minimum wage.[6] That support is only increasing: a nationwide poll in 2002 found that 77 percent of likely voters support raising the minimum wage from $5.15 to $8 per hour, and 79 percent favor regular cost-of-living adjustments to the minimum wage.[7]

Endnotes

[1] Based on the Consumer Price Index for Urban Wage Earners and Clerical Workers computed by the U.S. Bureau of Labor Statistics.

[2] AFL-CIO, "Minimum Wage: Myths and Realities," 2003.

[3] Economic Policy Institute, "Step Up, Not Out: The Case for Raising the Federal Minimum Wage for Workers in Every State," 2001.

[4] Ibid.

[5] Economic Policy Institute, "The Impact of the 1996-97 Minimum Wage Increase," 1998.

[6] TechnoMetrica Market Intelligence Poll for *Investor's Business Daily/Christian Science Monitor*, November 2001.

[7] Lake Snell Perry and Associates for the Ms. Foundation, "Raise the Floor: Wages and Policies That Work For All Of Us," January 2002.

Minimum Wage

Center for Policy Alternatives
1875 Connecticut Avenue NW, Suite 710
Washington, DC 20009
202-387-6030
www.stateaction.org

AFL-CIO
815 16th Street NW
Washington, DC 20006
202-637-5000
www.aflcio.org

Coalition on Human Needs
1120 Connecticut Avenue NW
Washington, DC 20036
202-223-2532
www.chn.org

Economic Policy Institute
1660 L Street NW
Washington, DC 20036
202-775-8810
www.epinet.org

Minimum Wage

Fair Minimum Wage Act

SECTION 1. SHORT TITLE

This Act shall be called the "Fair Minimum Wage Act."

SECTION 2. FINDINGS AND PURPOSE

(A) FINDINGS—The legislature finds that:

1. The current minimum wage is insufficient to keep families out of poverty or allow them to become self-sufficient.

2. Because of inflation coupled with inaction by the federal government, the value of the federal minimum wage has plummeted over the years.

3. State services are strained by the need to provide public assistance to families of workers who are paid at or near the current minimum wage.

(B) PURPOSE—This law is enacted to increase the wages of low-income workers, promote the economic strength of the state, and take pressure off state social service programs.

SECTION 3. FAIR MINIMUM WAGE

After section XXX, the following new section XXX shall be inserted:

1. Every employer shall pay not less than the [STATE] minimum wage designated in this section to each employee in every occupation.

2. The minimum wage for all employees at least 18 years of age shall be $6.15 per hour, beginning on July 1, 2004.

3. On September 30, 2005, and on each succeeding September 30, the Secretary [of Labor] shall calculate an adjusted minimum wage rate in direct proportion to any increase or decrease in the U.S. Department of Labor's Consumer Price Index for Urban Wage Earners and Clerical Workers (CPI-W), or a successor index, for the prior period of July 1 to June 30. That adjusted minimum wage shall take effect on the following January 1.

4. The minimum wage for employees under 18 years of age shall be 50 cents less than the minimum wage for employees who are at least 18 years of age.

5. For employees engaged in occupations in which gratuities are customarily recognized as part of the remuneration for employment, employers are entitled to an allowance for gratuities in an amount not to exceed 40% of the minimum wage rate. The Secretary [of Labor] shall require each employer desiring an allowance for gratuities to provide substantial evidence that the amount claimed was actually received by the employee in the period for which the claim of exemption is made, and no part thereof was returned to the employer.

SECTION 4. EFFECTIVE DATE

This Act shall take effect on July 1, 2004.

Prescription
Drug Marketing

Doctors concede that one of the major reasons they meet with drug detailers is to receive gifts. The more doctors rely on detailers for information about prescription medicines, the less likely they are to prescribe drugs in a manner consistent with patient needs.

Prescription Drug Marketing

Summary

- Prescription drug prices are skyrocketing.
- Drug manufacturers' marketing to doctors, called "detailing," induces doctors to prescribe the most expensive medicines.
- Gifts play a major role in detailing.
- Drug manufacturers are rapidly escalating their marketing to doctors.
- When detailers cause doctors to change which drugs they prescribe, patients often suffer for it.
- The drug industry's voluntary code of ethics for marketing isn't working.
- Vermont and Maine have enacted laws that require the disclosure of prescription drug marketing practices.

Prescription drug prices are skyrocketing.

Prescription drug spending is the fastest growing component of health care spending in the U.S.[1] In just five years, prices for the most-prescribed drugs increased by nearly 30 percent.[2] Rising drug prices are preventing patients from getting the medicines they need, driving up health insurance costs, and making government health programs unaffordable.

Drug manufacturers' marketing to doctors, called "detailing," induces doctors to prescribe the most expensive medicines.

Drug manufacturers spent more than $16 billion on direct marketing to doctors in the United States during 2001.[3] That amounts to more than $19,000 per physician per year.[4] This money is largely spent on visits to doctors by drug manufacturer sales representatives, called "detailers." The job of a detailer is to promote the latest, most expensive brand name drugs. Studies consistently prove that the practice of detailing causes doctors to prescribe the newest drugs, even when overwhelming medical evidence shows that less expensive, tried and true remedies would be much cheaper, just as effective, and often safer.[5]

Gifts play a major role in detailing.

Nearly all physicians accept gifts from drug detailers.[6] Those gifts, worth billions of dollars, run the gamut from free pens, pads and drug samples to high-priced meals, trips, fees and honoraria. Doctors concede that one of the major reasons they meet with drug detailers is to receive gifts.[7] As a result, the average doctor meets with detailers several times every month.[8] Many doctors see drug detailers in their office every day.

Drug manufacturers are rapidly escalating their marketing to doctors.

Drug companies increased spending on marketing to doctors by 74 percent between 1997 and 2001, according to the U.S. General Accounting Office.[9] The drug industry employed 87,892 detailers in 2001, an increase of 110 percent from the 41,855 employed in 1996. During that period, the drug industry sales force grew from one detailer for every 19 doctors to one detailer for every nine physicians in America.[10]

When detailers cause doctors to change which drugs they prescribe, patients often suffer for it.

The more doctors rely on drug detailers for information about prescription medicines, the less likely they are to prescribe drugs in a manner consistent with patient needs, according to numerous medical studies.[11] In order to promote the newest, most expensive drugs, detailers often provide information to doctors that is biased or misleading. And when patients are among the one in four Americans who do not have prescription drug insurance coverage, these expensive prescriptions become unaffordable.

The drug industry's voluntary code of ethics for marketing isn't working.

Lavish drug company gifts to doctors in the 1980s led the Pharmaceutical Research and Manufacturers of America (PhRMA) to adopt voluntary ethical guidelines in 1990. These guidelines prohibited gifts to doctors worth over $100. In recent years, PhRMA has recognized the continuing problem of unethical marketing practices and issued a slightly revised voluntary ethical code in 2002, again with a $100 limit. But industry self-regulation has failed.

Vermont and Maine have enacted laws that require the disclosure of drug manufacturers' marketing practices.

In 2002, Vermont enacted legislation that requires drug companies to file annual reports with the state disclosing the value, nature and purpose of any gift, payment or subsidy worth over $25 provided in connection with marketing activities to any physician, hospital, nursing home, pharmacist, or health plan administrator. Maine enacted a similar law in 2003.

This policy summary relies in large part on information from the National Legislative Association on Prescription Drug Pricing.

Endnotes

[1] U.S. General Accounting Office, "Prescription Drugs: FDA Oversight of Direct-to-Consumer Advertising Has Limitations," October 2002.

[2] Families USA, "Out-of-Bounds: Rising Prescription Drug Prices for Seniors," July 2003.

[3] U.S. General Accounting Office, "Prescription Drugs: FDA Oversight of Direct-to-Consumer Advertising Has Limitations," October 2002.

[4] There were 836,156 physicians in the U.S. in 2001 according to American Medical Association, "Total Physicians By Race/Ethnicity—2001," January 2003.

[5] Dana Katz, Arthur Caplan, and Jon Merz, "All Gifts Large and Small: Toward an Understanding of the Ethics of Pharmaceutical Industry Gift-Giving," *American Journal of Bioethics*, Summer 2003; Ashley Wazana, "Physicians and the Pharmaceutical Industry: Is a Gift Ever Just a Gift?," *Journal of the American Medical Association*, January 19, 2000.

[6] Ibid.

[7] Ibid.

[8] Ibid.

[9] U.S. General Accounting Office, "Prescription Drugs: FDA Oversight of Direct-to-Consumer Advertising Has Limitations," October 2002.

[10] Tyler Chin, "Drug firms score by paying doctors for time," *American Medical News*, May 6, 2002.

[11] "All Gifts Large and Small" and "Physicians and the Pharmaceutical Industry."

Prescription Drug Marketing

For more information...

Center for Policy Alternatives
1875 Connecticut Avenue NW, Suite 710
Washington, DC 20009
202-387-6030
www.stateaction.org

AARP
601 E Street, NW
Washington, DC 20049
202-434-2277
www.aarp.org

Alliance for Retired Americans
888 16th Street NW
Washington, DC 20006
888-373-6497
www.retiredamericans.org

National Legislative Association on Prescription Drug Pricing
Box 58
Stockbridge, VT 05772
802-234-5553
www.nlarx.org

USAction
USAction
1341 G Street NW, 10th floor
Washington, DC 20005
202-624-1730
www.citizen.org

Prescription Drug Marketing

Prescription Drug Ethical Marketing Act

SECTION 1. SHORT TITLE

This Act shall be called the "Prescription Drug Ethical Marketing Act."

SECTION 2. FINDINGS AND PURPOSE

(A) FINDINGS—The legislature finds that:

1. Prescription drug spending is the fastest growing component of health care spending in the United States.

2. Drug manufacturers' marketing to doctors, called "detailing," is causing doctors to prescribe the most expensive medicines, even when less expensive drugs are as effective or safer.

3. Gifts from prescription drug detailers to doctors play a major role in persuading doctors to change which drugs they prescribe.

(B) PURPOSE—This law is enacted to lower prescription drug costs for individuals, businesses and the state, and to protect the health of residents, by deterring the practice of unethical gift-giving by drug manufacturers.

SECTION 3. PRESCRIPTION DRUG ETHICAL MARKETING

After section XXX, the following new section XXX shall be inserted:

(A) DEFINITIONS—in this section:

1. "Pharmaceutical marketer" means a person who, while employed by or under contract to represent a manufacturer or labeler, engages in pharmaceutical detailing, promotional activities, or other marketing of prescription drugs in this state to any physician, hospital, nursing home, pharmacist, health benefit plan administrator, or any other person authorized to prescribe or dispense prescription drugs.

2. "Secretary" means the Secretary of the Department of [HEALTH], or the Secretary's designee(s).

3. "Manufacturer" means a manufacturer of prescription drugs as defined in 42 U.S.C. Section 1396r-8 (k)(5), including a subsidiary or affiliate of a manufacturer.

4. "Labeler" means an entity or person that receives prescription drugs from a manufacturer or wholesaler and repackages those drugs for later retail sale, and that has a labeler code from the Food and Drug Administration under 21 C.F. R. Section 207.20.

Prescription Drug Marketing

(B) DISCLOSURE OF MARKETING PRACTICES

1. On or before January 1 of each year, every manufacturer and labeler that sells prescription drugs in the state shall disclose to the Secretary the name and address of the individual responsible for the company's compliance with the provisions of this section.

2. On or before February 1 of each year, every manufacturer and labeler that sells prescription drugs in the state shall disclose to the Secretary the value, nature and purpose of any gift, fee, payment, subsidy or other economic benefit provided in connection with detailing, promotional or other marketing activities by the company, directly or through its pharmaceutical marketers, to any physician, hospital, nursing home, pharmacist, health benefit plan administrator, or any other person in [STATE] authorized to prescribe or dispense prescription drugs. Disclosure shall cover the prior year and disclosure shall be made on a form and in a manner prescribed by the Secretary.

3. On or before March 1 of each year, the Secretary shall report to the Governor and [General Assembly] on the disclosures made under this section.

4. The following shall be exempt from disclosure:

   a. Any gift, fee, payment, subsidy or other economic benefit the value of which is less than 25 dollars.

   b. Free samples of prescription drugs to be distributed to patients.

   c. The payment of reasonable compensation and reimbursement of expenses in connection with a bona fide clinical trial conducted in connection with a research study designed to answer specific questions about vaccines, new therapies, or new ways of using known treatments.

   d. Scholarship or other support for medical students, residents and fellows to attend a bona fide educational, scientific or policy-making conference of an established professional association if the recipient of the scholarship or other support is selected by the association.

(C) ADMINISTRATION AND ENFORCEMENT

1. This section shall be enforced by the Secretary, who shall promulgate such regulations as are necessary to implement and administer compliance, including regulations describing bona fide clinical trials in section (B)4c and bona fide conferences in section (B)4d.

2. If a manufacturer or labeler violates this section, the Secretary may bring an action in court for injunctive relief, costs, attorneys fees, and a civil penalty of up to $10,000 per violation. Each unlawful failure to disclose shall constitute a separate violation.

SECTION 4. EFFECTIVE DATE

This Act shall take effect on July 1, 2004. Initial disclosure shall be made on or before February 1, 2005 for the six-month period July 1, 2004 to December 31, 2004.

Prescription
Drug Pricing

Through free market negotiations each state can substantially lower drug prices for both the 70 million Americans who lack access to prescription drug insurance coverage and the state Medicaid program.

Prescription Drug Pricing

Summary

- A health crisis is sweeping this country, threatening the lives of millions of Americans and the solvency of state health programs—soaring prices for prescription drugs.
- One in four Americans—70 million—do not have insurance covering prescription drugs.
- Drug manufacturers sell identical pharmaceuticals to different purchasers at widely varying prices.
- Through free market negotiations, each state can substantially lower drug prices for both the uninsured and for the state Medicaid program.
- In recent years, at least 26 states have implemented programs to lower drug prices.
- The Fair Market Drug Pricing Act is based on voluntary negotiations with drug companies and doesn't cost taxpayers a dime.

A health crisis is sweeping this country, threatening the lives of millions of Americans and the solvency of state health programs—soaring prices for prescription drugs.

Drug prices are out of control, rising twice as fast as the inflation rate. The problem is literally an epidemic, as many Americans, especially seniors on fixed incomes, are forced to risk their health by sharing drugs, skipping doses, or doing without medicine altogether because it is simply too expensive. At the same time, skyrocketing drug prices could compel states to make cuts in critical medical assistance programs.

One in four Americans—70 million—do not have insurance covering prescription drugs.[1]

Not counting Medicare beneficiaries, more than 52 million Americans younger than 65 years old lack prescription drug coverage.[2] More than 10 million children are among the uninsured.

Drug manufacturers sell identical pharmaceuticals to different purchasers at widely varying prices.

On average, uninsured Americans pay about twice as much as the federal government pays for the same drugs. Uninsured families are charged far more for prescriptions than their insured neighbors, even in the same pharmacy. Similarly, state Medicaid programs pay a price, fixed by federal law, which is 20 to 40 percent higher than the federal government pays. Drug manufacturers make a healthy profit even on the lowest prices they charge the federal government.

Through free market negotiations, states have substantially lowered drug prices for Medicaid and other state programs.

Prior to 2001, only California authorized the use of preferred drug lists, and negotiating supplemental rebates to lower prescription drug prices paid by the state Medicaid program. Since 2001, at least 26 states have initiated these policies (AL, CT, FL, GA, HA, IN, IL, KY, LA, ME, MD, MA, MI, MN, NC, NM, OH, SC, SD, TN, TX, UT, VT, VA, WA and WV), saving states over one billion dollars per year.

INEQUITIES IN PRESCRIPTION DRUG PRICES

If the retail cost for a particular dosage and quantity of a brand name prescription drug is $100, on average:

- An uninsured resident pays $100 for that prescription.
- Medicaid and large HMOs pay $65.
- Federally-qualified health centers pay $54 (called the "340B" price).
- The federal government (largely, the U.S. Departments of Defense and Veterans Affairs) pays $46 or less.[3]

Drug manufacturers make a healthy profit on all of these prices.

Through free market negotiations, states have also lowered drug prices for uninsured residents.

In 2000, Maine enacted legislation that directs the state to use its bulk purchasing power to negotiate steep drug discounts for the uninsured. This law, called Maine Rx, was challenged in the courts and finally upheld in 2003 by the U.S. Supreme Court.[4] Hawaii enacted a version of Maine Rx in 2002. In 2003, Illinois, South Dakota, and Washington all enacted plans which direct the states to use their purchasing power to negotiate lower drug prices for individual residents.

The Fair Market Drug Pricing Act combines the approaches of several laws to lower drug prices for both state programs and state residents.

The Fair Market Drug Pricing Act is most similar to the law enacted in Hawaii. The Act:

■ Directs the state Secretary of Health (or similar cabinet Secretary) to negotiate voluntary drug discounts or rebates from prescription drug manufacturers and labelers.

■ Gives the Secretary the leverage to negotiate with drug companies in much the same way HMOs and health insurance companies negotiate— allowing the Secretary to place on the state Medicaid "prior authorization" list the products of any drug company that refuses to offer a substantial discount that is at least as favorable as the "340B" price.

■ Directs the Secretary to set up and administer an Rx Card program, passing negotiated discounts to the people who need them—uninsured seniors on Medicare, and residents earning less than 300 percent of the poverty level.

■ Empowers the Secretary to combine drug pricing negotiations for Medicaid, the Rx Card program, and any other state health programs, to maximize the Secretary's market clout.

■ Directs the Secretary to seek a Medicaid waiver from the U.S. Department of Health and Human Services to set up a prescription drug discount program modeled after the highly successful "Healthy Maine" program.

The Fair Market Drug Pricing Act is based on a free market approach to pharmaceutical prices— states engage in voluntary negotiations with drug companies.

If the companies don't want to participate, they don't have to negotiate.

The Fair Market Drug Pricing Act doesn't cost taxpayers a dime.

On the contrary, it will save each state tens or hundreds of millions of dollars per year, depending on the size of the state's Medicaid budget.

Endnotes

[1] U.S. Department of Health and Human Services, "Prescription Drug Coverage, Spending, Utilization and Prices," April 2000.

[2] Ibid.

[3] U.S. Department of Health and Human Services, "Prescription Drug Coverage, Spending, Utilization and Prices," April 2000, and see William von Oehsen, *Pharmaceutical Discounts Under Federal Law: State Program Opportunities*, 2001.

[4] *PhRMA v. Walsh*, U.S. Supreme Court Docket No. 01-188, decided May 19, 2003.

Prescription Drug Pricing

For more information...

Center for Policy Alternatives
1875 Connecticut Avenue NW, Suite 710
Washington, DC 20009
202-387-6030
www.stateaction.org

Alliance for Retired Americans
888 16th Street NW
Washington, DC 20006
888-373-6497
www.retiredamericans.org

American Association of Retired Persons
601 E Street NW
Washington, DC 20049
202-434-2277
www.aarp.org

National Conference of State Legislatures
7700 East First Place
Denver, CO 80230
303-364-7700
www.ncsl.org

National Legislative Association on Prescription Drug Pricing
Box 58
Stockbridge, VT 05772
802-234-5553
www.nlarx.org

Public Citizen
215 Pennsylvania Avenue SE
Washington, DC 20003
202-546-4996
www.citizen.org

USAction
1341 G Street NW, 10th floor
Washington, DC 20005
202-624-1730
www.usaction.org

Prescription Drug Pricing

Fair Market Drug Pricing Act

Summary: The Fair Market Drug Pricing Act lowers prices for the state Medicaid program and for uninsured state residents by directing the state Secretary of [HEALTH] to negotiate discounts and rebates from drug companies, and administer the Rx Card program, passing negotiated discounts to the uninsured.

SECTION 1. SHORT TITLE

This Act shall be called the "[STATE] Fair Market Drug Pricing Act."

SECTION 2. FINDINGS AND PURPOSE

(A) FINDINGS—The legislature finds that:

1. The State of [STATE] pays substantially more than the fair market price for many prescription drugs used in the Medicaid program. Considering the large volume of drugs purchased, the state will receive better drug prices by entering into voluntary negotiations with drug companies for supplemental rebates above and beyond the federally-designated rebates.

2. A number of states, including California, Florida, Illinois, Louisiana and Michigan, currently have programs to negotiate supplemental rebates. As a result, those states receive better Medicaid drug prices than [STATE].

3. In this time of economic difficulty, [STATE] needs to maximize its financial resources in order to provide as much health coverage as possible for low-income residents. Now more than ever, [STATE] needs to lower the prices it pays for prescription drugs.

4. At the same time, approximately one in four [STATE] residents are uninsured or underinsured for prescription drug coverage, and do not qualify for Medicaid.   These uninsured or underinsured residents pay excessive prices for prescription drugs.   In many cases, these excessive drug prices have the effect of denying residents access to medically necessary care, thereby threatening their health and safety.

5. Among these uninsured and underinsured residents, many require repeated doctor or medical clinic appointments, having gotten sicker because they cannot afford to take the drugs prescribed for them. Many are admitted to or treated at hospitals each year because they cannot afford the drugs prescribed for them that could have avoided the need for hospitalization. Many others enter expensive institutional care settings because they cannot afford the prescription drugs that could have supported them outside of an institution. In each of these circumstances, uninsured and underinsured residents too often become Medicaid recipients because of their inability to afford prescription drugs. Therefore, helping secure lower drug prices for the uninsured and underinsured directly benefits and supports Medicaid.

6. The state government is the only agent that, as a practical matter, can play an effective role as a market participant on behalf of all residents who are uninsured, underinsured or are Medicaid beneficiaries. The state already provides drugs and acts as a prescription benefits manager for a variety of programs, and should expand that role to negotiate voluntary drug rebates, using these funds to maintain and expand Medicaid services while offering lower drug prices to the uninsured who do not qualify for Medicaid.

(B) PURPOSE—Recognizing that the state already acts as a prescription benefits manager for a variety of health plans and assistance programs, this law is enacted to cover new populations by expanding the state's role as a participant in the prescription drug marketplace, negotiating voluntary rebates from drug companies, and using the funds to make prescription drugs more affordable to the state Medicaid program and to state residents. Such a program will improve public health and welfare, promote the economic strength of our society, and both directly and indirectly benefit the state Medicaid program.

Prescription Drug Pricing

SECTION 3. FAIR MARKET DRUG PRICING

After section XXX, the following new section XXX shall be inserted:

(A) DEFINITIONS—In this section:

1. "Secretary" means the Secretary of the Department of [HEALTH], or the Secretary's designee(s).

2. "Department" means the Department of [HEALTH].

3. "Manufacturer" means a manufacturer of prescription drugs as defined in 42 U.S.C. Section 1396r-8 (k)(5), including a subsidiary or affiliate of a manufacturer.

4. "Labeler" means an entity or person that receives prescription drugs from a manufacturer or wholesaler and repackages those drugs for later retail sale, and that has a labeler code from the Food and Drug Administration under 21 Code of Federal Regulations, 207.20 (1999).

5. "Participating retail pharmacy" means a retail pharmacy or other business licensed to dispense prescription drugs in this state that (a) participates in the state Medicaid program, or (b) voluntarily agrees to participate in the Rx Card program.

6. "Wholesaler" means a business licensed under [CITE EXISTING STATE LAW SECTION] to distribute prescription drugs in this state.

(B) NEGOTIATED DRUG DISCOUNTS AND REBATES

1. Drug discount and rebate agreements. The Secretary shall negotiate discount prices or rebates for prescription drugs from drug manufacturers and labelers. A drug manufacturer or labeler that sells prescription drugs in this state may voluntarily elect to negotiate: (a) supplemental rebates for the Medicaid program over and above those required under 42 U.S.C. Section 1396r-8, (b) discount prices or rebates for the Rx Card program, and (c) discount prices or rebates for any other state program that pays for or acquires prescription drugs.

2. Rebate amounts. In negotiating rebate terms, the Secretary shall take into consideration: the rebate calculated under the Medicaid rebate program pursuant to 42 U.S.C. Section 1396r-8, the price provided to eligible entities under 42 U.S.C. Section 256b, and any other available information on prescription drug prices, discounts and rebates.

3. Failure to agree.
    a. The Secretary shall prompt a review of whether to place a manufacturer's or labeler's products on the prior authorization list for the state Medicaid program and take similar actions involving prior authorization or formularies for any other state-funded or operated prescription drug program, if:
        (1) the Secretary and a drug manufacturer or labeler fail to reach agreement on the terms of a supplemental Medicaid rebate or a discount or rebate for the Rx Card program, and
        (2) the discounts or rebates offered by the manufacturer or labeler are not as favorable to the state as the prices provided to eligible entities under 42 U.S.C. Section 256b.

    b. Any prior authorization must meet the requirements of 42 U.S.C Section 1396r-8(d)(5) and be done in accordance with [CITE EXISTING STATE LAW SECTION]. The Secretary shall promulgate rules creating clear procedures for the implementation of this section.

Prescription Drug Pricing

c. The names of manufacturers and labelers that do not enter into rebate agreements are public information and the Department shall release this information to the public and actively distribute it to doctors, pharmacists, and other health professionals.

(C) RX CARD

1. Rx Card program established. The Department shall establish the Rx Card program as a state pharmaceutical assistance program under 42 U.S.C. Section 1396r-8(c)(1)(C)(i)(III), to provide discounts to participants for drugs covered by a rebate agreement. Using funds from negotiated rebates, the Department shall contract with wholesalers and/or participating retail pharmacies to deliver discounted prices to Rx Card participants.

2. Amount of discount. The drug discounts received by Rx Card participants shall be calculated by the Secretary on a quarterly basis. That calculation shall provide discounts approximately equal to the average amount of the negotiated drug rebate minus an amount to cover the reasonable administrative costs of the Rx Card program.

3. Eligibility for participation.
a. An individual is eligible to participate in the Rx Card program if s/he is a resident of the state and is eligible for participation in the Medicare program or has a net family income below 300 percent of the federal poverty level.

b. An individual is ineligible to participate in the Rx Card program if s/he is eligible for assistance under the state's Medicaid program or is covered by an insurance policy that provides benefits for prescription drugs equal to or greater than the benefits provided under the Rx program, as delineated by rules promulgated by the Secretary.

c. The Department shall establish simple procedures for enrolling Rx Card participants and shall undertake outreach efforts to build public awareness of the program and maximize enrollment by eligible residents.

4. Operation.
a.The Secretary shall adopt rules requiring disclosure by participating retail pharmacies to Rx Card program participants of the amount of savings provided as a result of the Rx Card program. The rules must protect information that is proprietary in nature.

b. A participating retail pharmacy shall verify to the Department the amounts charged to Rx Card participants and non-participants, and shall provide the Department with utilization data necessary to calculate rebates from manufacturers and labelers. The Department shall protect the confidentiality of all information subject to confidentiality protection under state or federal law, rule or regulation. The Department may not impose transaction charges on wholesalers or participating retail pharmacies that submit claims or receive payments under the program.

c. Wholesalers and/or participating retail pharmacies shall be paid in advance for Rx Card discounts or shall be reimbursed by the Department on a weekly basis.

d. The Department may require a wholesaler or participating retail pharmacy to segregate drugs under the Rx Card program from other drug inventory. The Department may require a wholesaler or participating retail pharmacy to maintain records of acquisition and disposition of drugs under the Rx Card program separately from the wholesaler's or pharmacy's other records.

Prescription Drug Pricing

(D) ADMINISTRATION

1. Discrepancies in rebate amounts. Disputes or discrepancies in rebate amounts must be resolved using the process established in this subsection.

a. If there is a discrepancy in the manufacturer's or labeler's favor between the amount claimed by a pharmacy and the amount rebated by the manufacturer or labeler, the Department, at the Department's expense, may hire a mutually agreed-upon independent auditor. If a discrepancy still exists following the audit, the manufacturer or labeler shall justify the reason for the discrepancy or make payment to the Department for any additional amount due.

b. If there is a discrepancy against the interest of the manufacturer or labeler in the information provided by the Department to the manufacturer or labeler regarding the manufacturer's or labeler's rebate, the manufacturer or labeler, at the manufacturer's or labeler's expense, may hire a mutually agreed-upon independent auditor to verify the accuracy of the data supplied to the Department. If a discrepancy still exists following the audit, the Department shall justify the reason for the discrepancy or provide a refund to the manufacturer or labeler.

c. Following the procedures established in paragraph (a) or (b), either the Department or the manufacturer or labeler may request a hearing. Supporting documentation must accompany the request for a hearing.

2. Annual summary report. The Department shall report the enrollment and financial status of the Rx Card program and report savings from supplemental Medicaid rebates to the legislature by February 1 each year.

3. Coordination with other programs. Where the Secretary finds that it is beneficial to both the Rx Card program and another state program to combine drug pricing negotiations to maximize drug rebates, the Secretary shall do so.

4. Rulemaking. The Department shall adopt rules to implement the provisions of this section.

5. Waivers. The Department may seek any waivers of federal law, rule or regulation necessary to implement the provisions of this section.

SECTION 4. MEDICAID WAIVER DISCOUNT PLAN

In addition to the Rx Card program established in Section 3 of this Act, the [Department of HEALTH] shall seek a Section 1115 Medicaid waiver to establish a pharmacy discount program modeled after the Healthy Maine Prescriptions Program. If the waiver is approved, the Department shall implement that program following consultation with the [insert appropriate legislative oversight committees].

SECTION 5. SEVERABILITY

The provisions of this Act shall be severable, and if any phrase, clause, sentence, or provision is declared to be invalid or is preempted by federal law or regulation, the validity of the remainder of this Act shall not be affected. The Secretary shall administer the provisions of this Act in a manner that benefits the largest number of residents while preventing it from being preempted by federal law or regulation. This includes, if necessary, separating Medicaid from non-Medicaid negotiations and preferred drug list decisions, or limiting participation in the Rx Card program to a smaller segment of residents.

SECTION 6. EFFECTIVE DATE—This Act shall take effect on July 1, 2004 and discounts to participants in the Rx Card program shall begin by January 1, 2005.

Privatizing Prisons

The for-profit prison industry has expanded rapidly in the past decade, capitalizing on soaring incarceration rates. Little evidence exists to support the claim that privatizing prisons cuts costs.

Privatizing Prisons

Summary

- The for-profit prison industry has expanded rapidly in the past decade, capitalizing on soaring incarceration rates.
- The business of incarceration is booming, with revenue passing the $1 billion mark in 1998.
- The industry argues that privatizing prisons cuts costs, but there is little evidence to support this claim.
- When profit is a primary motivation, quality of services and public safety can be jeopardized.
- Private prison companies ensure profitability by courting political influence and supporting stricter sentencing laws.
- States have used a variety of approaches to halt the privatization of prisons.
- Public opinion supports government-run prisons over private ones.

The for-profit prison industry has expanded rapidly in the past decade, capitalizing on soaring incarceration rates.

The United States is experiencing the largest prison build-up in recorded history, more than quadrupling its prison population since 1980. The number of prisoners in private prisons grew more than 2,000 percent between 1987-96, soaring from 3,122 to 78,000.[1] By 2002, nearly 94,000 inmates were housed in private prisons.

The business of incarceration is booming, with revenue passing the $1 billion mark in 1998.

Two companies dominate the for-profit incarceration industry—Corrections Corporation of America (CCA) and Wackenhut Corporation. These two companies control 75 percent of the for-profit incarceration market.[2]

The industry argues that privatizing prisons cuts costs, but there is little evidence to support this claim.

CCA advertises that privately-managed prisons can save states up to 20 percent on the cost of incarceration. Yet a study by the U.S. Bureau of Justice Assistance found that these savings "have simply not materialized."[3] In fact, some research has concluded that for-profit prisons cost more than public prisons.[4] Furthermore, cost estimates from privatization advocates are misleading because private facilities often refuse to accept inmates that

cost the most to house. In Texas, for example, private prisons will not accept inmates with serious or chronic health problems. And costs of transportation, classification and most monitoring activities are not included in per diem rates—those costs are still covered by the state.

When profit is a primary motivation, quality of services and public safety can be jeopardized.

CCA-owned facilities in various states have experienced numerous incidents of violence and inmate escapes. At the Northeast Ohio Correction Center, 17 inmates were stabbed, two were murdered, and six escaped during the first 15 months of operation. In other states, inadequate supervision and lax security measures have jeopardized public safety.[5]

Private prison companies ensure profitability by courting political influence and supporting stricter sentencing laws.

Corporate-owned prisons need a steady flow of inmates to maintain profits. To protect their profit margins, prison companies exert political influence by contributing thousands of dollars to state political campaigns. Lobbyists for private prisons support tough-on-crime legislation that ensures the continued need for prison space, including mandatory minimum sentences, life terms for "three strikes," and sentencing juveniles as adults.[6]

States have used a variety of approaches to halt the privatization of prisons.

In recent years, states have addressed the problem in different ways:

■ Banning privatization of state and local facilities:

Louisiana enacted a moratorium on private prisons in 2001. In 2000, Illinois and New York enacted laws banning the privatization of prisons, correctional facilities, and any services related to their operation.

■ Banning speculative private prison construction:

For-profit prison companies have built new prisons before they were awarded privatization contracts, in order to lure state contract approval. In 2001, Wisconsin's joint budget committee recommended language to ban all future speculative prison construction in the state.

■ Banning exportation and importation of prisoners:

To ensure that the state retains control over the quality and security of correctional facilities, North Dakota passed a bill in 2001 banning the export of Class A and AA felons outside the state. Similarly, Oregon allowed an existing exportation law to sunset in 2001, effectively banning the export of prisoners. Several states have considered banning the importation of prisoners to private facilities.

■ Requiring standards comparable to state prisons:

New Mexico enacted legislation that transfers supervision of private prisons to the state Secretary of Corrections, ensuring that private prisons meet the same standards as public facilities. In 2001, Nebraska legislation requiring private prisons to meet public prison standards was overwhelmingly approved by the legislature, but pocket-vetoed by the Governor.

Public opinion supports government-run prisons over private ones.

A majority of voters oppose the privatization of prisons, with Democrats, Republicans and Independents equally against it. The public fears that privately-run prisons are more likely to cut corners, placing profits ahead of public safety. Nearly 60 percent agree that government is best suited to protect public safety—providing necessary security and preventing prisoners from escaping.[7]

This policy summary relies in large part on information from the American Federation of State, County and Municipal Employees.

Endnotes

[1] Brigette Sarabi and Edwin Bender, "The Prison Payoff: The Role of Politics and Private Prisons in the Incarceration Boom," Western States Center & Western Prison Project, November 2000.

[2] American Federation of State, County and Municipal Employees, "The Evidence is Clear: Crime Shouldn't Pay," 2001.

[3] James Austin and Garry Coventry, "Emerging Issues on Privatized Prisons, Bureau of Justice Assistance," February 2001.

[4] Dennis Cunningham, "Projected FY 2000 Cost of DOC Operated Medium Security Beds Compared to Private Prison Contracts," 4th Annual Privatizing Correctional Facilities Conference, September 24, 1999.

[5] "Private Adult Correctional Facilities: Fines, Failures and Dubious Practices," Ontario Public Service, 2000.

[6] "The Prison Payoff."

[7] Lake Snell Perry & Associates, "Private Prisons Survey," August 1999.

Privatizing Prisons

For more information...

Center for Policy Alternatives
1875 Connecticut Avenue NW, Suite 710
Washington, DC 20009
202-387-6030
www.stateaction.org

American Federation of State, County and Municipal Employees
1625 L Street NW
Washington, DC 20036
202-429-1000
www.afscme.org

Service Employees International Union
1313 L Street NW
Washington, DC 20005
202-898-3200
www.seiu.org

Western Prison Project
P.O. Box 40085
Portland, OR 97240
503-335-8449
www.westernprisonproject.org

Prison Moratorium Project
388 Atlantic Avenue, 3rd Floor
Brooklyn, NY 11217
718-260-8805
www.nomoreprisons.org

Public Safety and Justice Campaign
P.O. Box 36006
Charlotte, NC 28236
704-376-9206
www.stopprivateprisons.org

Privatizing Prisons

Stopping the Privatization of Prisons

Banning the Use of Private Prisons by State and Local Governments:
(Language based upon laws enacted in Illinois and New York.)

> Neither the state nor any municipality or county shall contract with a private contractor or private vendor for the provision of services related to the operation of an adult or juvenile correctional facility.

Banning Importation of Inmates from Other States and the Federal Government into a Private Facility:
(Language based upon legislation introduced in California, Montana, North Carolina, and Utah.)

> A person charged or convicted in any court outside [STATE] may not be confined in a private correctional facility in [STATE].

Banning Exportation of Inmates to Prisons in Other States:
(Language based upon legislation introduced in Alaska.)

> A person charged or convicted in [STATE] must be housed in a correctional facility in the state.

Banning Speculative Construction of Prisons:
(Language based upon legislation introduced in Montana, New York and North Carolina.)

> An individual, corporation, partnership, association or other private organization or entity may not construct a private correctional facility in [STATE] unless authorized by the [Department of Corrections].

Banning Private Prisons:

> An individual, corporation, partnership, association or other private organization or entity may not own a private correctional facility in [STATE].

Racial Profiling

Racial profiling is a widely recognized problem, yet only 15 states have taken action to curtail the practice. Racial profiling must be ended, not only to stop discrimination, but to bridge the lack of trust between law enforcement agencies and communities of color.

Racial Profiling

Summary

- Discriminatory racial profiling is a widely recognized problem in communities across the country.
- States are beginning to recognize the need to address this discriminatory practice.
- Racial profiling of African Americans and Latinos is widespread. And in the aftermath of September 11, profiling of Arabs and South Asians has increased.
- Until recently, few states or federal agencies collected data on the incidence of racial profiling.
- The practice of racial profiling must be ended, not only to curtail discrimination, but to bridge the lack of trust between law enforcement agencies and communities of color.
- In recent years, over 20 states have enacted laws against racial profiling.

Discriminatory racial profiling is a widely recognized problem in communities across the country.

Numerous studies over the past few years have validated what many have known for decades: law enforcement agents at all levels consistently use race, ethnicity, national origin, and religion when choosing which individuals should be stopped and searched.[1]

States are beginning to recognize the need to address this discriminatory practice.

The practice of racial profiling occurs when law enforcement officers target suspects on the basis of race, national origin, ethnicity, or religion. Racial profiling is not just an issue of who gets stopped, but why individuals are stopped, and how they are treated. In 1999, the federal government and New Jersey came to an unprecedented agreement that state troopers could no longer use race as a factor in highway traffic stops. This decision came about after an investigation of police records revealed that three-fourths of the cars searched on state highways were driven by African Americans or Latinos.

Racial profiling of African Americans and Latinos is prevalent at all levels of law enforcement today.

A U.S. Department of Justice report states that in 1999, African Americans were 20 percent more likely to be stopped than white Americans, and that police were more than twice as likely to search the car of an African American or Hispanic driver than a white driver. Studies in Colorado, Massachusetts and Los Angeles in 2002 confirm that racial profiling continues to be a serious problem.[2]

In the aftermath of September 11, racial profiling of Arabs and South Asians has increased.

Since the terrorist attacks, individuals who are or appear to be of Arab or South Asian descent have been targeted for special scrutiny. Over 8,000 Arab men were called in for questioning after the September 11 attack, but this did not lead to the announcement of suspects in that attack or any other terrorist activity. In addition, many Arabs and South Asians have been asked to leave airplanes for no reason other than their appearance. Many Sikh Americans have been asked to remove their turbans in airports, a violation of their religious practices.

Until recently, few states or federal agencies collected data on the incidence of racial profiling.

The U.S. Department of Justice first issued voluntary guidelines for collection of racial profiling data in 2000. At least nine states are collecting such data today.

The practice of racial profiling must be ended, not only to curtail discrimination, but to bridge the lack of trust between law enforcement agencies and communities of color.

Policymakers typically underestimate the burden placed on innocent people stopped by law enforcement officers because of racial profiling. The Department of Justice reports that African Americans are 50 percent more likely than whites to be stopped more than once. These incidents lead to a reasonable fear of police officers, and risk the alienation of communities while doing little to serve the purposes of law enforcement.

In recent years, over 20 states have enacted laws against racial profiling.

These states (AR, CO, CT, FL, IL, KY, LA, MD, MA, MN, MO, MT, NE, NV, NJ, NC, OK, TX, UT, VA, WA, WV) typically require law enforcement agencies to develop and enforce policies to prevent racial profiling. Twelve of them (CO, CT, IL, MD, MO, NE, NC, OK, TX, UT, WA, WV) also require law enforcement officials to collect information, including the race and gender of each driver stopped by police, and what actions were taken.[3]

Endnotes

[1] "Wrong Then, Wrong Now: Racial Profiling Before and After September 11, 2001," Leadership Conference on Civil Rights. Leadership Conference on Civil Rights Education Fund, Criminal Justice Reform Project, February 2003.

[2] Ibid.

[3] Institute on Race and Justice, Northeastern University.

Racial Profiling

Center for Policy Alternatives
1875 Connecticut Avenue NW, Suite 710
Washington, DC 20009
202-387-6030
www.stateaction.org

American Civil Liberties Union
125 Broad Street, 18th Floor
New York, NY 10004
212-344-3005
www.aclu.org

National Association for the Advancement of Colored People
4805 Mt. Hope Drive
Baltimore, MD 21215
410-486-9100
www.naacp.org

North Carolina Department of Crime Control and Public Safety
4701 Mail Service Center
Raleigh, NC 27699
919-733-5027
www.nccrimecontrol.org

Racial Profiling Prevention Act

SECTION 1. SHORT TITLE

This Act shall be called the "[STATE] Racial Profiling Prevention Act."

SECTION 2. RACIAL PROFILING PREVENTION AND DATA COLLECTION

After section XXX, the following new section XXX shall be inserted:

(A) DEFINITIONS—In this section:

1. "Law enforcement agency" means the sheriff's office of any county, the police department of any city or municipality, or the state police.

2. "Law enforcement officer" means a sworn officer of a law enforcement agency.

3. "Racial profiling" means the detention, interdiction or other disparate treatment of an individual solely on the basis of their actual or perceived race, color, ethnicity, national origin, age, gender, religion, or sexual orientation.

(B) PROHIBITION AGAINST RACIAL PROFILING

1. No law enforcement officer shall engage in racial profiling.

2. Every law enforcement agency shall adopt a written policy that prohibits the stopping, detention or search of any person when such action is solely motivated by considerations of actual or perceived race, color, ethnicity, national origin, age, gender, religion, or sexual orientation, and the action would constitute a violation of the person's civil rights.

(C) DATA COLLECTION

1. Every law enforcement agency shall, using the form developed by the [Attorney General], record and retain the following information:

   a. The number of people stopped for traffic violations.

   b. Characteristics of race, color, ethnicity, gender, religion and age of such people, provided the identification of such characteristics shall be based on the observation and perception of the law enforcement officer responsible for reporting the stop, and the information shall not be required to be provided by the person stopped.

   c. The nature of the alleged traffic violation that resulted in the stop.

   d. Whether a warning or citation was issued, an arrest made, or a search conducted as a result of the stop.

Racial Profiling

  e. Any additional information that the [Attorney General] deems appropriate.

2. Every law enforcement agency shall promptly provide to the local [State's Attorney], or, in the case of the state police, to the Attorney General:

  a. A copy of each complaint received alleging racial profiling.

  b. Written notification of the review and disposition of such complaint.

3. Every law enforcement agency shall provide to the [Attorney General] an annual report of the information recorded pursuant to this section, in such a form as the [Attorney General] may prescribe. The [Attorney General] shall compile this information and report it to the Governor and legislature, including any observations or recommendations.

4. If a law enforcement agency fails to comply with the provisions of this section, the [Attorney General] may order an appropriate penalty in the form of withholding state funds from such law enforcement agency.

(D) REPORTING FORMS—The [Attorney General] shall develop and prescribe two forms:

1. A form, in both printed and electronic format, to be used by law enforcement officers when making a traffic stop to record personal information about the operator of the motor vehicle stopped, the location of the stop, the reason for the stop, and other information that is required by this section.

2. A form, in both printed and electronic format, to be used to report complaints by people who believe they were subjected to a motor vehicle stop by a law enforcement officer solely on the basis of their actual or perceived race, color, ethnicity, national origin, age, gender, or sexual orientation.

SECTION 3. EFFECTIVE DATE

This Act shall take effect on July 1, 2004. The forms described in section (D) shall be developed and distributed by October 1, 2004. The collection of data described in section (C) shall begin when the [Attorney General] certifies that the process is in place, but no later than January 1, 2005.

Safe Staffing
for Hospital Care

Over the past decade, hospitals have reduced nurse staffing levels, lowering the quality of health care provided and endangering the lives of patients.

Safe Staffing for Hospital Care

Summary

- Over the past decade, hospitals have reduced per-patient staffing levels by 13 percent.
- With reduced hospital staffing levels, fewer nurses are burdened with greater workloads.
- Substandard working conditions are causing experienced nurses to leave hospital jobs, exacerbating the staffing problem.
- As nurse staffing levels decline, hospital patients needlessly die.
- California has established comprehensive standards for nurse staffing.
- In recent years, six states have prohibited mandatory overtime for hospital nurses.

Over the past decade, hospitals have reduced per-patient staffing levels by 13 percent.[1]

Similarly, the proportion of registered nurses employed in hospitals decreased from 68 percent in 1988 to 59 percent in 2000. The problem is not a shortage of nurses. In fact, the supply of RNs exceeds demand—only 2.2 of the 2.7 million registered nurses in America are practicing in the profession, and only 1.3 million of those are working in hospitals.[2]

With reduced hospital staffing levels, fewer nurses are burdened with greater workloads.

Hospital managers fill gaps by requiring nurses to work mandatory overtime. A national survey found that nurses worked an average of 8½ weeks of overtime in 2000.[3] Mandatory overtime may ensure that a nurse is on duty, but it does not ensure that quality health care is provided.

Substandard working conditions are causing experienced nurses to leave hospital jobs, exacerbating the staffing problem.

Nurses remaining in hospital jobs have been stretched to the limit, and as a result they experience high levels of stress, chronic fatigue, and work-related injuries. A 2002 study of 168 Pennsylvania hospitals, for example, found that nurses with heavier workloads are more likely to report burnout and job dissatisfaction.[4] Increasingly unable to provide the quality of care their patients need, experienced nurses have been leaving hospitals for less frustrating jobs.

As nurse staffing levels decline, hospital patients needlessly die.

Understaffing is a contributing factor in 24 percent of all accidental patient deaths and injuries, according to data reported to the Joint Commission on Accreditation of Healthcare Organizations.[5] Similarly, a large-scale study published in the fall 2002 edition of the *Journal of the American Medical Association* found that every general surgery patient added to a hospital nurse's workload increases the patient's risk of death within 30 days by an average of seven percent.[6] A nationwide study by the *Chicago Tribune* found that tens of thousands of hospital patients die each year from hospital-acquired infections, largely because low staffing levels have made it difficult for hospital staff to execute proper infection control procedures.[7] In fact, according to a recent survey, more than 60 percent of nurses believe there are not enough RNs on hospital staffs to provide high-quality care, and 45 percent think the quality of care provided in their hospital has deteriorated over the previous year.[8]

California has established comprehensive standards for nurse staffing.

In order to guarantee adequate nurse staffing levels, California enacted legislation in 1999 to mandate a series of specific patient-to-nurse ratios in all hospital nursing units. The regulations to implement this legislation will take effect in January 2004.

A few other states now require specific ratios in specialty areas such as intensive care or labor and delivery units, but none require ratios in every patient care unit in every hospital as California has done.

In recent years, six states have prohibited mandatory overtime for hospital nurses.

Maine and Oregon enacted laws in 2001 to ban mandatory overtime, except during an emergency. Maryland, Minnesota, New Jersey and Washington followed suit in 2002. Some of these laws apply only to licensed nurses while others apply to all healthcare staff who directly serve patients. In each of the six states, voluntary overtime is permitted and healthcare workers are protected from retaliation if they refuse overtime assignments.

This policy summary is based in large part on information from the Service Employees International Union.

Endnotes

[1] HCIA-Sachs, "The Comparative Performance of U.S. Hospitals: The Sourcebook," 2001.

[2] U.S. Department of Health and Human Services, "The Registered Nurse Population: National Sample Survey of Registered Nurses," 2001.

[3] Service Employees International Union, survey of registered nurses, 2000.

[4] Linda Aiken et al., "Hospital Nurse Staffing and Patient Mortality, Nurse Burnout and Job Dissatisfaction," *Journal of the American Medical Association*, Fall 2002.

[5] Joint Commission of Accreditation of Healthcare Organizations, "Health Care at the Crossroads," August 7, 2002.

[6] Linda Aiken et al., "Hospital Nurse Staffing and Patient Mortality, Nurse Burnout and Job Dissatisfaction," *Journal of the American Medical Association*, Fall 2002.

[7] Michael Berens, "Infection Epidemic Carves Deadly Path; Poor Hygiene, overwhelmed Workers Contribute to Thousands of Deaths," *Chicago Tribune*, July 21, 2002.

[8] Linda Aiken and Sean Clarke, "Nurses' Reports On Hospital Care," *Health Affairs*, May/June 2001.

Safe Staffing for Hospital Care

For more information...

Center for Policy Alternatives
1875 Connecticut Avenue NW, Suite 710
Washington, DC 20009
202-387-6030
www.stateaction.org

Service Employees International Union
1313 L Street NW
Washington, DC 20005
202-898-3200
www.seiu.org

American Nurses Association
600 Maryland Avenue SW
Suite 100 West
Washington, DC 20024
1-800-274-4262
www.nursingworld.org

Safe Staffing for Hospital Care

Safe Staffing for Hospital Care Act

SECTION 1. SHORT TITLE

This Act shall be called the "Safe Staffing for Hospital Care Act."

SECTION 2. FINDINGS AND PURPOSE

(A) FINDINGS – The legislature finds that:

1. [STATE] has a substantial interest in assuring that delivery of healthcare services to patients in healthcare facilities located within this state is adequate and safe and that healthcare facilities retain sufficient nursing staff so as to promote optimal healthcare outcomes.

2. Recent changes in our healthcare delivery system are resulting in a higher acuity level among patients in healthcare facilities. Inadequate hospital staffing results in dangerous medical errors and patient infections.

3. Inadequate and poorly monitored nurse staffing practices can adversely impact the health of patients who enter hospitals and outpatient emergency and surgical centers.

4. A substantial number of nurses indicate that hospital-patient acuity measurements are inadequate and that many hospitals rarely, if ever, staff according to an acuity measurement tool.

5. Establishing staffing standards will ensure that healthcare facilities throughout the state operate in a manner that guarantees the public safety and the delivery of quality healthcare services.

6. Hospital nurses work substantial overtime hours and nurses working 12-hour shifts work the most additional overtime hours per week.

7. Mandatory overtime and lengthy work hours for direct-care nurses constitute a threat to the health and safety of patients, adversely impact the general wellbeing of nurses and result in greater turnover, which increases long-term shortages of nursing personnel.

(B) PURPOSE – This law is enacted to protect the health and safety of the residents of [STATE] by ensuring adequate protection and care for patients in healthcare facilities.

SECTION 3. SAFE STAFFING FOR HOSPITAL CARE

After section XXX, the following new section XXX shall be inserted:

(A) FACILITY STAFFING STANDARD

1. Each facility licensed pursuant to this statute shall ensure that it is staffed in a manner that provides sufficient, appropriately qualified nursing staff of each classification in each department or unit within the facility in order to meet the individualized care needs of patients.

Safe Staffing for Hospital Care

2. As a condition of licensing, each healthcare facility licensed pursuant to [citation] shall annually submit to the [appropriate agency] a documented staffing plan together with a written certification that the staffing plan is sufficient to provide adequate and appropriate delivery of healthcare services to patients for the ensuing year. The staffing plan must:

a. Meet the minimum requirements set forth in subsection 3.
b. Be adequate to meet any additional requirements provided by other laws or regulations.
c. Employ and identify an approved acuity system for addressing fluctuations in actual patient acuity levels and nursing care requirements requiring increased staffing levels above the minimums set forth in the plan.
d. Factor in other unit or department work, such as discharges, transfers and admissions, and administrative and support tasks, that is expected to be done by direct-care nurses in addition to direct nursing care.
e. Identify the assessment tool used to validate the acuity system relied on in the plan.
f. Identify the system that will be used to document actual staffing on a daily basis within each department or unit.
g. Include a written assessment of the accuracy of the prior year's staffing plan in light of actual staffing needs.
h. Identify each nurse staff classification referenced therein together with a statement setting forth minimum qualifications for each such classification.
i. Be developed in consultation with the direct-care nursing staff within each department or unit or, where such staff is represented, with the applicable recognized or certified collective bargaining representative(s) of the direct-care nursing staff.

3. The healthcare facility's staffing plan must incorporate, at a minimum, the following direct-care nurse-to-patient ratios: pediatric recovery room—1 to 1, operating room circulating nurse—1 to 1, special procedures (e.g. cath lab, radiology, endoscopy)—1 to 1, trauma—1 to 1, burn unit— 1 to 2, critical care—1 to 2, labor and delivery—1 to 2, adult recovery room—1 to 2, emergency room—1 to 3, oncology/chemotherapy—1 to 3, intermediate care unit—1 to 3, telemetry—1 to 3, mother/baby couplets and normal post-partum—1 to 4, pediatrics—1 to 4, psychiatric unit—1 to 4, adult medical-surgical unit—1 to 6.

4. The [appropriate agency] shall adopt regulations that establish minimum, specific, numerical direct-care nurse-to-patient ratios for other healthcare facility nursing departments and units that must be incorporated into the staffing plan.

5. The minimum numbers of direct-care nurse-to-patient staff set forth in the preceding paragraphs shall constitute the minimum numbers of direct-care nursing staff that shall be assigned to and be present within a nursing department or unit. Where the approved acuity system adopted by the facility indicates that additional staff is required, the healthcare facility must staff at the higher staffing level.

6. The skill mix reflected in a staffing plan must assure that all of the following elements of the nursing process are performed in the planning and delivery of care for each patient:

a. Assessment, nursing diagnosis, planning, intervention, evaluation and patient advocacy.
b. Registered nurses must constitute at least 50 percent of the direct-care nurses included in the staffing plan.
c. The skill mix may not incorporate or assume that nursing care functions required by licensing law or regulations or accepted standards of practice to be performed by a licensed nurse are to be performed by unlicensed personnel.

7. The [Department of Health] shall adopt regulations prescribing the method by which it will approve a healthcare facility's acuity system. Such regulations may include a system for class approval of acuity systems.

Safe Staffing for Hospital Care

(B) COMPLIANCE WITH PLAN AND RECORDKEEPING

1. As a condition of licensing, a healthcare facility must at all times staff in accordance with its staffing plan and the staffing standards set forth herein, provided, however, that nothing herein shall be deemed to preclude a healthcare facility from implementing higher direct-care nurse-to-patient staffing levels.

2. No nurse shall be assigned, or included in the count of assigned nursing staff for purposes of compliance with minimum staffing requirements, in a nursing department or unit or a clinical area within the healthcare facility without appropriate licensing, prior orientation, and verification that the nurse is capable of providing competent nursing care to the patients therein.

3. As a condition of licensure, each healthcare facility licensed under this section shall maintain accurate daily records showing:

    a. The number of patients admitted, released and present in each nursing department or unit within the facility.
    b. The individual acuity level of each patient present in each nursing department or unit within the facility.
    c. The identity and duty hours of each direct-care nurse in each nursing department or unit within the facility.

4. As a condition of licensure, each healthcare facility shall maintain daily statistics, by nursing department and unit, of mortality, morbidity, infection, accident, injury and medical errors.

5. All records required to be kept under this subsection shall be maintained for a period of seven years.

6. All records required to be kept under this subsection shall be made available upon request to the [oversight agency] and to the public, provided, however, that information released to the public shall not contain the name or other personal identifying information, apart from acuity level, about any individual patient.

(C) MANDATORY OVERTIME AND EXCESSIVE DUTY HOURS

1. Except during a state of emergency declared by the Governor, a healthcare facility may not mandate or otherwise require, directly or indirectly, a healthcare employee to work or be in on-duty status in excess of any one of the following:

    a. The scheduled work shift or duty period.
    b. 12 hours in a 24-hour period.
    c. 80 hours in a 14 consecutive-day period.

"Mandate" means any request which, if refused or declined by the healthcare employee, may result in discharge, discipline, loss of promotion, or other adverse employment consequence. Nothing in this subsection is intended to prohibit a healthcare employee from voluntarily working overtime.

2. Except during a state of emergency declared by the Governor:

    a. No healthcare employee may work or be in on duty status more than 16 hours in any 24-hour period.
    b. Any healthcare employee working 16 hours in any 24-hour period must have at least 8 consecutive hours off duty before being required to return to duty.
    c. No healthcare employee may be required to work or be on-duty more than 7 consecutive days without at least one consecutive 24-hour period off duty within that time.

Safe Staffing for Hospital Care

3. A work shift schedule or overtime program established pursuant to a collective bargaining agreement negotiated on behalf of the healthcare employees by a bona fide labor organization may provide for mandatory on-duty hours in excess of that permitted under this subsection, provided adequate measures are included in the agreement to ensure against excessive fatigue on the part of the affected employees.

(D) EMPLOYEE RIGHTS

1. As a condition of licensure, each healthcare facility licensed under [insert statutory citation] shall adopt and disseminate to direct-care nursing staff a written policy that complies with the requirements set forth in paragraphs (2) and (3) below, detailing the circumstances under which a direct-care nurse may refuse a work assignment.

2. At a minimum, the work assignment policy shall permit a direct-care nurse to refuse an assignment for which:

    a. The nurse is not prepared by education, training or experience to safely fulfill the assignment without compromising or jeopardizing patient safety, the nurse's ability to meet foreseeable patient needs, or the nurse's license.
    b. The nurse has volunteered to work overtime but determines that his or her level of fatigue and/or decreased alertness would compromise or jeopardize patient safety, the nurse's ability to meet foreseeable patient needs, or the nurse's license.
    c. The assignment otherwise would violate requirements set forth in this section.

3. At a minimum, the work assignment policy shall contain procedures for the following:

    a. Reasonable requirements for prior notice to a nurse's supervisor regarding the nurse's request and supporting reasons for being relieved of an assignment or continued duty.
    b. Where feasible, an opportunity for the supervisor to review the specific conditions supporting the nurse's request, and to decide whether to remedy the conditions, to relieve the nurse of the assignment, or to deny the nurse's request to be relieved of the assignment or continued duty.
    c. A process which permits the nurse to exercise the right to refuse the assignment or continued on-duty status when the supervisor denies the request to be relieved if:
        (1) The supervisor rejects the request without proposing a remedy, or the proposed remedy would be inadequate or untimely.
        (2) The complaint and investigation process with the [regulatory agency] would be untimely to address the concern.
        (3) The employee in good faith believes that the assignment meets conditions justifying refusal.

4. An employee is deemed to act in good faith if the employee reasonably believes that the information reported or disclosed is true, and that a violation has occurred or may occur. A healthcare facility covered by this section shall not penalize, discriminate or retaliate in any manner against an employee with respect to compensation, terms, conditions or privileges of employment, who in good faith, individually or in conjunction with another person or persons:

    a. Reports a violation or suspected violation of this section to a public regulatory agency, a private accreditation body, or management personnel of the healthcare facility,
    b. Initiates, cooperates or otherwise participates in an investigation or proceeding brought by a regulatory agency or private accreditation body concerning matters covered by this section,
    c. Informs or discusses with other employees, with representative(s) of the employees, with patients or patient representatives, or with the public, violations or suspected violations of this section, or
    d. Otherwise avails himself or herself of the rights set forth in this section.

Safe Staffing for Hospital Care

(E) ENFORCEMENT

1. This section may be enforced by a private cause of action under [appropriate section of state law].

2. This section shall be enforced by [appropriate state agency], which shall promulgate such regulations as are necessary to implement and administer compliance. Regulations shall include procedures to receive, investigate, and attempt to resolve complaints, and bring actions in any court of competent jurisdiction to recover appropriate relief for aggrieved employees.

3. No healthcare facility shall discharge, demote, harass or otherwise take adverse actions against any individual because such individual seeks to enforce this section, or testifies, assists or participates in any manner in an investigation, hearing or other proceeding to enforce this section.

4. In any action under this section in which an employee prevails:

a. The employee shall be awarded monetary relief, including back pay in an amount equal to the difference between the employee's actual earnings and what the employee would have earned but for the healthcare facility's unlawful practices, and an additional amount in punitive damages, as appropriate.
b. The healthcare facility shall be enjoined from continuing to violate the provisions of this section and may be ordered to take such additional affirmative steps as are necessary to ensure an end to the unlawful practices.
c. The healthcare facility shall pay a reasonable attorney's fee, reasonable expert witness fees, and other costs of the action.

SECTION 4. EFFECTIVE DATE

This Act shall take effect on July 1, 2004.

Self-Sufficiency

Standard

The Federal Poverty Measure, developed in the 1960s, is based on outdated methodology and data. States are adopting the Self-Sufficiency Standard as an alternative that assesses a family's real costs of living, state-by-state.

Self-Sufficiency Standard

Summary

- At $18,400 for a family of four, the Federal Poverty Measure is the same for Sioux Falls as it is for New York City.
- The Federal Poverty Measure, developed in the 1960s, is based on outdated methodology and data.
- The one-size-fits-all approach to poverty measurement does not even come close to assessing accurately the income needs of working families today.
- The Self-Sufficiency Standard provides an alternative to the Federal Poverty Measure, assessing a family's real costs of living, state by state.
- The Self-Sufficiency Standard has already been calculated for 34 states.
- States are adopting the Self-Sufficiency Standard as an official measure of the cost-of-living.
- Voters understand that basic costs for families far exceed the Federal Poverty Measure.

At $18,400 for a family of four, the Federal Poverty Measure is the same for Sioux Falls, South Dakota as it is for New York City. [1]

Despite overwhelming evidence to the contrary, the Federal Poverty Measure assumes that living costs are the same across the continental United States. (It is higher for Alaska and Hawaii.) The poverty measure utterly fails to assess accurately both poverty and the income needs of working families. Yet this measure is used to determine eligibility for numerous programs for low-income Americans, including TANF, food stamps, child care, Medicaid, and other work supports.

The Federal Poverty Measure, developed in the 1960s, is based on outdated methodology and data.

The official U.S. measure of poverty was developed in 1963. It is based on the thrifty food plan, published by the U.S. Department of Agriculture, which estimated that a family of two adults and two children spent about $1,033 per year on food. A 1955 household food consumption survey estimated that a typical family spent one-third of its income on food. So $1,033 was multiplied by three to establish the baseline poverty measure for 1963 at $3,100 for a family of four. Today's poverty measure of $18,400 for a family of four is essentially the 1963 measure adjusted for inflation.

The one-size-fits-all approach to poverty measurement does not even come close to assessing accurately the income needs of working families today.

The Federal Poverty Measure has never been updated to account for social and economic changes. For most families today, food costs constitute less than one-fifth of their budgets. Housing, transportation and utilities are a much bigger percentage of family costs today than they were 40 years ago. Moreover, the poverty measure was calculated based on a two-parent family model with one stay-at-home parent. That model doesn't accurately describe contemporary families, and is particularly off-base for low-income families with a single working parent. For working families, there are costs associated with employment—transportation and child care—that the Federal Poverty Measure either underestimates or ignores entirely.

Because of the way it is calculated, the Federal Poverty Measure is far below the income needed just to survive.

In almost any city, town or suburb, an annual income of $18,400—the poverty measure for a family of four—is nowhere near enough to cover housing, food, clothing, child care, transportation, and taxes. For example, in one of the least expensive areas of the nation, Southwest Tennessee, a family of four needs about $29,000 a year just to survive. In contrast, in a more expensive area like Trenton, New Jersey, a family needs at least $53,000.

The Self-Sufficiency Standard provides an alternative to the Federal Poverty Measure, assessing a family's real cost of living, state by state.

The Self-Sufficiency Standard is calculated for 70 different family types, and for each jurisdiction within a state. By including the costs of housing, food, child care, health care, transportation, and taxes (including tax credits), the Self-Sufficiency Standard provides an accurate measure of the income needs of families at the most minimal level—no Happy Meals, take-out pizza, or cable TV are figured in the calculation.

The Self-Sufficiency Standard has already been calculated for 34 states.

Wider Opportunities for Women (WOW) has calculated the Self-Sufficiency Standard for 34 states (AL, AZ, CA, CO, CT, DE, FL, GA, HI, IL, IN, IA, KY, LA, MD, MA, MS, MO, MT, NE, NV, NJ, NY, NC, OK, PA, SD, TN, TX, UT, VA, WA, WV, WI) and the District of Columbia.[2] In a number of states, the process of calculating a Standard has convinced agencies to use it as a policy tool for making more effective program decisions for low-income families.

States are adopting the Self-Sufficiency Standard as an official measure of the cost-of-living.

The state of Connecticut first legislated the calculation of a self-sufficiency measurement in 1998, and in 2001 the state required this measurement to be recalculated biannually. Since then, the Self-Sufficiency Standard has been used to expand job training opportunities to low-income and displaced workers, by accurately defining who "underemployed" and "at-risk" workers are. In Pennsylvania, welfare and workforce development caseworkers are using the Self-Sufficiency Standard as a counseling tool to help clients understand what jobs or career paths will pay wages that will help them move toward self-sufficiency. In Illinois and Pennsylvania, as well as Seattle, Tulsa and the

District of Columbia, Workforce Investment Boards (WIB) are using the Self-Sufficiency Standard to determine who is eligible for training services through One-Stop job sites. Using the Standard to determine eligibility—rather than the Lower Living Standard Income Level, the minimum measure that may be used by WIBs—steers training services to those who need it most.

Voters understand that basic costs for families far exceed the Federal Poverty Measure.[3]

A poll of registered voters in Massachusetts found that over 63 percent believed families in the state need more than $40,000 annually to meet their basic needs. This figure is in sync with the Self-Sufficiency Standard for Massachusetts, but not the Federal Poverty Measure.

The goal of any family support program must be to help families achieve economic independence.

Policymakers on both sides of the aisle say that government must move families to self-sufficiency. The Self-Sufficiency Standard, a benchmark that provides an accurate measure of the income a family requires to meet its most basic needs—food, shelter, health care, child care, transportation, taxes, and other necessities—is absolutely essential to translate good intentions into a workable program.

This policy summary relies in large part on information from Wider Opportunities for Women.

Endnotes

[1] U.S. Department of Health and Human Services, 2002 Federal Poverty Guidelines.

[2] To review a Self-Sufficiency Standard report for any of the 34 states, see www.sixstrategies.org.

[3] Opinion Dynamics Corporation, "A Survey of Voter Attitudes: Welfare, Self-Sufficiency and Making Ends Meet," April 2001.

Self-Sufficiency Standard

For more information...

Center for Policy Alternatives
1875 Connecticut Avenue NW, Suite 710
Washington, DC 20009
202-387-6030
www.stateaction.org

Economic Policy Institute
1660 L Street NW, Suite 1200
Washington, DC 20036
202-775-8810
www.epinet.org

Wider Opportunities for Women
1001 Connecticut Avenue NW, Suite 930
Washington, DC 20036
202-464-1596
www.sixstrategies.org

Self-Sufficiency Standard

Establishment of a Self-Sufficiency Standard Act

SECTION 1. SHORT TITLE

This Act shall be called "Establishment of a Self-Sufficiency Standard Act."

SECTION 2. ESTABLISHMENT OF A SELF-SUFFICIENCY STANDARD

(A) DEFINITION—In this section, "self-sufficiency standard" means a calculation of the income an employed adult requires to meet his or her family's needs, including, but not limited to, housing, food, dependent care, transportation, and medical costs.

(B) SELF-SUFFICIENCY STANDARD

1. The [Office of Policy and Management] shall contract with a private consultant to develop a self-sufficiency standard by January 1, 2005. This standard shall take into account geographical variations in costs, the age and number of children in a family, and any state or federal public assistance benefit received by a family.

2. Not later than March 1, 2005, the [Office of Policy and Management] shall distribute the self-sufficiency standard to all state agencies that counsel individuals who are seeking education, training or employment. Those state agencies shall use the self-sufficiency standard to assist individuals in establishing personal financial goals and estimating the amount of income such individuals may need to support their families.

3. The self-sufficiency standard shall not be used to analyze the success or failure of any program or determine eligibility or benefit levels for any state or federal public assistance program.

SECTION 3. EFFECTIVE DATE

This Act shall take effect on July 1, 2004.

NOTE: After a self-sufficiency standard is established, the state can apply the measurement as a substitute for the Federal Poverty Measure in appropriate situations. For example, Connecticut has used the self-sufficiency standard to define the terms "at-risk worker" and "underemployed worker," as follows:

1. "At-risk worker" means a worker who may lose employment due to factors including, but not limited to, an announced layoff, business shut-down or relocation, a new job skill requirement for which the worker is not trained, a change or reduction in wages, hours or benefits such that the worker must seek other employment in order to meet the self-sufficiency standard calculated by the [Office of Policy and Management], or a change or reduction in available transportation such that the worker is forced to seek new employment.

2. "Underemployed worker" means a worker whose education and skill level limits such worker's earning capacity to an hourly wage below 100 percent of the self-sufficiency standard calculated by the [Office of Policy and Management].

Self-Sufficiency Standard

Connecticut also used the self-sufficiency standard and the revised definitions of "at-risk" and "underemployed" based on the measurement to define the mission of a state workforce development plan:

The plan shall, at a minimum, include:

a. Determination of whether individuals are eligible to receive assistance under Subtitle B of the Workforce Investment Act of 1998, P.L. 105-220, as from time to time amended;
b. Outreach, intake and orientation to the information and other services available through the one-stop delivery system;
c. A uniform assessment procedure for screening adults and dislocated workers which shall include, but not be limited to, initial assessment of skill levels, aptitudes, abilities and supportive service needs based on the self-sufficiency standard calculated by the [Office of Policy Management].

[The plan shall include] development of incumbent worker, vocational and manpower training programs, including customized job training programs to enhance the productivity of state businesses and to increase the skills and earnings of underemployed and at-risk workers, and other programs administered by the regional workforce development boards. The [State Department of Labor], in collaboration with the regional workforce development boards, shall implement any incumbent worker and customized job training programs developed by the [Commission] pursuant to this subdivision.

The recommendations shall be consistent with the workforce development plan, for (1) job-related vocational, literacy, language or numerical skills training; (2) underemployed and at-risk workers.

Sentencing
Reform

Since the early 1990s, the number of inmates in state prisons has almost doubled. This unprecedented increase was caused not by a rise in crime rates, but by "tough-on-crime" legislation.

Sentencing Reform

Summary

- State prison populations and spending on corrections have skyrocketed.
- The unprecedented increase in the prison population has been caused not by a rise in crime rates, but by "tough-on-crime" legislation.
- A massive racial disparity has resulted from sentencing laws.
- States have been reforming harsh drug sentencing laws.
- States have been curtailing the use of mandatory minimum sentencing.
- States have been relaxing Three-Strikes-And-You're-Out laws.
- Sentencing reform can help balance state budgets.
- The public strongly supports sentencing reform.

State prison populations and spending on corrections have skyrocketed.

From 1990 to mid-2002, state prison populations almost doubled from nearly 685,000 to more than 1.2 million.[1] Including federal prisons and local jails, the total number of people held behind bars in the United States now exceeds 2 million, far more than the number of inmates in China (1.4 million) or Russia (920,000). This staggering increase in the number of prisoners was accompanied by similar increases in cost. During the 1990s, aggregate state spending on corrections more than doubled from $17.2 billion to almost $35 billion.

The unprecedented increase in the number of prisoners has been caused not by a rise in crime rates, but by "tough-on-crime" legislation.

In fact, both violent and property crime rates declined more than 50 percent during the 1990s. By 2002, crime rates were at their lowest levels in 30 years. But because a wave of harsh anti-crime laws—mostly enacted over a decade ago—curtailed parole and imposed strict mandatory minimum sentencing, 25 state prison systems are operating at or above capacity.

A massive racial disparity has resulted from sentencing laws.

In 2002, African Americans, who comprise only 12 percent of the U.S. population, represented about 45 percent of all prisoners with sentences of one year or more. That same year, about 10 percent of all black males in America between the ages of 25 and 29

were in prison. At the state level, this disparity can be astonishing. For example, a recent report by the Justice Policy Institute revealed that while African Americans make up only 28 percent of Maryland's population, they account for 90 percent of people incarcerated for drug offenses in that state.

States have been reforming harsh drug sentencing laws.

Of the 1.2 million inmates in state prisons, about 250,000 are imprisoned for drug offenses. Half of those—about 125,000—are nonviolent offenders who would be appropriate candidates for diversion to drug treatment programs. A growing body of research shows that treatment, rather than incarceration, is the most effective tactic to fight drug abuse—a tactic which can also save billions of taxpayer dollars. Putting this strategy into effect in 2002, Hawaii and Washington replaced prison sentences with treatment for first-time nonviolent drug offenders. Kansas, Missouri, Nebraska and Texas followed suit in 2003.

States have been curtailing the use of mandatory minimum sentencing.

Mandatory sentencing laws have resulted in disproportionately long prison terms, ranging from five years for simple possession of crack cocaine to 20 years for distribution of any narcotic. Many of the offenders subject to mandatory sentencing are guilty of relatively minor crimes for which they should be held accountable—but for which long prison terms are unjustified. In a sweeping reform effort, eighteen states have rolled back mandatory minimum sentences or restructured other harsh penalties. For example, Michigan repealed almost all of its mandatory minimum drug sentencing statutes in 2002, and Delaware reduced mandatory minimums and provided judges more latitude in sentencing in 2003.

States have been relaxing Three-Strikes-And-You're-Out laws.

Approximately 65 percent of the inmates serving two- or three-strikes sentences were convicted of non-violent, fairly minor crimes.[2] Three-Strikes-And-You're-Out is an effective slogan, but no evidence proves that it works to prevent crime. Both Indiana and Kansas have relaxed their three-strikes laws.

Sentencing reform can help balance state budgets.

States save tens of millions of dollars when they reform their sentencing rules. For example, Michigan is saving taxpayers $41 million a year, Washington is saving $45 million a year, and Texas is saving $30 million over two years through the adoption of sentencing reforms.[3]

The public strongly supports sentencing reform.

Public attitudes toward crime and corrections have been shifting for more than a decade. Eighty-nine percent of Americans now favor treatment instead of incarceration for first-time drug offenders. Seventy-six percent also oppose mandatory life imprisonment for anyone convicted of a non-violent felony for the third time.[4]

This policy summary relies in large part on information from the Sentencing Project.

Endnotes

[1] Bureau of Justice Statistics, "Prisoners in 2002," U.S. Department of Justice, July 2003.

[2] U.S. Department of Justice, "Three Strikes and You're Out: A Review of State Legislation," September 1997.

[3] Judith A. Green, "Positive Trends in State-Level Sentencing and Corrections Policy," Families Against Mandatory Minimums, November 2003.

[4] ABC News Poll, March 2002.

Sentencing Reform

Center for Policy Alternatives
1875 Connecticut Avenue NW, Suite 710
Washington, DC 20009
202-387-6030
www.stateaction.org

Families Against Mandatory Minimums
1612 K Street NW, Suite 700
Washington, DC 20006
202-822-6700
www.famm.org

The Sentencing Project
514 10th Street NW, Suite 1000
Washington, DC 20004
202-628-0871
www.sentencingproject.org

Sentencing Reform

Drug Treatment Instead of Incarceration Act

SECTION 1. SHORT TITLE

This Act shall be called the "Drug Treatment Instead of Incarceration Act."

SECTION 2. FINDINGS AND PURPOSE

(A) FINDINGS—The legislature finds that:

1. Substance abuse treatment is a proven public safety and health measure. Nonviolent drug-dependent criminal offenders who receive treatment are much less likely to abuse drugs and commit future crimes, and are likely to live healthier, more stable, and more productive lives.

2. When nonviolent persons convicted of drug possession or drug use are provided appropriate community-based treatment instead of incarceration, communities are healthier and safer, while taxpayer dollars are saved.

(B) PURPOSE—This law is enacted to enhance public safety by reducing drug-related crime, to improve public health by reducing drug abuse and drug dependence through proven and effective drug treatment strategies, and to halt the wasteful expenditure of millions of dollars each year on the incarceration and re-incarceration of nonviolent drug offenders who would be better placed in community-based treatment.

SECTION 3. DRUG TREATMENT INSTEAD OF INCARCERATION

(A) DEFINITIONS—In this section:

1. "Rehabilitative treatment program" means the least restrictive rehabilitative treatment program appropriate, as determined by clinical assessment. Such a program shall include drug treatment provided by a certified community drug treatment program. Such a program may include one or more of the following: outpatient treatment, halfway house treatment, narcotic replacement therapy, drug education or prevention courses, vocational training, family counseling, literacy training, community service, and inpatient or residential drug treatment as needed to address severe dependence, special detoxification, or relapse situations.

2. "Nonviolent drug offense" means an offense involving the possession or sale of a controlled substance, as defined in [insert appropriate citation], and which offense did not involve the use, attempted use, or threatened use of physical force against another person.

(B) APPROPRIATE ASSIGNMENT OF NONVIOLENT DRUG OFFENDERS

1. After arraignment, the court shall direct that a clinical assessment be performed of all persons charged with a nonviolent drug offense, with the consent of the person arrested. Such clinical assessment shall form the basis for all orders pursuant to this section.

Sentencing Reform

2. There shall be a presumption that any person who would otherwise be arraigned for a nonviolent drug offense for the first time shall, prior to the entry of a guilty plea, be ordered by the court to participate in and complete a rehabilitative drug treatment program. This section shall apply to all first-time felony and all misdemeanor drug offenders.

3. Upon application by the defendant, and upon good cause shown, the court may allow a repeat nonviolent felony drug offender to plead guilty to the drug offense and subsequently order the person to participate in and complete a rehabilitative treatment program. The repeat nonviolent felony drug offender shall be sentenced in accordance with applicable provisions of the criminal code, but such sentence shall be suspended following the defendant's participation in and completion of appropriate rehabilitative treatment.

4. Paragraphs (B)(2) and (B)(3) shall not apply to any person who:
   a. Has been convicted within the previous five years of a felony involving the use, attempted use, or threatened use of physical force against another person.
   b. In addition to the conviction of the nonviolent drug offense, has been charged and/or convicted in the same proceeding of a felony not related to the use of drugs.
   c. Refuses participation in a clinical assessment or rehabilitative treatment program.
   d. Has two separate convictions for nonviolent drug offenses, has participated in two separate courses of rehabilitative treatment under this section, and is found by the court by clear and convincing evidence to be unsuitable for any available form of rehabilitative treatment.

5. If, during the course of rehabilitative treatment, the treatment provider determines that the defendant is unsuitable for the treatment being provided, but may be suitable for other rehabilitative treatment programs, the court may modify the terms of its order to ensure that the person receives the alternative treatment or program.

6. Nothing in this section precludes a defendant from declining to participate in a clinical assessment or rehabilitative treatment program. A person who declines participation shall be prosecuted and sentenced in accordance with otherwise applicable provisions of the criminal code.

(C) SUBSEQUENT PROSECUTION

1. Where any person participating in a rehabilitative treatment program pursuant to section (B) is arrested for an offense other than a nonviolent drug offense or violates a non-drug-related condition of the order directing that person to a rehabilitative treatment program, or non-drug-related condition of probation, the District Attorney may move to proceed with prosecution, at which time the court shall conduct a hearing. If the alleged violation is proven, the court may modify its order or the conditions of probation, or may direct prosecution to proceed.

2. Where any person participating in a rehabilitative treatment program pursuant to section (B) is arrested for a nonviolent drug possession offense, or violates a drug-related condition of the order directing that person to a rehabilitative treatment program, or a drug-related condition of probation, the District Attorney may move to proceed with prosecution, and the court shall conduct a hearing. If the alleged violation is proved, and the state proves by clear and convincing evidence that such person poses a danger to the safety of other persons, the court may direct prosecution to proceed. Otherwise, the court may order that the rehabilitative treatment program be intensified or modified.

3. Where the court directs prosecution to proceed, in no event shall any person who has failed to successfully complete a rehabilitative treatment offense pursuant to this section receive a sentence that exceeds the sentence to which the person would have been subject had the person declined to participate in the rehabilitative treatment program.

4. Where the court directs prosecution of a first-time felony or any misdemeanor nonviolent drug offense to proceed because the defendant has failed to successfully complete a rehabilitative treatment program pursuant to this section, notwithstanding any other provision of law, the trial court shall not sentence the defendant to a term that exceeds 30 days in jail.

5. Where a defendant has two separate convictions for a nonviolent possession offense, has participated in two separate courses of drug treatment, and is found by the court, by clear and convincing evidence to be unsuitable for any available form of drug treatment, the defendant is not eligible for continued probation under section (B). Notwithstanding any other provision of law, the trial court shall not sentence the defendant to a term that exceeds 90 days in jail.

6. At any time after completion of treatment, a defendant subject to section (B)(2) may petition the court for dismissal of the charges. If the court finds that the defendant successfully completed the prescribed course of treatment and substantially complied with the conditions of probation, the charges against the defendant will be dismissed in accordance with section [insert appropriate citation].

7. At any time after completion of treatment, a defendant sentenced pursuant to (B)(3) may petition the court for dismissal of the charges. If the court finds the defendant successfully completed the prescribed course of treatment, the conviction on which the sentence was based shall be set aside. The plea entered by the defendant will be withdrawn and the charges dismissed.

SECTION 4. SUBSTANCE ABUSE TREATMENT TRUST FUND

(A) ESTABLISHMENT OF FUND—A special fund to be known as the "Substance Abuse Treatment Trust Fund" is created within the [Department of Justice].

1. Upon passage of this Act, $XXXXX shall be appropriated from the General Fund to the Substance Abuse Treatment Trust Fund for the 2003-04 fiscal year.

2. There is hereby continuously appropriated from the General Fund to the Substance Abuse Treatment Trust Fund an additional $XXXXXX annually. These funds shall be transferred to the Substance Abuse Treatment Trust Fund on July 1 of each fiscal year.

3. Nothing in this section shall preclude additional appropriations by the legislature to the Substance Abuse Treatment Trust Fund.

(B) FUNDING ALLOCATION

1. Monies deposited in the Substance Abuse Treatment Trust Fund shall be distributed annually by the [CONTROLLER] through the [State Department of CORRECTIONS] to counties to cover the costs of placing persons in and providing drug treatment programs under this Act.

2. Such monies shall be allocated to counties through a fair and equitable distribution formula as determined by the Department as necessary to carry out the purposes of this Act. That includes, but is not limited to, per capita arrests for controlled substance possession violations and substance abuse treatment caseload.

Sentencing Reform

3. The Department may reserve a portion of the fund to pay for direct contracts with drug treatment service providers in counties or areas in which the Department has determined that demand for drug treatment services is not adequately met by existing rehabilitative treatment programs. However, nothing in this section shall be interpreted or construed to allow any entity to use funds from the Substance Abuse Treatment Trust Fund to supplant funds from any existing fund source or mechanism currently used to provide substance abuse treatment.

(C) ACCOUNTABILITY AND EVALUATION

1. The Department shall annually conduct a study to evaluate the effectiveness and financial impact of the programs that are funded pursuant to the requirements of this Act.

2. The study shall include, but not be limited to, a study of the implementation process, a review of incarceration costs, crime rates, prison and jail construction, welfare costs, the adequacy of funds appropriated, and any other impacts or issues the Department can identify.

SECTION 5. SEVERABILITY

The provisions of this Act shall be severable, and if any phrase, clause, sentence or provision is declared to be invalid or is preempted by federal law or regulation, the validity of the remainder of the Act shall not be affected.

SECTION 6. EFFECTIVE DATE

This Act shall take effect on July 1, 2004 and its provisions shall be applied prospectively.

Smart Growth

Building Codes

Smart growth is a strategy to discourage development projects that harm the environment and encourage projects that enhance the quality of life in a region.

Smart Growth Building Codes

Summary

- **Sprawling land development is devouring the American countryside at an alarming rate—about 365 acres per hour.**
- **Every year about 1.2 million new housing units are created in the United States, while 200,000 units are abandoned or destroyed.**
- **Smart growth is a strategy to discourage development projects that harm the environment and encourage projects that enhance the quality of life in a region.**
- **One key tactic to promote smart growth is to reform out-of-date building codes.**
- **New Jersey has led the nation in promoting smart building codes.**
- **New Jersey has successfully encouraged redevelopment in cities, while keeping land development profitable.**
- **Revitalization of existing communities is a win-win situation for developers, residents, taxpayers and the environment.**
- **Three states have followed New Jersey's success with smart building codes.**

Sprawling land development is devouring the American countryside at an alarming rate—about 365 acres per hour.

Across the nation, urban areas have expanded at approximately twice the rate of population growth.[1] In some places, like Chicago and Los Angeles, urban sprawl has advanced ten times faster than population growth. Phoenix is encroaching on the surrounding desert at a rate of one acre per hour.[2] As new development outpaces population growth, people become overly dependent on automobiles, increasing both air and water pollution. This pattern of development also destroys farmland, forests and wetlands.

Every year about 1.2 million new housing units are created in the United States, while 200,000 units are abandoned or destroyed.

The majority of these new housing units are built on the urban fringe, while older downtowns are left with underutilized and deteriorating buildings. Development on the fringe remains attractive to developers because of fewer obstacles to construction, cheaper land, and the potential to assemble large parcels.

Smart growth is a strategy to discourage development projects that harm the environment and encourage projects that enhance the quality of life in a region.

Smart growth addresses a broad range of goals, including neighborhood livability, environmental protection, mixing land uses, promoting sustainable development, and providing multiple transportation choices, while keeping open space open. It attempts to improve the quality of life by putting the needs of existing communities first, and focusing new development in areas that already have an infrastructure of roads, sewers, power lines, and schools.

One key tactic to promote smart growth is to reform out-of-date building codes.

Building codes have generally been written with an eye toward new construction. As a result, it is often much harder for developers to comply with building codes when rehabilitating existing buildings than when undertaking new construction. For this reason, inflexible building codes tend to encourage sprawl projects on undeveloped land over revitalization projects in cities and towns. States can reverse this trend by adopting rehabilitation building codes that provide greater flexibility to safely renovate existing structures.

New Jersey has led the nation in promoting smart building codes.

In 1997, New Jersey implemented new rehabilitation guidelines that have since been endorsed by the federal government and the National Association of Home Builders. These provisions encourage the redevelopment of existing buildings by ensuring that a newly renovated property meets an acceptable threshold of safety without requiring unnecessary additional measures.[3]

New Jersey has successfully encouraged redevelopment in cities, while keeping land development profitable.

Over the years, the New Jersey law has seen numerous success stories. For example, after standing vacant for eight years, a Jersey City building was renovated to provide 24 apartments for low- and moderate-income senior citizens, and a day care center. The project directors estimated that because of building code changes they saved nearly $400,000—about one-quarter of total project costs. Local governments have also enjoyed savings on publicly-funded renovations, allowing them to provide more community centers, government offices, and affordable housing units for less.[4]

Revitalization of existing communities is a win-win situation for developers, residents, taxpayers and the environment.

A growing number of American families are moving back into urban centers, seeking the community, amenities and diversity that urban life brings. Making the redevelopment of existing buildings more practical for builders doesn't simply open up new markets for developers. It benefits whole regions by encouraging mixed-income neighborhoods that raise living standards for all, expanding tax bases that bring increased funding for local schools, and preventing sprawl and pollution to help protect the environment.

Three states have followed New Jersey's success with smart building codes.

In 2000, Maryland adopted legislation modeled after the New Jersey building code. Rhode Island, whose rehabilitation code went into effect in May 2002, exempts existing commercial buildings from certain construction requirements. California's new building code promotes the preservation, rehabilitation and restoration of historic properties.

This policy summary relies in large part on information provided by the State Environmental Resource Center.

Endnotes

[1] "The State of the Cities 2000," U.S. Department of Housing and Urban Development, 2000.

[2] Charles Schmidt, "The Specter of Sprawl," National Institute of Environmental Health Sciences, 1998.

[3] National Association of Home Builders Research Center, "Nationally Applicable Recommended Rehabilitation Provisions," 1997.

[4] William Connolly, "Rules That Make Sense—New Jersey's Rehabilitation Subcode," 2003.

Smart Growth Building Codes

For more information...

Center for Policy Alternatives
1875 Connecticut Avenue NW, Suite 710
Washington, DC 20009
202-387-6030
www.stateaction.org

Smart Growth America
1200 18th Street NW, Suite 801
Washington, DC 20036
202-207-3355
www.smartgrowthamerica.org

State Environmental Resource Center
106 East Doty Street, Suite 200
Madison, WI 53703
608-252-9800
www.serconline.org

Smart Growth Building Codes

Smart Building Rehabilitation Code Act

SECTION 1. SHORT TITLE

This Act shall be called the "Smart Building Rehabilitation Code Act."

SECTION 2. FINDINGS AND PURPOSE

(A) FINDINGS—The legislature finds that:

1. In this era of rapid population growth, while new residential and commercial development consumes agricultural land, forests and other undeveloped land, thousands of existing buildings in our communities are not being fully utilized or are abandoned.

2. The rehabilitation of existing buildings is often hampered by inflexible building codes.

3. The state should model its rehabilitation code after the Nationally Applicable Recommended Rehabilitation provisions developed by the United States Department of Housing and Urban Development and the National Association of Home Builders Research Center.

(B) PURPOSE—This law is enacted to revitalize urban areas, preserve the environment, enhance the economic vitality of the state, and protect public health, safety and welfare.

SECTION 3. SMART BUILDING REHABILITATION CODE

After section XXX, the following new section XXX shall be inserted:

(A) DEFINITIONS—In this section:

1. "Addition" means an increase in building area, aggregate floor area, height, or number of stories of a building or structure.

2. "BRC" means the [STATE] Building Rehabilitation Code.

3. "Change of occupancy" means a change in the purpose or level of activity within a structure that involves a change in application of the requirements of the local building code.

4. "Construction permit application" means any application made to a local jurisdiction for a permit or other government approval for a rehabilitation project.

5. "Department" means the Department of [Housing and Community Development].

6. "Existing building" means any building or structure that was erected and occupied or issued a certificate of occupancy at least one year before a construction permit application for that building or structure was made to a local jurisdiction.

7. "Local jurisdiction" means any county, city or municipality in [STATE].

Smart Growth Building Codes

8. "Modification" means the:
   a. Reconfiguration of any space;
   b. Addition or elimination of any door or window;
   c. Reconfiguration or extension of any system; or
   d. Installation of any additional equipment.

9. "Reconstruction" means:
   a. The reconfiguration of a space which affects an exit or element of the egress access shared by more than a single occupant;
   b. The reconfiguration of space such that the work area is not permitted to be occupied because existing means of egress and fire protection systems, or their equivalent, are not in place or continuously maintained; or
   c. Extensive modifications.

10. "Rehabilitation project" means any construction work undertaken in an existing building that includes repair, renovation, modification, reconstruction, change of occupancy, or addition.

11. "Renovation" means the change, strengthening or addition of load bearing elements; or refinishing, replacement, bracing, strengthening, upgrading or extensive repair of existing materials, elements, components, equipment or fixtures. "Renovation" does not include reconfiguration of space or interior and exterior painting.

12. "Repair" means the patching, restoration or minor replacement of materials, elements, components, equipment or fixtures for the purposes of maintaining these materials, elements, components, equipment or fixtures in good or sound condition.

(B) ADOPTION OF THE BUILDING REHABILITATION CODE

1. The Department, in cooperation with the Building Rehabilitation Code Advisory Council, the Department of [Licensing and Regulation], and the State Fire Marshal, shall adopt by regulation the [STATE] Building Rehabilitation Code. The BRC shall be modeled on the nationally applicable recommended rehabilitation provisions developed by the United States Department of Housing and Urban Development and the National Association of Home Builders Research Center.

2. The purpose of the Building Rehabilitation Code is to encourage and facilitate the rehabilitation of existing buildings by reducing the costs and constraints on rehabilitation resulting from existing procedures and standards.

3. As provided under the [Administrative Procedure Act], the Department shall:
   a. Submit to the Joint Committee on [Administrative, Executive, and Legislative Review] the proposed regulations to adopt the BRC by December 31, 2004; and
   b. Adopt the BRC as soon as possible thereafter.

4. The Department, in cooperation with the Building Rehabilitation Code Advisory Council, shall review the BRC and adopt any necessary or desirable revisions at least every three years.

5. Except as otherwise permitted in this title, and notwithstanding any relevant provisions of existing state building codes, mechanical codes, plumbing codes, fire prevention codes, and electrical codes adopted thereunder, the BRC shall apply to all rehabilitation projects for which a construction permit application is received by a local jurisdiction or Planning Commission after adoption of the BRC.

Smart Growth Building Codes

6. By October 1, 2004:

   a. The Department of [Licensing and Regulation], the State Board of [Heating, Ventilation, Air-Conditioning, and Refrigeration Contractors], the State Board of [Plumbing], and the Board of [Boiler Rules] shall submit proposed changes to their regulations to make the [Mechanical Code, the Plumbing Code, the Boiler Safety Code, and the Elevator Code] consistent with the BRC;

   b. The [State Police] and State [Fire Prevention Commission] shall submit proposed changes to their regulations to make the [State Fire Prevention Code] consistent with the BRC; and

   c. The Department shall submit proposed changes to its regulations to make the [Building Performance Standards, the Safety Glazing Code, the Energy Code, and the Accessibility Code] consistent with the BRC.

7. A local jurisdiction may adopt local amendments to the BRC that apply only to the local jurisdiction.

8. Only a local jurisdiction that does not amend the BRC shall be eligible for any funding appropriated in conjunction with this chapter.

(C) MINIMUM PROVISIONS OF THE BUILDING REHABILITATION CODE

1. The BRC shall, at a minimum:

   a. Maintain a level of safety consistent with existing codes, and provide for multiple categories of work with multiple compliance standards;

   b. Be enforceable by local officials using existing enforcement procedures;

   c. Apply to repair, renovation, modification, reconstruction, change of occupancy, or addition to an existing building;

   d. Provide an expedited review process for proposed amendments to the BRC submitted by a local government or an organization that represents local governments; and

   e. Contain provisions that provide an opportunity for a person proposing a complex rehabilitation project involving multiple codes, prior to the submission of a construction permit application, to meet with local officials or their designees responsible for permit approval and enforcement in construction related laws and regulations that may be applicable to the rehabilitation project.

2. The meeting provided under subsection 1(e) of this subsection shall, to the extent possible, include the officials responsible for permit approval and enforcement in the following areas, as may be applicable to the rehabilitation project: [building code; mechanical code; plumbing code; electrical code; fire prevention code; boiler safety code; energy code; elevator code; and local historic preservation ordinances].

3. The purpose of the meeting provided for under subsection 1(e) of this section shall be to anticipate and expedite the resolution of problems a complex rehabilitation project may have in complying with the applicable laws and regulations and the BRC.

(D) ADVISORY COUNCIL

1. There shall be a [STATE] Building Rehabilitation Code Advisory Council comprised of 28 members as follows:

   a. The Secretary of [Housing and Community Development] or designee;

   b. The Secretary of [Licensing and Regulation] or designee;

   c. The State Fire Marshal or designee;

   d. The State [Historic Preservation Officer] or designee;

   e. The Director of the [Governor's Office for Individuals with Disabilities] or designee;

   f. The Director of the [Department of the Environment] or designee; and

Smart Growth Building Codes

g. Twenty-two members appointed by the Governor, including a representative of the [State Fire Prevention Commission]; four representatives of the building trades who are directly involved in or have experience in code setting or enforcement, including plumbers, electricians, heating, ventilation, air-conditioning and refrigeration contractors, and boiler operators; two architects whose practice involves a significant portion of rehabilitation projects; a professional construction engineer; two contractors specializing in rehabilitation construction; two representatives of county government; two representatives of municipal government; two building code officials serving local government; a commercial or industrial building owner or developer; a multifamily building owner or developer; two local fire officials; and two members of the general public.

2. From among the members of the Council, the Governor shall designate a chairman. The composition of the Council should reflect the race, gender and geographic diversity of the population of the State.

3. The term of an appointed member is four years. The terms of appointed members shall be staggered. The Governor shall specify five appointed members to serve a first term of one year; five appointed members to serve a first term of two years; six appointed members to serve a first term of three years; and six appointed members to serve a first term of four years.

4. At the end of a term, a member continues to serve until a qualified successor is appointed. A member who is appointed after a term has begun serves only for the rest of the term and until a successor is appointed and qualifies. An appointed member may serve no more than two terms.

5. A member shall serve without compensation and shall be reimbursed for expenses in accordance with the [Standard State Travel Regulations].

6. The Council shall:
   a. Advise the Department on the development, adoption and revisions to the BRC;
   b. Provide technical advice on the interpretation of the BRC to property owners, design professionals, contractors, local jurisdiction code officials, and local jurisdiction code appeal boards;
   c. To the extent possible, develop the BRC to seek to avoid increased costs to local jurisdictions arising from implementation of the BRC;
   d. To the extent provided in the State budget, provide training on the BRC for code officials and other public and private construction-related professionals.

7. The Council shall have an Executive Director, appointed by the Secretary of [Housing and Community Development]. The Executive Director shall be a special appointee in the [State Personnel Management System].

SECTION 4. PLANNING AND ZONING AUTHORITY NOT AFFECTED

This Act does not supersede the planning, zoning or subdivision authority of local jurisdictions.

SECTION 5. SEVERABILITY

The provisions of this Act shall be severable, and if any phrase, clause, sentence or provision is declared to be invalid or is preempted by federal law or regulation, the validity of the remainder of this Act shall not be affected thereby.

SECTION 6. EFFECTIVE DATE—This Act shall take effect on July 1, 2004.

TANF

As the nation struggles through its current economic difficulties, TANF becomes increasingly important. States have a number of options to improve TANF and strengthen the social safety net.

TANF

Summary

- As the nation struggles through its current economic difficulties, TANF becomes increasingly important.
- Poverty is on the rise, and the poor are becoming poorer.
- In 2002, the number of families living in poverty increased.
- Just as the economic downturn has caused former TANF recipients to lose their jobs, lifetime limits on cash assistance are going into effect.
- Americans support TANF expansion.
- States have a number of options to improve TANF and strengthen the social safety net.

As the nation struggles through its current economic difficulties, TANF becomes increasingly important.

The Temporary Assistance to Needy Families (TANF) block grant program was enacted by Congress in 1996 as a replacement for the previous welfare system. It was designed to move Americans from welfare to work, finding jobs for poor parents and reducing the number of families receiving cash assistance. TANF caseloads fell throughout the 1990s, largely because a robust economy generated millions of new jobs. But as the national economy fell into recession in 2001, state TANF programs were expected to hold up the social safety net.

Poverty is on the rise, the poor are becoming poorer, and people of color are disproportionately affected.

The poverty rate rose to 12.1 percent in 2002 from 11.7 percent in 2001, adding 1.7 million to the ranks of the poor. The number of people in poverty grew to 34.6 million last year, including 12.1 million children. Over the past few years, income disparities have widened, and the poorest families experienced the largest losses in income. By 2001, the average poor person had fallen further below the poverty line than at any time since 1979. Poverty levels for families of color were disproportionately higher. In 2002, nearly one in four African Americans (24.1 percent) and more than one in five Hispanics (21.8 percent) lived in poverty, compared to one in 12 non-Hispanic whites (8.0 percent). Blacks saw the largest increase in their poverty rate.[1]

In 2002, the number of families living in poverty increased.

The number of families in poverty increased from 6.8 million in 2001 (or 9.2 percent of all families) to 7.2 million (or 9.6 percent) in 2002. Almost 75 percent of children in poverty have parents who work, and these are the very families that TANF was intended to support.[2] Explanations for the rise in family poverty include extremely low wages, insufficient benefits, and the growing unemployment rate. The jobless rate of low-income single mothers rose faster than the overall rate between 2000 and 2002, averaging 12.3 percent last year.[3]

Just as the economic downturn has caused former TANF recipients to lose their jobs, lifetime limits on cash assistance are going into effect.

Former TANF recipients, even the "success" stories, are the first to lose their jobs in an economic downturn. They have the least job seniority and hold the most expendable positions. Just when poor families most need support, the five-year lifetime limit on cash assistance is taking effect. Thirty-seven states have TANF lifetime limits that have gone into effect already, while only seven states have no lifetime limits on cash assistance.

Americans support TANF expansion.

According to an August 2001 survey by the Feldman Group, 67 percent of American voters support adjusting TANF to help people improve their education and learn new skills, in order to earn enough money to move out of poverty, a policy also favored by a majority of Republicans (56 percent). Ninety-five percent favor allowing TANF recipients to fulfill their work requirements through education and training. Respondents also saw the value in suspending work requirements for TANF recipients who are primary caretakers of young children. Seventy-one percent want to allow a parent with a child under three to receive cash assistance in order to stay home with the child, and 64 percent support a proposal to give cash assistance to parents with children younger than six.

At no cost to the state, At-Home Infant Care is an option that allows parents the flexibility to care for their young children at home.

Two states, Minnesota and Montana, operate TANF-funded At-Home Infant Care (AHIC) programs. AHIC allows qualifying parents to stay home with young children while receiving 90-100 percent of the childcare subsidy the state would otherwise pay if those parents were employed. The program helps young children get the parental attention and affection they need to ensure proper physical and emotional development, and acknowledges that caring for infants is a full-time job.

States also have other options to improve TANF and strengthen the social safety net.

States can:

■ Extend time limits for assistance under TANF and/or use state maintenance of effort funds to provide cash benefits to families who are cut off from federal funding.

■ Invest in low-wage workers and laid-off workers by allowing them to obtain additional education and training *and* count the education programs as a work activity under TANF. Education will help workers find new, better jobs so they can become economically self-sufficient.

■ Address shortfalls in state unemployment insurance programs that deny eligibility to many of the newly unemployed.

■ Adopt or expand state Earned Income Tax Credit (EITC) programs that target the working poor.

■ Take advantage of various new state options under the food stamp program, which is primarily paid for by federal funds.

Endnotes

[1] Economic Policy Institute, "Income Picture," September 2003.

[2] Children's Defense Fund, "The State of Children in America's Union," 2002.

[3] Economic Policy Institute, "Falling Through the Safety Net: Low-income Single Mothers in the Jobless Recovery," April 2003.

TANF

Center for Policy Alternatives
1875 Connecticut Avenue NW, Suite 710
Washington, DC 20009
202-387-6030
www.stateaction.org

Center on Budget and Policy Priorities
820 First Street NE, Suite 510
Washington, DC 20002
202-408-1080
www.cbpp.org

Center for Law and Social Policy
1015 15th Street NW, Suite 400
Washington, DC 20005
202-906-8000
www.clasp.org

Children's Defense Fund
25 E Street NW
Washington, DC 20001
202-628-8787
www.childrensdefense.org

National Conference of State Legislatures
444 North Capitol Street NW, Suite 515
Washington, DC 20001
202-624-5400
www.ncsl.org

Welfare Information Network
The Finance Project
1000 Vermont Avenue NW, Suite 600
Washington, DC 20005
202-628-4200
www.welfareinfo.org

At-Home Infant Care Act

SECTION 1. SHORT TITLE

This Act shall be called the "At-Home Infant Care Act."

SECTION 2. FINDINGS AND PURPOSE

(A) FINDINGS – The legislature finds that:

1. Young children need as much parental attention and affection as possible to ensure proper physical and emotional development.

2. Current state laws do not provide a practical opportunity for TANF recipients to stay home and take care of their young children.

3. The state should adopt an At-Home Infant Care program similar to those operated in Minnesota and Montana.

(B) PURPOSE – This law is enacted to improve the health and welfare of young children by allowing TANF recipients to act as full-time caregivers for their young children.

SECTION 3. AT-HOME INFANT CARE

After section XXX, the following new section XXX shall be inserted:

(A) DEFINITIONS – In this section:

1. "Parent" means a birth parent, stepparent, adoptive parent, foster parent, or guardian who is acting *in loco parentis*.

2. "Secretary" means the Secretary of the Department of [Social Services], or the Secretary's designee(s).

(B) AT-HOME INFANT CARE PROGRAM

1. The Secretary shall operate an At-Home Infant Care program for qualifying low-income families to receive a payment in lieu of childcare assistance when a parent provides full-time childcare for the family's infant under two years of age.

2. In order to qualify for the At-Home Infant Care program:

    a. The family must be at or below 150 percent of the federal poverty level.
    b. The family must not have previously received a total of 24 months of At-Home Infant Care assistance under this section.

c. The family must have fulfilled the following work requirements for one out of the three months prior to entering the program:

    (1) 120 hours a month for two-parent families, which may be the contribution of one or both parents;

    (2) 60 hours a month for single-parent families; or

    (3) 40 hours a month for single-parent families who are attending postsecondary education or training.

3. A parent must be 18 years of age or older or, if under 18 years of age, have received a high school diploma or its equivalent.

4. The maximum rate of assistance allowed is equal to the amount of childcare assistance for infant family care for the appropriate district, as established by the Secretary by regulation. The family may not receive childcare subsidies for any other children in the family.

5. Family members may participate in education and work activities as long as one or both parents provide care full time for the infant.

6. The Secretary shall, by regulation, establish procedures for the program.

(C) FUNDING

Childcare payments through the At-Home Infant Care program shall be funded by available moneys from federal or private sources, and any state appropriations specifically for that purpose.

SECTION 4. EFFECTIVE DATE

This Act shall take effect on July 1, 2004.

Tobacco
Taxes

States can raise hundreds of millions of dollars in new revenue, and save thousands of lives, by increasing tobacco taxes.

Tobacco Taxes

Summary

- States can raise hundreds of millions of dollars in new revenue by increasing tobacco taxes.
- Higher tobacco taxes save thousands of lives by reducing teen smoking, as well as adult tobacco use.
- The experience of states that have increased tobacco taxes shows that cigarette smuggling is only a minor problem.
- Americans strongly support increasing state tobacco taxes.
- In 2002 and 2003, 31 states increased their tobacco taxes.

States can raise hundreds of millions of dollars in new revenue by increasing tobacco taxes.

Every state that has significantly raised its cigarette tax rate has experienced a major increase in state revenue. California's 50-cent per pack increase raises more than $500 million a year. Annual tobacco tax revenues have increased by $68 million in Maryland, $167 million in New Jersey, and $341 million in Michigan.[1] Early reports from New York City (which increased its local cigarette tax from 8 cents to $1.50 per pack), Ohio (from 24 to 50 cents), Massachusetts (from 76 cents to $1.51), and other states that increased their cigarette tax in 2002 show substantial revenue increases that are often larger than expected.[2]

Higher tobacco taxes save thousands of lives by reducing teen smoking, as well as adult tobacco use.

Research has consistently documented that cigarette price increases reduce smoking, especially among young people. Internal tobacco industry documents show that, since at least the early 1980s, companies have fully understood that tax increases reduce their sales, especially among youth, and they regularly admit this in their filings with the U.S. Securities and Exchange Commission. Indeed, the reason cigarette companies oppose state cigarette tax increases is precisely because they decrease pack sales.

The experience of states that have increased tobacco taxes shows that cigarette smuggling is only a minor problem.

Smuggling and tax avoidance are relatively insignificant problems, according to all major studies. Recent studies have found that cigarette smuggling, cross-border cigarette purchases, and Internet sales account for five to ten percent of all cigarette sales, at most.[3] Similarly, a California study found that after the state's 50-cent cigarette tax increase went into effect in 1999, no more than five percent of all continuing smokers were avoiding the state's cigarette tax.[4] It is also worth noting that any real or imagined problems with smuggling and tax avoidance after New York's 55-cent tax increase in 2000 were not significant enough to stop the state from increasing its cigarette tax again, by 39 cents in 2002, to $1.50 per pack—or to prevent New York City from increasing its supplementary local cigarette tax from eight cents to $1.50 per pack the same year.

Americans strongly support increasing state tobacco taxes.

Poll after poll has shown strong support for increased tobacco taxes in every region of the country. More than 30 different state polls conducted across the country in 2002 and 2003 have found that Americans favor large tobacco tax increases—raising cigarette taxes by 50 or 75 cents per pack. Even in the tobacco-growing state of Kentucky, 60 percent of voters favored a 75-cent per pack tax increase. In most states, voters favor the tax increase by at least a two-to-one margin. Every poll in every state found at least majority support among Democrats, Republicans and Independents. For example, in Nebraska, 67 percent of Democrats and 70 percent of Republicans favored a tax increase of 50 cents per pack. And in nearly every state where the question was asked, a large majority preferred increasing state tobacco taxes over any other measure that would significantly increase taxes or cut programs.

CENTER FOR POLICY ALTERNATIV

Recent State Experiences with Cigarette Tax Increases[6]

State	Date	Tax Increase Amount (per pack)	New State Tax (per pack)	State Consumption Decline	Revenue Increase (percent)	New Annual Revenue (millions)
Alaska	10/97	71¢	$1.00	-13.5%	+202%	$28.7
California	1/99	50¢	87¢	-18.9%	+90.7%	$555.4
Hawaii	7/98	20¢	$1.00	-8.1%	+19.9%	$6.4
Illinois	12/97	14¢	58¢	-8.9%	+19.0%	$77.4
Maine	11/97	37¢	74¢	-15.5%	+66.7%	$30.8
Maryland	7/99	30¢	66¢	-16.3%	+52.5%	$68.0
Massachusetts	10/96	25¢	76¢	-14.3%	+28.0%	$64.1
Michigan	5/94	50¢	75¢	-20.8%	+139.9%	$341.0
New Hampshire	7/99	15¢	52¢	-10.4%	+27.1%	$19.6
New Jersey	1/98	40¢	80¢	-16.8%	+68.5%	$166.6
New York	3/00	55¢	$1.11	-20.2%	+57.4%	$365.4
Oregon	2/97	30¢	68¢	-8.3%	+77.0%	$79.8
Rhode Island	7/97	10¢	71¢	-1.5%	+16.2%	$8.6
South Dakota	7/95	10¢	33¢	-5.6%	+40.4%	$6.1
Utah	7/97	25¢	51.5¢	-25.7%	+71.0%	$17.6
Vermont	7/95	24¢	44¢	-16.3%	+84.2%	$11.7
Wisconsin	11/97	15¢	59¢	-6.5%	+25.8%	$52.9

In 2002 and 2003, 31 states increased their tobacco taxes.

Increasing tobacco taxes is one of the most popular revenue enhancing measures in state legislatures across the nation. Since the beginning of 2002, the average state cigarette tax has increased from 43 to 73 cents per pack. Twenty-eight state legislatures (AR, CT, DE, GA, HI, ID, IL, IN, KS, LA, MD, MA, MI, MT, NE, NV, NJ, NM, NY, OH, PA, RI, SD, TN, UT, VT, WV, WY) raised cigarette taxes. Also, Arizona, Oregon and Washington increased tobacco taxes by statewide referendum. Most of the tax increases were quite large—40 cents or more per pack. Seven states (AZ, CT, IN, KS, OH, PA, VT) more than doubled their tobacco taxes. Tennessee raised its tax for the first time in 33 years. Tobacco taxes now range from Virginia's 2.5 cents per pack to New Jersey's $2.05. Sixteen state tobacco taxes are $1 per pack or more.[5]

This policy summary relies in large part on information from the Campaign for Tobacco-Free Kids.

Endnotes

[1] Orzechowski and Walker, "Tax Burden on Tobacco," 2003.

[2] See, e.g., Michael Cooper, "Cigarette Tax, Highest in Nation, Cuts Sales in City," *New York Times,* August 6, 2002; Paul Hampel, "Illinois Cigarette Tax Hike Cuts Sales But Not Revenue, *St. Louis Post-Dispatch,* August 9, 2002; "Mass. New 75-Cent Cigarette Tax Brings in $38.5 Million in August," *Associated Press,* September 11, 2002; Andrew Welsh-Huggins, "Cigarette Tax Raises More Money Than Expected," *Associated Press,* September 20, 2002.

[3] Matthew Farelly, "State Cigarette Excise Taxes: Implications for Revenue and Tax Evasion," RTI International, 2003; Yurekli and Zhang, "The Impact of Clean Indoor-Air Laws and Cigarette Smuggling on Demand for Cigarettes: An Empirical Model," *Health Economics,* 2000.

[4] Sherry Emery, "Was there significant tax evasion after the 1999 50 cent per pack cigarette tax increase in California?," *Tobacco Control,* June 2002.

[5] American Lung Association, "State Legislated Actions on Tobacco Issues," August 2002.

[6] Orzechowski and Walker, "Tax Burden on Tobacco," 2002. There is not yet sufficient data to calculate revenue changes for the numerous tobacco tax increases in 2002 and 2003, but preliminary data demonstrates that the trends in this chart have continued.

Tobacco Taxes

For more information...

Center for Policy Alternatives
1875 Connecticut Avenue NW, Suite 710
Washington, DC 20009
202-387-6030
www.stateaction.org

Campaign for Tobacco-Free Kids
1400 Eye Street NW, Suite 1200
Washington, DC 20005
202-296-5469
www.tobaccofreekids.org

The American Lung Association
61 Broadway, 6th Floor
New York, NY 10006
212-315-8700
www.lungusa.org/tobacco

American Cancer Society
901 E Street NW, Suite 510
Washington, DC 20004
202-661-5700
www.cancer.org

Tobacco Tax Revenue Act

SECTION 1. SHORT TITLE

This Act shall be called the "Tobacco Tax Revenue Act."

SECTION 2. DEFINITIONS

After subsection XXX, the following new subsection XXX shall be inserted:

1. "Other tobacco product" means:
   a. Any cigar or roll for smoking, other than a cigarette, made in whole or in part of tobacco; or
   b. Any other tobacco or product containing tobacco, other than a cigarette, that is intended for human consumption by smoking, by insertion into the mouth or nose, or by other means.

2. "Wholesaler" means, unless the context requires otherwise:
   a. A person who acts as a wholesaler as defined in [citation to state law referring to cigarette wholesalers]; or
   b. A person who:
      (1) Holds other tobacco products for sale to another person or entity for resale; or
      (2) Sells other tobacco products to another person or entity for resale.

3. "Wholesale price" means the price for which a wholesaler sells other tobacco products to a retailer, exclusive of any discount, trade allowance, rebate, or other reduction.

SECTION 3. TOBACCO TAX RATES

Section XXX is hereby repealed and the following new section XXX is inserted:

1. Except as otherwise provided in this section, the tobacco tax rate for cigarettes is:
   a. $1.50 for each package containing 20 or fewer cigarettes, whether sold or provided as a free sample.
   b. 7.5 cents for each cigarette in a package containing more than 20 cigarettes, whether sold or provided as a free sample.

2. The tobacco tax rate for other tobacco products is 45 percent of the wholesale price of the other tobacco products, whether sold or provided as a free sample.

3. The requirement under this subsection includes:
   a. Cigarettes and other tobacco products in vending machines or other mechanical dispensers.
   b. Cigarettes and other tobacco products generally referred to as "floor stock" in packages that already bear stamps issued by the [Comptroller] but for an amount less than the full tax imposed.
   c. Cigarettes and other tobacco products delivered to consumers in the state by mail, common carrier, or other delivery service.

4. No cigarette or other tobacco product shall be sold or delivered to a consumer without a tax stamp issued by the [Comptroller] showing that the tax has been paid.

Tobacco Taxes

5. All cigarettes and other tobacco products held for sale by any person that bear a tax stamp issued by the [Comptroller] in a value less than the full tax imposed must be stamped with the additional stamps necessary to make the aggregate value equal to the full tax imposed. However, in lieu of the additional stamps necessary to make the aggregate tax value equal to the full tax imposed, the [Comptroller] may provide an alternate method of collecting the additional tax.

6. The [Comptroller] shall establish, by regulation, a system of administering, collecting and enforcing the tobacco tax on other tobacco products. Regulations adopted under this section may include:
    a. Self-assessment, filing of returns, and maintenance and retention of records by wholesalers or retailers.
    b. Payment of the tax by:
        (1) A wholesaler who sells other tobacco products to a retailer or consumer in the state; or
        (2) A retailer or consumer who possesses other tobacco products in the state on which the tobacco tax has not been paid.
        (3) Any other provision that the [Comptroller] considers necessary to efficiently and economically administer, collect and enforce the tax.

SECTION 4. EFFECTIVE DATE

This Act shall take effect on July 1, 2004.

Unemployment Insurance -

Alternative Base Period

The Unemployment Insurance (UI) program
needs to be reformed to provide a better
safety net for the unemployed.

Unemployment Insurance - Alternative Base Period

Summary

- Only 40 percent of all unemployed workers collected benefits in 2002, and the percentage is even smaller for low-wage workers.
- The single most important reform that would bring more low-wage workers into the Unemployment Insurance (UI) system is the alternative base period (ABP).
- The ABP enables workers who fail to qualify for UI using the typical base period to receive benefits based on more recent wages.
- Adopting ABPs does not significantly deplete UI trust funds.
- Eighteen states and the District of Columbia have adopted ABPs to promote UI eligibility expansion.

Only 40 percent of all unemployed workers collected benefits in 2002, and the percentage is even smaller for low-wage workers.[1]

The unemployment insurance (UI) program was created in 1935, based on a Depression-era model of factory employment. Over the past six decades, changes in the labor market—such as increased use of part-time and temporary employment, and rapid job turnover—have eroded the UI safety net so that less than half of the unemployed receive UI benefits.

All states use a base period, or a base year, to determine whether unemployed workers have earned enough wages to qualify for UI benefits.

A base period is typically four calendar quarters—January through March, April through June, July through September, and October through December. Most states define their base periods as the first four of the last five completed calendar quarters. In other words, workers filing UI claims cannot use wages earned in the current quarter (the "filing quarter") or the most recently completed quarter (the "lag quarter") to calculate eligibility or benefit amounts.

The single most important reform that would bring more low-wage workers into the UI system is the alternative base period (ABP).

Some workers fail to qualify for UI because they do not have enough qualifying weeks of wages using the traditional base period. Calculating eligibility with the ABP allows the inclusion of more recent wages from the lag and/or filing quarters in order to meet the state's eligibility requirements.

Among the workers who fail eligibility requirements for UI benefits, one in five would qualify through ABPs.

Calculating eligibility requirements with the ABP expands UI coverage to low-wage and part-time workers—especially women, new entrants to the labor market (including former welfare recipients), and re-entrants to the workforce, who are concentrated in these jobs. Seasonal workers, including those in the building and construction trades, benefit the most from ABPs, because these workers often earn wages concentrated in fewer quarters of their base periods. In addition, because more recent wages are used, ABPs sometimes result in higher weekly UI benefits.

Adopting ABPs does not significantly deplete UI trust funds.

On average, the benefits paid out of UI trust funds have increased by four to six percent in states with ABPs. Given the comparably large numbers of workers who benefit from ABPs, this cost is justified. Furthermore, the cost estimates do not take into account that a fair proportion of newly-included recipients would have remained unemployed and filed valid UI claims at a later date, when their wages fell into the traditionally defined base period.

How Most States Define Their Base Periods[2]

Traditional Base Period

First Quarter	Second Quarter	Third Quarter	Fourth Quarter	Completed Lag Quarter	Filing Quarter

The Alternative Base Period Allowed in Connecticut, District of Columbia, Georgia, Hawaii, Maine, Michigan, New Hampshire, New Mexico, New York, North Carolina, Ohio, Oklahoma, Rhode Island, Virginia, Washington and Wisconsin

Alternative Base Period

First Quarter	Second Quarter	Third Quarter	Fourth Quarter	Completed Lag Quarter	Filing Quarter

The Alternative Base Period in Massachusetts, New Jersey and Vermont

Alternative Base Period

First Quarter	Second Quarter	Third Quarter	Fourth Quarter	Completed Lag Quarter	Filing Quarter

Eighteen states and the District of Columbia have adopted ABPs to promote UI eligibility expansion.

In 2003, New Mexico and Virginia adopted the ABP. A total of 18 states (CT, GA, HI, ME, MA, MI, NH, NJ, NM, NY, NC, OH, OK, RI, VT, VA, WA, WI) and DC, responsible for one-third of the nation's UI claims, have adopted ABPs.

This policy summary relies in large part on information from the National Employment Law Project.

Endnotes

[1] National Employment Law Project, "What Is An Alternative Base Period and Why Does My State Need One?" 2003.

[2] Illustrations courtesy of the National Employment Law Project.

Unemployment Insurance - Alternative Base Period

For more information...

Center for Policy Alternatives
1875 Connecticut Avenue NW, Suite 710
Washington, DC 20009
202-387-6030
www.stateaction.org

AFL-CIO
Building and Construction Trades Department
815 16th Street NW, Suite 600
Washington, DC 20006
202-647-1461
www.buildingtrades.org

Center on Budget and Policy Priorities
820 First Street NE, Suite 510
Washington, DC 20002
202-408-1080
www.cbpp.org

National Employment Law Project
55 John Street, 7th Floor
New York, NY 10038
212-285-3025
www.nelp.org/ui/

Economic Policy Institute
1660 L Street NW, Suite 1200
Washington, DC 20036
202-775-8810
www.epinet.org

Unemployment Insurance - Alternative Base Period

Alternative Base Period Act

SECTION 1. SHORT TITLE

This Act shall be called the "Alternative Base Period Act."

SECTION 2. ALTERNATIVE BASE PERIOD

After section XXX, the following new section XXX shall be inserted:

1. If an individual does not have sufficient qualifying weeks or wages in the base period to qualify for unemployment insurance benefits, the individual shall have the option of designating that the base period shall be the "alternative base period," which means:

   a. The last four completed calendar quarters immediately preceding the individual's benefit period, or

   b. The last three completed calendar quarters immediately preceding the benefit period and, of the calendar quarter in which the benefit period commences, the portion of the quarter which occurs before the commencing of the benefit period.

2. The [unemployment insurance agency] shall inform the individual of the option under this section.

3. If information regarding weeks and wages for the calendar quarter or quarters immediately preceding the benefit period is not available from the regular quarterly reports of wage information, and the [unemployment insurance agency] is not able to obtain the information using other means pursuant to state or federal law, the [unemployment insurance agency] may base the determination of eligibility for unemployment insurance benefits on the affidavit of an individual with respect to weeks and wages for that calendar quarter. The individual shall furnish payroll documentation, if available, in support of the affidavit. A determination of unemployment insurance benefits based on an alternative base period shall be adjusted when the quarterly report of wage information from the employer is received, if that information causes a change in the determination.

SECTION 3. EFFECTIVE DATE

This act shall take effect on July 1, 2004.

Unemployment Insurance

for Domestic Violence Survivors

Allowing domestic violence survivors to take advantage of unemployment insurance (UI) will help them maintain economic independence from their abusers while trying to escape violence.

Unemployment Insurance for Domestic Violence Survivors

Summary

- **1.5 million women are physically or sexually assaulted by an intimate partner each year.**
- **Every day, domestic violence follows women to work—at least one quarter of survivors report losing a job due, at least in part, to the violence in their lives.**
- **Nearly all employed domestic violence survivors experience work-related problems as a result of their abuse.**
- **Maintaining an independent source of income is critical for women who are trying to escape domestic violence.**
- **Unemployment insurance (UI) is needed to help domestic violence survivors maintain economic independence from their abusers.**
- **Twenty-four states explicitly provide UI benefits to women who lose their jobs as a result of domestic violence.**

1.5 million women are physically or sexually assaulted by an intimate partner each year.

In addition to women who experience domestic violence, millions more children are affected.

Every day, domestic violence follows women to work—at least one quarter of survivors report losing a job due, at least in part, to the violence in their lives.

According to a series of studies, between 24 and 52 percent of domestic violence victims report that they lost a job due, at least in part, to domestic violence.[1]

Nearly all employed domestic violence survivors experience work-related problems as a result of their abuse.

Ninety-six percent report some type of work-related problem due to the violence they suffer in their personal relationships.[2] For example, a perpetrator may stalk a victim at her workplace—making harassing phone calls, waiting outside, or coming into the workplace and verbally or physically assaulting her.

Maintaining an independent source of income is critical for women who are trying to escape domestic violence.

Job loss, or the threat of job loss, prevents many battered women from escaping violent relationships. Women who suffer domestic violence are often dependent upon their abusers to provide food and shelter for themselves and their children. Without an income source separate from their abusers, many women are unable to escape the violence in their homes. Survivors should not have to choose between violence and poverty. The 1990 National Family Violence Survey found that levels of "abusive violence" to women with annual incomes below $10,000 are more than 3.5 times those found when incomes exceed $40,000.

Unemployment insurance (UI) is needed to help domestic violence survivors maintain economic independence from their abusers.

Unemployment insurance helps battered women find and maintain safety for themselves and their children. UI benefits allow women who lose or leave their jobs because of an abusive relationship to secure the basic necessities for themselves and their children.

Twenty-four states explicitly provide UI benefits to women who lose their jobs as a result of domestic violence.

In 2003, six states (IN, KS, NM, OK, SD and TX) adopted provisions recognizing domestic violence as "good cause" for leaving work, preserving eligibility for UI. Three states provide UI eligibility to domestic violence survivors as a result of court rulings. Seven other states provide UI to workers who have been separated from their jobs for personal reasons, including domestic violence.

State Laws Explicitly Recognizing UI for Domestic Violence	Courts Directing UI for Domestic Violence	States Allowing Use of UI for Personal Reasons, Including Domestic Violence
CA, CO, CT, DE, IN, KS, ME, MA, MN, MT, NE, NH, NJ, NM, NY, NC, OK, OR, RI, SD, TX, WA, WI, WY	AK, FL, PA	AL, HI, NV, OH, SC, UT, VA

This policy summary relies in large part on information from the National Employment Law Project.

Endnotes

[1] General Accounting Office, "Domestic Violence and Wefare," 1999.

[2] Robin Runge, Rebecca Smith and Richard McHugh, "Unemployment Insurance and Domestic Violence: Learning from our Experiences," 2002.

Unemployment Insurance for Domestic Violence Survivors

For more information...

Center for Policy Alternatives
1875 Connecticut Avenue NW, Suite 710
Washington, DC 20009
202-387-6030
www.stateaction.org

National Coalition Against Domestic Violence
1532 16th Street NW
Washington, DC 20036
202-745-1211
www.ncadv.org

National Employment Law Project
55 John Street, 7th Floor
New York, NY 10038
212-285-3025
www.nelp.org

National Network to End Domestic Violence
660 Pennsylvania Avenue SE, Suite 303
Washington, DC 20003
202-543-5566
www.nnedv.org

National Organization for Women
Legal Defense and Education Fund
1522 K Street NW, Suite 550
Washington, DC 20005
202-326-0040
www.nowldef.org

Unemployment Insurance for Domestic Violence Survivors

Unemployment Insurance for Domestic Violence Survivors Act

SECTION 1. SHORT TITLE

This Act shall be called the "Unemployment Insurance for Domestic Violence Survivors Act."

SECTION 2. UNEMPLOYMENT INSURANCE FOR DOMESTIC VIOLENCE SURVIVORS

(A) DEFINITIONS—In this section:

1. "Domestic violence" means abuse committed against an employee or an employee's dependent child by:
   a. A current or former spouse of the employee.
   b. A person with whom the employee shares parentage of a child in common.
   c. A person who is cohabitating with, or has cohabitated with, the employee.
   d. A person who is related by blood or marriage.
   e. A person with whom the employee has or had a dating or engagement relationship.

2. "Abuse" means:

   a. Causing, or attempting to cause, physical harm.
   b. Placing another person in fear of imminent serious physical harm.
   c. Causing another person to engage involuntarily in sexual relations by force, threat or duress, or threatening to do so.
   d. Engaging in mental abuse, which includes threats, intimidation, stalking and acts designed to induce terror.
   e. Depriving another person of medical care, housing, food or other necessities of life.
   f. Restraining the liberty of another.

(B) ELIGIBILITY FOR UNEMPLOYMENT INSURANCE

1. An individual shall not be disqualified from receiving unemployment insurance benefits if the individual establishes to the satisfaction of the [Commissioner] that the reason the individual left work was due to domestic violence, including:

   a. The individual's reasonable fear of future domestic violence at or en route to or from the individual's place of employment.
   b. The individual's need to relocate to another geographic area in order to avoid future domestic violence.
   c. The individual's need to address the physical, psychological and legal impacts of domestic violence.
   d. The individual's need to leave employment as a condition of receiving services or shelter from an agency which provides support services or shelter to victims of domestic violence.
   e. Any other situation in which domestic violence causes the individual to reasonably believe that termination of employment is necessary for the future safety of the individual or the individual's family.

2. An individual may demonstrate the existence of domestic violence by providing one of the following:

   a. A restraining order or other documentation of equitable relief issued by a court of competent jurisdiction;

Unemployment Insurance for Domestic Violence Survivors

b. A police record documenting the abuse;

c. Documentation that the abuser has been convicted of one or more of the criminal offenses enumerated in [cite appropriate criminal law section];

d. Medical documentation of the abuse;

e. A statement provided by a counselor, social worker, health worker, member of the clergy, shelter worker, legal advocate, or other professional who has assisted the individual in addressing the effects of the abuse on the individual or the individual's family; or

f. A sworn statement from the individual attesting to the abuse.

3. No evidence of domestic violence experienced by an individual, including the individual's statement and corroborating evidence, shall be disclosed by the [Department] unless consent for disclosure is given by the individual.

4. For an individual who left work due to domestic violence, requirements to pursue suitable work must reasonably accommodate the individual's need to address the physical, psychological, legal and other effects of the domestic violence.

(C) TRAINING PROGRAM

1. The [Commissioner of Employment and Training] shall implement a training curriculum approved by the [Governor's Commission on Domestic Violence and the Human Resources Division].

2. All senior management personnel of the [Division of Employment and Training] shall be trained in this curriculum not later than 60 days from the effective date of this section. The [Commissioner] shall develop an ongoing plan for employees of the [Division] who interact with claimants to be trained in the nature and dynamics of domestic violence, so that employment separations stemming from domestic violence are reliably screened and adjudicated, and so that victims of domestic violence are able to take advantage of the full range of job services provided by the [Division].

SECTION 3. EFFECTIVE DATE—This Act shall take effect on July 1, 2004.

Unemployment Insurance -

Options for Reform

Unemployment insurance (UI) is our nation's first line of defense in economic downturns, but millions of Americans are outside its safety net. UI reform is an urgent priority as benefit claims have reached levels not seen since the recession of the early 1990s. Several options for reform exist that would assist laid off workers.

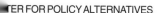

Unemployment Insurance - Options for Reform

Summary

- Unemployment insurance (UI) is our nation's first line of defense in economic downturns, but millions of Americans fall outside the program's safety net.
- With unemployment benefit claims reaching levels not seen since the recession of the early 1990s, UI reform remains an urgent priority.
- States must avoid cutting UI benefits.
- Many states still have UI trust funds sufficient to expand their UI safety nets.
- A number of states with ample UI trust funds have accumulated those balances while operating limited UI programs that pay below-average benefits to a lower than average proportion of their unemployed workers.
- Suggested UI reforms include: raising weekly UI benefit amounts, adopting alternative base periods, providing equitable coverage of part-time workers, adopting extended benefit triggers, or adding state benefit extensions.
- The public strongly supports measures assisting laid off workers.

Unemployment insurance (UI) is our nation's first line of defense in economic downturns, but millions of Americans fall outside the program's safety net.

By assisting laid off workers experiencing financial hardship while searching for employment, UI boosts the economy. But because UI programs in many states pay inadequate benefits and cover only a small proportion of unemployed workers, the UI safety net is eroded. As job losses have continued, some states face solvency challenges that can be used to attack benefit levels and program eligibility.

With unemployment benefit claims reaching levels not seen since the recession of the early 1990s, UI reform is an urgent priority.

The jobless rate is not expected to decline in coming months. State legislatures from New Mexico to Maine have already taken steps to improve UI in response to worsening economic conditions. States need to improve benefit levels and expand eligibility now, while the need is greatest.

States with low trust fund balances must avoid cutting UI benefits.

Some states, including IL, MA, MO, NY, ND, PA, TX and WV, will be under financial pressure to cut benefits in the coming months. Other states will join this list if job losses and UI claims continue.

Many states have UI trust funds sufficient to expand their UI safety nets and help the sinking economy.

Regular state UI benefits are financed through state payroll taxes and paid from state trust fund accounts maintained in the U.S. Treasury. State trust fund levels were boosted by an $8 billion transfer of federal funds in 2002. Despite current unemployment rates, many state UI trust funds can adequately meet the needs of the jobless in 2004.

A number of states with ample UI trust funds have accumulated those balances while operating limited UI programs that pay below-average benefits to a lower than average proportion of their unemployed workers.

Among the more solvent states paying lower than average weekly UI benefits are AK, AR, GA and LA, as well as the District of Columbia. Other states with lower than recommended weekly UI benefit amounts are AL, MS, MT, SC, SD and TN. States with restrictive UI program eligibility and above-average trust fund reserves include AZ, CO, FL, GA, LA, MS, NH, NM, OK and VA.

A series of options are available for states to boost their economies through UI reform:

■ **Raising weekly UI benefit amounts.** Too many states provide inadequate weekly UI benefits. The accepted formula calls for UI benefits to replace about one half of lost wages up to a maximum of two-thirds of the state average weekly wage. Many states need to update their UI benefit levels in order to protect laid off workers' standards of living. California increased its maximum weekly benefit from $230 to $330 in 2002, and to $370 in 2003. Also in 2002, Michigan raised its maximum weekly benefit from $300 to $362. AL, GA, MD, NH, OR and VT enacted more modest benefit increases in 2002.

■ **Adopting alternative base periods (ABPs).** These provisions take more recent wages into account when calculating UI eligibility and benefit levels than traditionally defined methods. ABPs promote UI eligibility expansion, especially among women, new entrants to the labor market (including former welfare recipients), re-entrants to the workforce, and low-wage workers. In 2003, Hawaii, New Mexico, and Virginia adopted the ABP. A total of 18 states (CT, GA, HI, ME, MA, MI, NH, NJ, NM, NY, NC, OH, OK, RI, VT, VA, WA, WI) and DC, representing over one-third of the nation's UI claims, have adopted ABPs.

■ **Providing equitable coverage of part-time workers.** Part-time workers account for nearly 20 percent of the workforce, but in a majority of states they do not qualify for UI benefits. These workers are predominantly women and disproportionately low-income. In 2003, Maine, New Jersey, New Mexico, and North Carolina passed significant expansions of UI eligibility for unemployed workers who had held part-time jobs, while Washington passed a limited measure.

■ **Adopting extended benefit triggers.** States can adopt triggers that extend UI coverage for an additional 13 weeks under the temporary federal extensions and the federal-state extended benefits program. Recognizing the inadequacy of UI benefit duration, seven states (AK, CT, KS, OR, RI, VT, WA) have adopted the Total Unemployment Rate trigger, while North Carolina and Michigan adopted temporary triggers in order to pay an additional 13 weeks of benefits.

■ **State benefit extensions.** Responding to the need to address long-term unemployment beyond the 13 weeks provided by the temporary federal extension program, seven states passed measures to pay additional benefits under state programs (KS, MA, NH, NJ, NM, OR, UT).

The public strongly supports measures assisting laid off workers.

A 2001 poll by Lake Snell Perry & Associates found that 76 percent of Americans supported increasing UI benefits for laid off workers.

This policy summary relies in large part on information from the National Employment Law Project.

Unemployment Insurance - Options for Reform

For more information...

Center for Policy Alternatives
1875 Connecticut Avenue NW, Suite 710
Washington, DC 20009
202-387-6030
www.stateaction.org

National Employment Law Project
55 John Street, 7th Floor
New York, NY 10038
212-285-3025
www.nelp.org/ui/

AFL-CIO
815 16th Street NW
Washington, DC 20006
202-637-5000
www.aflcio.org

Center on Budget and Policy Priorities
820 First Street NE, Suite 510
Washington, DC 20002
202-408-1080
www.cbpp.org

Economic Policy Institute
1660 L Street NW, Suite 1200
Washington, DC 20036
202-775-8810
www.epinet.org

Unemployment Insurance - Options for Reform

Unemployment Insurance Eligibility for Part-Time Workers Act

SECTION 1. SHORT TITLE

This Act shall be called the "Unemployment Insurance Eligibility for Part-Time Workers Act."

SECTION 2. EXTENSION OF UNEMPLOYMENT INSURANCE TO PART-TIME WORKERS

After section XXX, the following new section XXX shall be inserted:

1. An unemployed individual shall not be disqualified for eligibility for unemployment compensation benefits solely on the basis that he or she is only available for part-time work.

2. If an individual restricts his or her availability to part-time work, he or she may be considered to be able to work and available for work pursuant to [cite appropriate section], if it is determined that all of the following conditions exist:

   a. The claim is based on the individual's part-time employment.
   b. The individual is actively seeking, and is willing to accept, work under essentially the same conditions that existed while the wage credits were accrued.
   c. The individual imposes no other restrictions, and is in a labor market in which a reasonable demand exists for the part-time services he or she offers.

SECTION 3. EFFECTIVE DATE

This Act shall take effect on July 1, 2004.

Universal
Health Insurance

More than 43 million Americans are without
health insurance and 28 million more are
underinsured. States are now taking the lead
in trying to provide health care for all.

Universal Health Insurance

Summary

- More than 43 million Americans are without health insurance and 28 million more are underinsured.
- Employers are not providing healthcare coverage to millions of their employees.
- Uninsured Americans die prematurely because they don't receive medical treatment when they need it.
- The current system for providing medical care to the uninsured drives up healthcare costs for everyone else.
- The healthcare situation is getting worse.
- With the federal government unlikely to act, states are taking the lead in trying to cover the uninsured.
- In 2003, California enacted a landmark law mandating that large and medium-sized employers extend health coverage to their workers.
- In 2003, Maine enacted an innovative plan to induce employers to expand health coverage.
- Americans strongly favor health care for all.

Over 43 million Americans are without health insurance and 28 million more are underinsured.[1]

As a nation, we are left with the obvious conclusion: the healthcare marketplace is unwilling and ill-equipped to cover the uninsured. Indeed, the increasing financial instability of the managed care industry and the rising cost of premiums and prescriptions cast doubt on whether any American's health care is secure. Congress seems incapable of repairing the system's structural flaws.

Employers are not providing healthcare coverage to millions of their employees.

The American healthcare system is based on the assumption that employers will provide health insurance coverage to employees. But 85 percent of those without health coverage are in families with working parents. Seventy percent of uninsured workers are not even offered health coverage by their employers. Of the rest, 84 percent cite the high cost of health insurance premiums as the reason for declining coverage. Only 55 percent of low-wage workers—those earning under $7 per hour—have access to job-based health insurance.[2]

Uninsured Americans die prematurely because they don't receive medical treatment when they need it.

Every year, 18,000 Americans die prematurely because they don't have health insurance, according to a comprehensive report by the National Academy of Sciences' Institute of Medicine. Since they receive inadequate health care and their major illnesses are diagnosed too late, the uninsured become sicker and die sooner. In one study conducted over a period of 17 years, the uninsured were 25 percent more likely to die than those with private insurance.[3]

The current system for providing medical care to the uninsured drives up healthcare costs for everyone else.

When the uninsured do receive care, it is often at hospital emergency rooms and urgent care clinics—costly and inefficient places to provide primary care. Facilities that treat the uninsured provide nearly $100 billion in healthcare services each year.[4] To pay for unreimbursed costs, these facilities have to increase costs to public and private insurance programs, driving up rates for everyone.

The healthcare situation is getting worse.

Health insurance costs have increased by double-digit percentages in three of the last four years, and are projected to rise more than 12 percent in 2004. Medical bills are now the primary cause of 50 percent of personal bankruptcies. And just during the past year, an additional 2.4 million Americans joined the ranks of the uninsured.[5]

With the federal government unlikely to act, states are taking the lead in trying to cover the uninsured.

Rather than abandon the uninsured, or conclude that the problem is too overwhelming to solve, states are experimenting with an assortment of plans, programs and remedies.

In 2003, California enacted a landmark law mandating that large and medium-sized employers extend health coverage to their workers.

California's new law will require companies to extend coverage to more than a million uninsured workers. This employer mandate "pay or play" program requires companies to cover at least 80 percent of monthly insurance premiums, or contribute to a state program that provides insurance coverage. Low-income workers will contribute not more than 5 percent of their wages toward insurance premiums.

In 2003, Maine enacted an innovative plan to induce employers to expand health coverage.

Maine's "Dirigo" plan allows enrollees, mostly individuals and smaller companies, to participate in a buying pool that offers the benefits of a larger group, thereby lowering and stabilizing insurance rates. Among its range of benefits, the Dirigo plan expands Medicaid to cover more low-income residents and provides subsidies to middle-income families, using a sliding scale based on ability to pay.

The Health Care for All campaign in Maryland provides a thoughtful universal healthcare policy model.

The plan requires all employers to make a "fair share" contribution—5% of payroll—either by helping their employees purchase coverage or by paying into a fund for the uninsured. It expands SCHIP and Medicaid eligibility to trigger federal matching funds, gives individuals and families access to group purchasing power through a small group health insurance consortium, and increases the state tobacco tax by 50 cents per pack to raise Medicaid and SCHIP provider reimbursement rates. The plan also creates a quasi-public insurer to provide comprehensive and affordable benefits.

The Health Care for All campaign also provides a strong organizing model.

For four years, the Maryland Citizen's Health Initiative has built support for the concept of universal coverage, reaching out to thousands of community groups, holding dozens of town meetings, and convening a task force of health policy experts, to create a plan informed by the public process. Over 1,000 health care, business, labor and civic organizations have endorsed the Health Care for All plan.[6]

Americans strongly favor health care for all.

An October 2003 ABC News/Washington Post Poll found that Americans prefer universal health care to the current health system by a margin of 2 to 1. Even more revealing is the fact that Americans favor guaranteeing health insurance for all, "even if it means raising taxes."[7] In spite of the public's clear commitment to universal health care, it remains one of the most woefully neglected policy priorities of our time.

This policy summary relies in large part on information from the Maryland Citizens' Health Initiative.

Endnotes

[1] U.S. Census Bureau, "Health Insurance Coverage in the United States: 2002."

[2] Families USA, "Going Without Health Insurance," March 2003.

[3] Institute of Medicine, "Care Without Coverage: Too Little, Too Late," National Academy of Sciences, 2002.

[4] Institute of Medicine, "Hidden Costs, Value Lost: Uninsurance in America," National Academy of Sciences, 2003.

[5] U.S. Census Bureau.

[6] http://www.healthcareforall.com.

[7] ABC News/Washington Post Poll, October 9-13, 2003.

Universal Health Insurance

For more information...

Center for Policy Alternatives
1875 Connecticut Avenue NW, Suite 710
Washington, DC 20009
202-387-6030
www.stateaction.org

Families USA
1334 G Street NW
Washington, D.C. 20005
202-628-3030
www.familiesusa.org

Henry J. Kaiser Family Foundation
2400 Sand Hill Road
Menlo Park, CA 94025
650-854-9400
www.kff.org

Maryland Citizens' Health Initiative
2600 St. Paul Street
Baltimore, MD 21218
410-235-9000
www.healthcareforall.com

Physicians for a National Health Program
332 S. Michigan, Suite 500
Chicago, IL 60604
312-554-0382
www.pnhp.org

Universal Health Care Action Network
2800 Euclid Avenue, Suite 520
Cleveland, OH 44115
216-241-8422
www.uhcan.org

Voter Registration - Election Day

Hundreds of thousands of Americans were unable to exercise their right to vote in the 2000 elections due to inefficient, poorly run or discriminatory voter registration systems. Election Day registration would ensure that all eligible citizens are able to exercise their right to vote.

Voter Registration - Election Day

Summary:

- Hundreds of thousands of Americans were unable to exercise their right to vote in the 2000 elections due to inefficient, poorly run, or discriminatory voter registration systems.
- Minority voters were disproportionately excluded from the voting process in the 2000 elections.
- Voter registration deadlines limit voter participation.
- Six states have enacted legislation allowing voters to register on Election Day.
- States with Election Day registration report higher turnout and few problems with fraud, administrative complexity, or excessive cost.
- The federal Help America Vote Act makes it easier for states to implement Election Day registration.

Hundreds of thousands of Americans were unable to exercise their right to vote in the 2000 elections due to inefficient, poorly run, or discriminatory voter registration systems.

Between 1.5 and 3 million votes were lost or not cast in 2000 because of problems with registration processes and voting lists.[1] According to an August 2001 congressional report, eligible voters in at least 25 states arrived at the polls and were unable to vote because their names had been illegally purged from the voter rolls or not added in time for Election Day.[2]

Minority voters were disproportionately excluded from the voting process in the 2000 elections.

According to national studies, many disfranchised voters were African Americans and Latinos who registered at state agencies pursuant to the National Voter Registration Act (NRVA). In fact, the 2000 election produced a record number of complaints about the failure of new NRVA registrants to be added to voting rolls in time for Election Day, according to the Federal Election Commission.[3]

Voter registration deadlines limit voter participation.

Thirty-seven states cut off registration opportunities 20 to 30 days before Election Day. Yet many voters do not take an interest in elections until a few weeks before Election Day, when political campaigns do most of their advertising and races inevitably tighten. A series of Gallup polls in 2000 found that the proportion of Americans giving "quite a lot" of thought to the election rose from 62 percent in early October, when voter registration usually closes, to 75 percent just before Election Day.[4] The 13 percent

who became more interested during the final month of the campaign generally could not vote unless they were already registered.

Six states have enacted legislation allowing voters to register on Election Day.

Idaho, Maine, Minnesota, New Hampshire, Wisconsin, and Wyoming allow eligible citizens to register to vote and cast a ballot on Election Day.[5] These states also allow voters whose names were improperly excluded from, or never added to, the rolls to correct the errors and vote.

States using Election Day registration have significantly higher voter turnout than the national average.

In 2000, when nationwide voter turnout totaled 59 percent, the six Election Day registration states had a combined turnout of 68 percent, with Maine boasting the highest voter turnout in the nation.[6] Researchers estimate that eliminating voter registration deadlines and implementing Election Day registration would produce an average seven percent rise in voter turnout.[7] In fact, according to a May 2001 poll, 64 percent of nonvoters said that Election Day registration would make them more likely to vote.[8]

States using Election Day registration report few problems with fraud or administrative complexity.

Where Election Day registration is practiced, state officials report minimal problems with fraud and no unusual administrative problems. Indeed, Election Day registration can help address one of the most frustrating administrative problems exposed during the 2000 election: incomplete or inaccurate registration lists that result in people being barred from voting. In the states that use Election Day registration, the additional work of adding new voters has proven manageable. To accommodate the new procedures, election officials in these states educate registration clerks on how to make reasonable estimates of voter turnout, ensuring that polling places are adequately staffed.

States implementing Election Day registration do not face substantially higher costs.

The most obvious costs associated with Election Day registration relate to increasing the number of polling place workers and training them to handle new registrations on Election Day. But, as the 2000 elections demonstrated, most states need to pay for more staffing at the polls and better training for poll workers anyway.

The federal Help America Vote Act (HAVA) makes it easier for states to implement Election Day registration.

Enacted by Congress in 2002, HAVA is designed to encourage all states to reform their voting processes. It includes a requirement that states begin using statewide computerized voter registration databases by January 1, 2006. Centralized databases will enable election officials to prevent duplicate registrations in different voting precincts, eliminating one possible argument against Election Day registration. HAVA also requires states to offer provisional ballots to voters claiming to be registered but not listed on the voter rolls. Election Day registration would make provisional ballots unnecessary and would be easier for officials to administer, providing certainty to citizens that their votes would, in fact, be counted.

States are moving toward implementation of Election Day registration.

In 2003, the Connecticut legislature passed an Election Day registration statute, but the bill was ultimately vetoed by the governor. Similarly, the California legislature approved a bill authorizing an Election Day registration pilot project in Alameda County, but Governor Gray Davis vetoed it before leaving office. Officials in Massachusetts, Nevada, North Carolina, and the District of Columbia are now advocating the adoption of Election Day registration as part of the overall HAVA implementation process.

This policy summary relies in large part on information from Demos.

Endnotes

[1] Caltech-MIT Voting Technology Project, "Voting - What Is, What Could Be," July 2001.

[2] Democratic Investigative Staff, U.S. House Committee on the Judiciary, "How to Make a Million Votes Disappear: Electoral Slight of Hand in the 2000 Presidential Election," August 20, 2001.

[3] Federal Election Commission, "The Impact of The National Voter Registration Act of 1993 on the Administration of Elections for Federal Office," July 2001.

[4] "The Gallup Poll: The Nine Weeks of Election 2000."

[5] A seventh state, North Dakota, does not require voter registration.

[6] U.S. Census Bureau, "Voting and Registration in the Election of November 2000," February 2002.

[7] Craig Leonard Brians and Bernard Grofman, "Election Day Registration's Effect on U.S. Voter Turnout," *Social Science Quarterly*, Vol. 82, No. 1, March 2001.

[8] "America's No-Shows," Medill School of Journalism and Medill News Service, Northwestern University, May 2001.

Voter Registration - Election Day

Center for Policy Alternatives
1875 Connecticut Avenue NW, Suite 710
Washington, DC 20009
202-387-6030
www.stateaction.org

Demos
220 Fifth Avenue, 5th Floor
New York, NY 10001
212-633-1405
www.demos-usa.org

Alliance for Better Campaigns
1990 M Street NW, Suite 200
Washington, DC 20036
202-659-1300
www.bettercampaigns.org

Voter Registration - Election Day

Election Day Registration Act

Summary: The Election Day Registration Act allows qualified residents to register to vote and cast ballots on the day of a regular national, state or local election.

SECTION 1. SHORT TITLE

This Act shall be called the "[STATE] Election Day Registration Act."

SECTION 2. FINDINGS AND PURPOSE

(A) FINDINGS—The legislature finds that:

1. Many individuals are unable to vote on Election Day because of inefficiencies and mistakes in the voter registration system.

2. Precincts with predominantly minority populations are most affected by inaccurate voting rolls.

3. Election Day registration would increase voter participation in elections, which strengthens our democratic institutions.

4. Election Day registration has been successfully tested in a number of states.

(B) PURPOSE—This law is enacted to improve the state's election process, enfranchise voters, and increase civic participation by [STATE] citizens.

SECTION 3. ELECTION DAY REGISTRATION

After section XXX, the following new section XXX shall be inserted:

ELECTION DAY REGISTRATION

1. An individual who is eligible to vote may register on Election Day by:

   a. Appearing in person at the polling place for the precinct in which the individual maintains residence.
   b. Providing proof of residence.
   c. Completing a registration form, and making an oath in the prescribed form.

2. An individual may prove residence for purposes of registering by showing any of the following items listing a valid address in the precinct:

   a. A [STATE] driver's license or [STATE] identification card issued by the [Department of Motor Vehicles].
   b. A residential lease or utility bill together with a photo identification card.
   c. A student identification card from a postsecondary educational institution in [STATE] accompanied by a current student fee statement.

3. Election Day registration provided in this section shall apply to all elections conducted under [cite elections code], including national, state, municipal and school district elections.

SECTION 4. EFFECTIVE DATE—This Act shall take effect on July 1, 2004.

Voting Rights
Restoration

An estimated 4.6 million Americans—1 in 50 adults—are currently barred from voting because of a felony conviction. States are moving to restore voting rights to many of those citizens, thereby reintegrating them into society, increasing voter participation, and strengthening democracy.

Voting Rights Restoration

Summary

- An estimated 4.6 million Americans—1 in 50 adults—are currently barred from voting because of a felony conviction.
- 1.6 million of those barred from voting are people with felony convictions who have completed their sentences.
- African-American and Latino communities are disproportionately affected by the disfranchisement of criminal offenders—13 percent of African-American men are barred from voting.
- Restoring the right to vote helps reintegrate former offenders into society, and by increasing voter participation, it strengthens democracy.
- States are moving to restore the right to vote to many citizens with felony convictions.

An estimated 4.6 million Americans—1 in 50 adults—are barred from voting because of a felony conviction.[1]

The number of inmates in state and federal prisons has increased more than six-fold, from less than 200,000 in 1970 to more than 1.4 million in 2002, largely due to drug prosecutions. Between 1985-95, the number of people in prison for drug offenses increased 306 percent for whites and 707 percent for African Americans.

1.6 million of those barred from voting are people with felony convictions who have completed their sentences.

Thirteen states permanently deny the right to vote to at least some citizens who have completed sentences for felony convictions. Of these, five permanently disfranchise everyone with a felony conviction.

African-American and Latino communities are disproportionately affected by the disfranchisement of criminal offenders—13 percent of African-American men are barred from voting.

More than one-third of the total disenfranchised population are black men. In seven states, more than one in four African-American men are permanently disfranchised. Given current rates of incarceration, three in ten of the next generation of black men are expected to be disfranchised at some point in their lives, and in states that permanently disfranchise citizens with a felony record, as many as 40 percent of black men may permanently lose their right to vote.

Restoring the right to vote helps reintegrate former offenders into society, and by increasing voter participation, it strengthens democracy.

Voting is integral to the fabric of our democracy—permanently disfranchised Americans can hardly feel a part of the process. Restoration of voting rights helps former offenders become productive members of society and strengthens our American institutions by increasing participation in the democratic process.

The United States is the only democracy in the world that disfranchises offenders who have completed their sentences.

In fact, many countries, including France, South Africa, Japan, Peru and Israel, allow incarcerated felons to vote. Germany mandates that corrections officials encourage prisoners to vote. Two states, Maine and Vermont, never strip away voting rights from their citizens—prisoners are eligible to vote.

States are moving to restore the right to vote to many citizens with felony convictions.

In 2003, Nevada amended its law to automatically re-enfranchise most first-time offenders on completion of their prison sentence or parole. Wyoming abandoned its permanent disfranchisement law and now allows persons convicted of nonviolent felonies to apply for reinstatement of their voting rights five years after release from prison or probation. And Alabama now requires its parole board to issue a "certificate of eligibility to vote" to most former offenders after completion of sentence, including any parole, probation or payment of fines.

Endnotes

[1] Jeff Manza and Christopher Uggen, "The Political Consequences of Felon Disenfranchisement Laws in the United States," August 31, 2001.

STATE DISENFRANCHISEMENT LAWS

Prisoners permitted to vote:

ME, VT

Voting restored after release from prison:

HI, ID, IL, IN, LA, MA, MI, MT, NH, ND, OH, OR, PA, SD, UT

Voting restored after release from prison and completion of parole (probationers may vote):

CA, CO, CT, NY

Voting restored after completion of sentence, including parole and probation:

AK, AR, GA, KS, MN, MO, NE, NJ, NM, NC, OK, RI, SC, TX, WV, WI

Voting restored after completion of sentence for first felony, permanently disenfranchised for at least some second felonies:

AZ, MD

Voting restored for certain ex-offenders convicted of felonies, others permanently disenfranchised:

AL, DE, NV, WY

Voting restored after completion of sentence, except those convicted of felonies before a certain date who are permanently disenfranchised:

TN (pre-1986 disenfranchised), WA (pre-1984 disenfranchised)

All convicted of felonies permanently disenfranchised:

FL, IA, KY, MS, VA

This policy summary relies in large part on information from Demos and The Sentencing Project.

Voting Rights Restoration

For more information...

Center for Policy Alternatives
1875 Connecticut Avenue NW, Suite 710
Washington, DC 20009
202-387-6030
www.stateaction.org

American Civil Liberties Union of Florida
4500 Biscayne Boulevard, Suite 340
Miami, FL 33137
305-576-2336
www.aclufl.org

Brennan Center for Justice
NYU School of Law
161 Avenue of the Americas, 12th Floor
New York, NY 10013
212-998-6730
www.brennancenter.org

DemocracyWorks
53 Oak Street
Hartford, CT 06106
860-727-1157
www.democracyworksct.org

Demos
220 5th Avenue, 5th Floor
New York, NY 10001
212-633-1405
www.demos-usa.org

Georgia Rural Urban Summit
P.O. Box 225
Decatur, GA 30031
404-522-4787
www.georgiasummit.org

New Jersey Policy Perspective
145 W. Hanover Street
Trenton, NJ 08618
609-393-1145
www.njpp.org

Progressive Leadership Alliance of Nevada
1101 Riverside Drive
Reno, NV 89509
775-348-7557
www.planevada.org

The Sentencing Project
514 10th Street NW, Suite 1000
Washington, DC 20004
202-628-0871
www.sentencingproject.org

Texas Criminal Justice Reform Coalition
1506 S. First Street
Austin, TX 78704
512-441-8123
www.protex.org/criminaljustice

Western Prison Project
P.O. Box 40085
Portland, OR 97240
503-335-8449
www.westernprisonproject.org

Voting Rights Restoration

Restoration of Voting Rights Act

Summary: The Restoration of Voting Rights Act allows persons who were disfranchised because of felony convictions to regain their right to vote after being discharged from a correctional institution.

SECTION 1. SHORT TITLE

This Act shall be called the "[STATE] Restoration of Voting Rights Act."

SECTION 2. FINDINGS AND PURPOSE

(A) FINDINGS—The legislature finds that:

1. [STATE] currently denies the right to vote to all persons who have been convicted of a felony and [insert what is applicable to the state].

2. The current disfranchisement law has a disproportionate impact on minorities, especially African-American and Latino men.

3. Voting is part of the fabric of our democracy. Restoring the right to vote helps reintegrate former felons into society and, by increasing voter participation, it strengthens democracy.

(B) PURPOSE—This law is enacted to help former felons become productive members of society, and strengthen democratic institutions by increasing participation in the voting process.

SECTION 3. RESTORATION OF VOTING RIGHTS

In Chapter XXX, Sections XXX are deleted and the following are inserted in lieu thereof:

(A) A person shall forfeit the right to vote in a federal, state or municipal election upon conviction of a felony and confinement to a federal or state correctional institution in the United States.

(B) A person who has been convicted of a felony and confined to a federal or state correctional institution in the United States shall be restored the right to vote in a federal, state or municipal election when that person has been discharged from confinement.

[NOTE: A stricter standard would be, "…has been discharged from confinement, and parole has been completed.]

(C) When a person is restored the right to vote, the [Department of Corrections] shall provide that person with a voter registration form, assistance in filling out the form, and a document certifying the person is eligible to vote, as part of the release process. The [Department of Corrections] shall deliver completed voter registration forms to the [Secretary of State].

Voting Rights Restoration

(D) The [Department of Corrections] shall, on or before the 1st and 15th days of each month, transmit to the [Secretary of the State] a list of the names, birth dates, and addresses of persons convicted of a felony who, during the preceding period, have become eligible to vote.

(E) The [Secretary of State] shall develop and implement a program to educate state and local election officials and corrections officals about the requirements of this section, ensuring that:

1. Eligible citizens are not kept off the voting rolls.
2. The language on voter registration forms does not mislead eligible citizens into believing they cannot register.
3. Pre-trial detainees who are eligible to register and vote are given the opportunity and assistance to do so.

SECTION 4. EFFECTIVE DATE

This Act shall take effect on July 1, 2004. Section 3, restoring voting rights to persons who have completed their [confinement], shall apply to all residents, whether those conditions were satisfied before or after July 1, 2004.